81

Published by Vision Sports Publishing in 2022

Vision Sports Publishing Ltd
19-23 High Street
Kingston upon Thames
Surrey
KT1 1LL
www.visionsp.co.uk

ISBN: 978-1913412-44-9

This book is an officially licensed publication

The views expressed in this book do not necessarily reflect the views, opinions or policies of Tottenham Hotspur Football and Athletic Co Ltd, nor those of any persons connected with the same.

Tottenham Hotspur Football and Athletic Co Ltd
Lilywhite House
782 High Road
London
N17 0BX
www.tottenhamhotspur.com

Editor: Jim Drewett
Art director: Doug Cheeseman
Editorial production: Ed Davis
Reprographics: Bill Greenwood
Print production: Ulrika Drewett
Commercial director: Toby Trotman
Club liaison: Jon Rayner

Photos: Getty Images, Shutterstock, Colorsport, Alamy, PA Photos, Offside, Mirrorpix, Reuters, Dail Mail
Memorabilia and clippings: Bob Goodwin, Neville Evans, Lee Hermitage/nwmfootball.com

Every effort has been made to contact the copyright holders of the photographs used in this book. If there are any errors or omissions the publishers will be pleased to receive information and will endeavour to rectify any outstanding permissions after publication.

Printed and bound in Slovakia by Neografia

A CIP Catalogue record for this book is available from the British Library

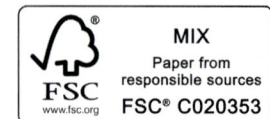

MIX
Paper from responsible sources
FSC® C020353

81

The year that changed our lives

by Steve Perryman with Julie Welch

TOTTENHAM
HOTSPUR

Foreword

by Ricky Villa

For Ossie and I to join Spurs was a huge gamble for both sides, but fortune favours the brave. We all took a calculated risk and we all got lucky. We found ourselves at a club that treated us perfectly, with a great manager and, in Stevie P, an outstanding captain. We proved to them that we were proud professionals, trustworthy and committed to the cause of putting Spurs back on the big stage where the club belonged.

Everything was very new to Ossie and me, of course. We came to a country where we didn't speak the language and didn't really know about the club or the league, and there was speculation in the papers that we wouldn't make it to Christmas. That is why I always say we were lucky because we came to the right place. Spurs gave us everything. I remember thinking what a wonderful stadium it was, and then there was the ticker-tape reception for our first home game – all the fans were laughing and waving. It was amazing.

When Ossie and I arrived in England we could tell how important the FA Cup was to everybody, and we were determined to help bring it back to White Hart Lane. I can play badly one day, but the next I can play well. I never play in between. For me, this is football. But when Keith substituted me in that first final against Manchester City I thought my dream of winning the FA Cup was over, and I was very sad.

But as I sat, head bowed, in the dressing room, I heard the Wembley roar. We had a second chance, and so did I. Getting that second chance meant everything. Now I say, 'Thank you' to Keith because he allowed me to play in the replay.

My first goal in the second match seemed very easy. Steve Archibald shot towards the goal and the goalie couldn't catch it and I scored from the rebound. Ossie says it was harder than I make out, though. The goal was in front of me, but the pressure was on. If I had missed, then it would have changed everything. The fans would have been saying, 'Take Ricky off!' But it didn't happen that way, of course.

My second goal was very, very, very easy! I wasn't thinking about scoring when I picked up the ball. I just started to run round one player, then two, then three and suddenly there was the keeper. I put the ball in the back of the net. Goal! To hear the fans sing my name, to know that I had put it right, meant the world to me. It was the most wonderful goal of my career, the sort of goal you dream of scoring – a winning goal that you've made yourself in an FA Cup Final.

The whole experience of playing in England was a fantastic period in my life. I take great pride in the fact that Ossie and I left a positive impression of Argentinian people. Ossie and I were part of one of the greatest Spurs sides in history and we helped make that history. Winning the FA Cup in 1981 meant Spurs were back where they belonged.

There's nothing quite like scoring the goal of the century in a Wembley final to make people remember you forever, and even now when I am back in England they still talk about it. I am so glad I made everyone happy.

I hope you enjoy this brilliant book that brings back so many happy memories.

Contents

The year that changed our lives

by Steve Perryman

The first time you lift a trophy for your club as captain is special. As a teenager about to sign schoolboy forms for Spurs I had watched at Wembley as the great Dave Mackay lifted the 1967 FA Cup, and I wondered if I would ever have that honour and privilege myself.

In September 1969 I made my debut at White Hart Lane against Sunderland. The 1-0 defeat wouldn't have greatly pleased Bill Nicholson, but he and 30,523 others were witnessing the start of a record that, with all the developments in the modern game, will most likely never be beaten. I was 17 years old and went on to make 855 appearances in the Spurs shirt.

By the time I was made captain of the club by Bill's successor, Terry Neill, I had been part of teams that won two League Cups and the UEFA Cup.

I was also there on that day in 1976 when Spurs were relegated to the Second Division. From then on I was determined to lead us back to where we belonged and put Tottenham Hotspur on the big stage again.

With Keith Burkinshaw now in charge, and me as his leader on the pitch, we started on the long road back to glory. That began in 1978 with two signings that astonished the world, when Ossie Ardiles and Ricky Villa joined us from Argentina. But there was plenty more to do and it wasn't until Steve Archibald and Garth Crooks joined us in the summer of 1980 that we had a team that was capable of competing for the biggest prizes.

The 1980/81 season was one of the most important in Tottenham Hotspur's history. The first step is always the hardest to take, and this is the story of how we took it, with all the twists of fate, the dramas and injustices, the great goals and the glory night that ended in the fulfilment of my schoolboy dreams.

I went up, to lift the FA Cup.

The memories remain strong and so does my affection for the great Spurs side created by Keith all those years ago. And while telling this story I want to thank all the people who supported my career, all the team-mates who were with me on the rollercoaster journey of the 1981 cup run, and all the fans who never lost faith in us as we took Tottenham Hotspur to the top again. All along I had the simple message given to me by Bill Nick to inspire me: 'Do it right'. And I believe I can say that I did do it right to the best of my ability. I cared and showed respect to the club, its supporters, its tradition and the state of our great game.

This is the story of the year that changed our lives...

"UP THE SPURS!"

TOTTENHAM

BACK ROW (left to right): Peter Shreeves (coach), John Lacy, Glenn Hoddle, Milija Aleksic, Barry Daines, Paul Miller, Ricardo Villa, Mike Varney (physio).
MIDDLE ROW: John Wallis (coach), Terry Yorath, Gerry Armstrong (now Watford), Graham Roberts, Gordon Smith, Peter Southey, Tony Galvin, Jimmy Holmes, Don McAllister.
FRONT ROW: Steve Archibald, Osvaldo Ardiles, Mark Falco, Steve Perryman, Tony Gibson, Chris Hughton, Garth Crooks.

24   25

9

81

MOMENT IN TIME

11th April 1981, Hillsborough
Wolverhampton Wanderers v Tottenham Hotspur
FA Cup semi-final, extra-time

"It was never a penalty.

It wasn't a foul. Kenny Hibbitt just went down because it was their last chance. Glenn hardly touched him. And the referee falls for it.

We had them well beaten. There was one minute to go. We were so close.

All those years we'd worked towards that moment. Fourteen years of hurt were about to come to an end. When you're on your way back from the deep disappointment of the relegation season. When you've been working your way up from the humiliation of being knocked out in the first round for five years in a row. When at last you've got a team with the firepower to put you on the big stage again. When you're one minute from Wembley, and then it gets snatched off you.

But on that bus, leaving that stadium, we knew it wasn't over. We knew we were going to win that replay. We were going to bring the glory days back to Tottenham. To our club, our fans, our Spurs family. We *knew* we were going to Wembley."

Steve Perryman

My road to Wembley

I grew up in West London and Wembley Stadium literally loomed large on the horizon. To play there was the ultimate schoolboy footballer's dream and I was no exception

Above: 'Que sera, sera'... Fresh-faced schoolboy international Steve Perryman, Wembley-bound for the first – but certainly not the last – time

Right: The 'old' Wembley Stadium on FA Cup Final day: the home of English football hosting the greatest day in the English football calendar

Growing up in the shadows of the Twin Towers, Wembley was always two different places for me. During my childhood in West London the stadium was almost on our doorstep. It was so familiar you hardly noticed it. We didn't talk about it the way most people did – in an awed way, like, 'Wow! Wembley!' To us it was just an everyday sight that you rode past on the bus on the way to somewhere else. In fact it probably impressed local people less than the greengrocers that the heavyweight boxing champion Henry Cooper and his twin brother had on the corner of Wembley High Street. The stadium was just a stage on the bus route. You went past it to get to the North Circular. That's how normal it was to us.

But the 'other' Wembley was different. It was the pinnacle of where you were trying to go. It was the Twin Towers, the hallowed turf, the '66 World Cup. It was the FA Cup Final that we watched every year on TV. My brothers and I loved the FA Cup. We had an interest in Brentford and QPR, our local clubs, and there was a lot of excitement when they sometimes got through to the third round. 'Where's that?' we'd ask if they drew a non-league club and then go and look it up on the map.

Growing up, we were part of the TV audience for the FA Cup Final. There weren't many live games shown back then so it was an enormous national event, like a royal wedding. This was the day you craved. Your only chance to see the biggest game in football as it

happened before your eyes. It was the very, very special game of the year. To get to that game you'd have had to win other special games. It was do or die. The replays only added to the excitement.

We'd watch the TV build-up that started in the morning, with all the traditional pre-match rituals like the walk up Wembley Way and the crowd singing *Abide With Me*. I felt the emotion of winning, I memorised every result, and the names of all the players. I learnt about the 'Matthews Final', when Blackpool came back from 3-1 down to beat Bolton Wanderers 4-3. I heard all about the Wembley hoodoo, when final after final had one or the other team either losing a player through injury or having to carry on with a player who could hardly walk. The one all Spurs fans know about was in 1961, the Double season, when Les Chalmers, the Leicester City right-back, had his leg caught accidentally in a tackle by Les Allen and spent the rest of the game hobbling up and down the wing.

I watched Bolton Wanderers beat the Manchester United team that had to be rebuilt following the 1958 Munich Air Crash, when Nat Lofthouse bundled over Harry Gregg, the United goalie, for Bolton's second goal. It wasn't like Lofthouse did it as the goalie took the ball, he hit him at least a second and a half after Gregg got hold of it. One-two-*hit*. I think he'd have got sent off now...

I knew that Elton John's uncle Roy Dwight scored the opening goal for Nottingham Forest when they won in 1959. I knew that Bert

> "There weren't many live games shown back then so the FA Cup Final was an enormous national event, like a royal wedding"

ENGLAND'S YOUNGSTERS MEET SCOTLAND

SCHOOLBOYS AT WEMBLEY

Their goal— to be stars

PROBABLE TEAMS

ENGLAND
Mervyn Cawston
Lawrence Millerchip
Richard Pitt
Melvyn Simmonds
Tommy Taylor (Capt.)
Mark Towers
David Spencer
Stephen Perryman
William Kenny
Leonard Cantello
George Jones

★

SCOTLAND
John McInally
Ian Donald
Lawrence Reekie
Norman Stevenson
John Gallacher (Capt.)
Gavin Scullion
Joseph Sloan
Joseph Cruickshand
Joseph Ward
Anthony McBride
Kenneth Watson

Above: Steve (front row, second left) fulfils every young footballer's dream, playing for England Schoolboys in 1967

Right: Spurs parade the FA Cup in 1967 – the club's fifth success in the competition, and the fifth major trophy of the Bill Nicholson era

Trautmann got his neck broken in the Manchester City v Birmingham final in 1956 but carried on in goal. It was all part of what the FA Cup Final stood for. Class. Style. Honour. Will to win. Triumph. It definitely had a shine on it, didn't it, the FA Cup?

I started experiencing *that* Wembley as a schoolboy. I went there to play for England Schoolboys against Scotland. Then, in February 1967, I made an appearance at the League Cup Final. It was QPR v West Brom, and the first of the League Cup Finals to be played there. The League Cup had only been going a few years, and most of the big clubs hadn't supported it at first. So to raise its profile the Football League came up with the idea of putting on an exhibition match between London and Birmingham Schoolboys before the big game. By the day of the final, though, it had been raining so much that that part of the programme was called off to protect the pitch. Instead we had to parade in line holding placards representing one of the clubs who had entered the competition that season. I was Carlisle United. I had the Carlisle kit on though in those days you wouldn't have known Carlisle United from anybody else playing in all blue. Instead of getting on the pitch to play, which would have been our dream at that point, we were walking round the dog track – you can imagine how cheated we felt.

But on 20th May I was back. It was the 1967 FA Cup Final – Chelsea v Tottenham Hotspur. I'd been training with Spurs most nights for a while by then, and a bit of loyalty was building up, but I hadn't yet signed for them and a lot of clubs were competing for my signature, including Chelsea.

I'd been at White Hart Lane one day towards the end of April when I turned a corner into the car park only to see Bill Nicholson walking towards me from the opposite direction. And he said: 'Steve, are you going to sign for us or not?'

'Well, Bill, er, er...'

'Because if you don't, you're not getting your cup final ticket.'

Tommy Docherty, the Chelsea manager, had already offered me and my whole family – Mum, Dad and my two brothers – a chauffeur-driven car to Wembley. From there I'd be conveyed to the team hotel, be part of the pre-match meal, get to listen to everything on the team bus and then attend the banquet after they'd won the cup.

Which they didn't, of course. And that tells you the different kind of mentality at Chelsea back then. All the glitz and glamour and a lot of hot air compared to Bill's straightforward, honest way of putting a bit of pressure on. That was the attitude that appealed to me, and it was his offer that I took up. My brother and I watched Tottenham win the FA Cup and that doesn't hurt the chances of you joining a particular club, does it? You're there watching it all, taking it all in, and you find yourself thinking, 'Some day I might be the one lifting that silverware.'

Once I was on Tottenham's books I would go past Wembley virtually every single day on the way to training. I wondered if I was ever going to play there as a professional footballer, although in fact that didn't take long. I was 19 when I took part in my first Wembley final – the 1971 League Cup Final when for the first time the competition drew a 100,000-capacity crowd at Wembley, and two goals by Martin Chivers did for Aston Villa. That was when, like London buses, the finals were all coming at once – we went on to be inaugural winners of the UEFA Cup in 1972. Back in 1963, Spurs had become the first British club to win in Europe by beating Atlético Madrid to take the European Cup Winners' Cup. Now our victory against Wolves made us the first British club to win two major European trophies. Ralph Coates' goal against Norwich won the League Cup again for us in 1973. Other sides might have dominated in the league in those days but Spurs were the great cup side and they were wonderful times for us. But we hadn't smelt an FA Cup Final since 1967 and that wasn't going to change any time soon.

"I watched Tottenham win the cup in 1967 and thought, 'Some day I might be the one lifting that silverware'"

Official Programme One Shilling

THE FOOTBALL ASSOCIATION CHALLENGE CUP COMPETITION

FINAL

SATURDAY MAY 20th 1967

CHELSEA
V
TOTTENHAM HOTSPUR

EMPIRE STADIUM

WEMBLEY

Stamps
of approval

100th F.A. CUP FINAL
9 May, 1981

HER MAJESTY Queen ELIZABETH THE QUEEN MOTHER

ARLINGTON COVER

THE 100th F.A. CUP FINAL
100
9 MAY 81 - WEMBLEY

TOTTENHAM HOTSPUR F.C.
v
MANCHESTER CITY F.C.
DAY OF EVENT COVER

The 100th Cup Final honoured by the presence of H.M. The Queen Mother resulted in a 1-1 draw. Both goals scored by Hutchinson of Manchester City. The replay on Thursday 14 May enabled Tottenham Hotspur to establish a new record, six appearances in F.A. Cup Finals — six wins, Tottenham Hotspur beating Manchester City 3-2. Receipts for the two matches totalled £12 million.

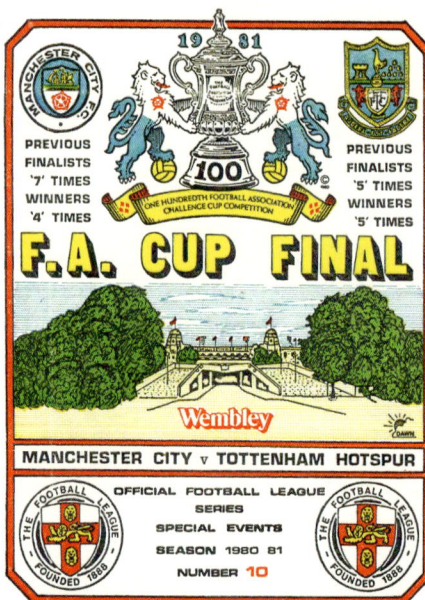

MANCHESTER CITY F.C.
PREVIOUS FINALISTS '7' TIMES WINNERS '4' TIMES

1981
100
ONE HUNDREDTH FOOTBALL ASSOCIATION CHALLENGE CUP COMPETITION

PREVIOUS FINALISTS '5' TIMES WINNERS '5' TIMES

F.A. CUP FINAL

Wembley

MANCHESTER CITY v TOTTENHAM HOTSPUR

THE FOOTBALL LEAGUE FOUNDED 1888

OFFICIAL FOOTBALL LEAGUE SERIES
SPECIAL EVENTS
SEASON 1980 81
NUMBER 10

THE FOOTBALL LEAGUE FOUNDED 1888

Tommy Hutchison scored for City after 30 mins. and after 80 mins. the ball was deflected off him for Spurs equaliser.

13½P

THE 100th F.A. CUP FINAL
100
9 MAY 81 - WEMBLEY

MATCH RESULT

MANCHESTER C. 1   TOTTENHAM H. 1
Hutchison   Hutchison (o.g.)
(After Extra Time)

The General Manager
Wembley Stadium Ltd
Empire Way,
Wembley, HA9 0DW

The Post Office produced a series of commemorative covers, stamps and postcards to mark the occasion, before and after the 100th FA Cup Final

Cover 1

1981

MANCHESTER CITY F.C.

PREVIOUS FINALISTS '7' TIMES
WINNERS '4' TIMES

100

ONE HUNDREDTH FOOTBALL ASSOCIATION CHALLENGE CUP COMPETITION

PREVIOUS FINALISTS '5' TIMES
WINNERS '5' TIMES

F.A. CUP FINAL

REPLAY

Wembley

MANCHESTER CITY v TOTTENHAM HOTSPUR

THE FOOTBALL LEAGUE FOUNDED 1888

OFFICIAL FOOTBALL LEAGUE SERIES
SPECIAL EVENTS
SEASON 1980 81
NUMBER 10

THE FOOTBALL LEAGUE FOUNDED 1888

THIS WAS THE FIRST EVER F.A. CUP REPLAY AT WEMBLEY.
City goalkeeper, Joe Corrigan, won 2 special trophies for his outstanding play.

Small Tortoiseshell

14p

WEMBLEY 730 PM 14 MY 81 MIDDX.

REPLAY MATCH RESULT

MANCHESTER C. 2   TOTTENHAM H. 3
Mackenzie, Reeves   Villa 2, Crooks

Cover 2

1981 FA CUP WINNERS

TOTTENHAM HOTSPUR

SPORTING LEGENDS - COMMEMORATIVE
MAY 14 1981

TOTTENHAM HOTSPUR 1   MANCHESTER CITY 1
Hutchison (o.g.)   Hutchison

TOTTENHAM HOTSPUR 3   MANCHESTER CITY 2
Villa (2)   MacKenzie
Crooks   Reeves

We will rise again

When I joined Spurs after the FA Cup triumph against Chelsea in 1967, I would never have believed that it would take 14 years to get back to the showpiece final again

Above: 'One of our own' – In his debut season at White Hart Lane, Steve's selfless midfield displays endeared him to the home faithful

Right: The end of an era. Jimmy Greaves (No.8) plays his final cup game for Spurs against Crystal Palace

If you look at how we got on in the FA Cup over the decade that followed, you get a good picture of the decline and fall of Tottenham Hotspur. In 1968 we lost to Liverpool in a fifth-round replay at Anfield. In 1969 we made it to the sixth round, where we went out to Manchester City at Maine Road. I was just a youth-team player then, but the following season I became part of the first-team squad and was in the side that played our third round game at Bradford City. On a skating rink of a pitch we should have got beaten but managed to earn a 2-2 draw. The replay at White Hart Lane was on ice as well, and we crushed them 5-0. Jimmy Greaves scored a brace that day. Three days later he found the net in our 2-1 win over Derby County – that was the last goal he ever scored for us.

Our fourth-round tie was home to Crystal Palace, which ended up in a disappointing draw. What happened after the replay at Selhurst Park is part of Tottenham Hotspur history. We lost 1-0, but it was the way we lost that drove Bill to act. He dropped five of us for the league game against Southampton three days later – Jimmy, Cyril Knowles, Joe Kinnear, Alan Gilzean and me. Bill kindly made a point of saying that in fact I was not dropped; I was being rested because I was playing so many games. Which was correct – that season I played for the A-team, the reserves, the first team, the England Youth team and in the FA Youth Cup games, and if someone had counted up the number of games I played that year it would probably have broken some kind of record. And in fact I didn't think I played that badly at Crystal

Palace and I'm normally a tough judge of myself. But he left out Jimmy and Gilly. The 'G-men'. Wow. What a brave decision that was.

Gilly, Knowlesy and Joe were brought back into the side in due course, and as for me I missed five games. It was the end of Jimmy's career at Tottenham, though. Bill gave our greatest-ever goalscorer the stark choice: 'Retire, see out your contract in the reserves, or move', and Jimmy opted to go to West Ham as the makeweight in the £200,000 deal that brought Martin Peters to us.

At the time, whatever was going on behind the scenes passed me by. I wasn't involved in the banter or the inside gossip. The naive 17-year-old me was just happy to turn up on time and play, avoid doing anything out of place and not make myself conspicuous. But Jimmy's game was all about scoring. He wasn't there for anything else. That season he'd played 33 games in all, 28 in the league, and scored 11 goals – one in three games. If you're scoring one in two then that counts as contributing in most people's eyes, but I suspect the cold, hard thinking was that if he was down to only one goal per three games then he didn't contribute enough. Whatever the case, something was going on that made Bill take that step, although the fact that Jimmy was being swapped for a 1966 World Cup winner sort of contained the outcry a bit. And well done Bill for his shrewdness in the transfer market. Can you imagine if he'd signed an out-and-out striker instead? Think of what pressure they'd have been under as a replacement for Jimmy Greaves. Some fans might have thought it was

> **"Jimmy's game was all about scoring. He wasn't there for anything else"**

Alan Mullery (left), Martin Peters (centre) and Steve Perryman formed a new and impressive midfield trio following Peters' arrival from West Ham. Surrounded by a wealth of experience, Perryman's game came on leaps and bounds

That season, our FA Cup campaign began with a 6-0 thrashing of tiddlers Margate. Sadly, I missed out on most of the fun. I rarely went off in games but around 10 minutes in I had a collision with a Margate player. My knee hit his, and it was the worst pain I've ever felt in my life. There was no question of staying on in the hope I'd run it off. I wasn't capable of running. Our fourth round opponents were Derby County, who had emerged under Brian Clough's management to win the 1972 League title. We got a very good 1-1 draw at the Baseball Ground and were 3-1 up with 10 minutes to go in the replay at the Lane. Then Roger Davies took over and spanked the life out of us.

Roger was one of the gems Cloughie's partner, Peter Taylor, had unearthed from non-league football. Mike England used to love saying how long it was since a number nine had scored against him. I don't know what number Roger was wearing that night but it was obvious he was Mike's man in terms of being the big chap up front. We went from 3-1 up to 5-3 down in extra time, and I don't quite know what happened in that last 10 minutes but when he scored that third goal we thought: 'That's done. Game over.' With Pat Jennings in your team then there must have been a mess up somewhere because it was rare for Pat to let a soft one in. I actually met Roger recently up in Derby. He's a nice man. I think that's the game that everyone wants to ask him about. That hat-trick is his *pièce de résistance*.

You could say 1973/74 was a watershed season for us, but for all the wrong reasons. In the League Cup we were knocked out by QPR in our first match, and the same thing happened in the FA Cup only this time to Leicester City. Things were slipping. Even so, we had some good results in Europe and got to the UEFA Cup Final – that could have made it a creditable season. But it wasn't to be. We drew 2-2 with Feyenoord in the home leg, so were already at a disadvantage when we went to Rotterdam the following week. When Chris McGrath had what appeared a perfectly good goal disallowed for offside, mayhem broke out on the terraces. As the rioting carried on during the half-time break, Bill appeared on the pitch to appeal to the fans for calm. His words were ignored, and some would say the episode was the straw that broke the camel's back for him. The 1974/75 season got under way, we lost four out of our first five games, and he called it a day.

wrong to get rid of Jimmy after everything he'd achieved for Spurs but you can't be sentimental in football. There's too much at stake. It's kill or be killed.

Gilly struck up a new scoring partnership with Martin Chivers and in 1971 we made it to the FA Cup sixth round, where after holding Liverpool to a draw at Anfield – a hell of a result – a 56,000 crowd saw us go down by a single goal at home. We felt a bit hard done by with that loss, but that was the season when our League Cup win over Aston Villa entitled us to a place in the following season's UEFA Cup and put us back on the big stage. Losing to Leeds in the FA Cup sixth round in 1972 was a disappointment, but victory over Wolves in the UEFA Cup was more than adequate compensation. It also meant we were back in Europe the following year, only for Liverpool to beat us in the semi-final on away goals.

"Spurs weren't in Europe any more. We weren't a great cup side any more."

Terry Neill took over. He'd been doing well as manager of Hull City, but before that he had spent 11 years playing centre-back for Arsenal – a lot of them as captain – so it was a bit of a shock appointment. Plus he had a job on his hands. As punishment for the Rotterdam riots UEFA ordered that our next two European games had to be played at least 250 kilometres from White Hart Lane, but the sanctions were immaterial. Spurs weren't in Europe any more. We weren't a great cup side any more. Over the next two seasons, we went out of the FA Cup as soon as we entered it. We lost to Nottingham Forest in 1975 and to Stoke in 1976. We drew 1-1 at home and got beaten 2-1 in the replay. Somehow it didn't matter very much that I scored my first FA Cup goal. We finished ninth in the league, which was a big improvement from the season before when we were fourth from bottom, but Terry didn't stay to build on it. He went back to Highbury, his spiritual home, and Keith Burkinshaw – who he had brought in as coach – took over.

For many Spurs fans, Keith's place in the pantheon of the club's managers is second only to Bill. Not that it seemed it would finish up that way in his first season in charge. If anything symbolised how bad things were it was our 1-0 away defeat to Cardiff in 1977. That was a shocker. If everyone's giving all they've got and you lose on the day that's one thing, but we lay down and died. It was the season we were relegated. Ten years on from beating Chelsea at Wembley, we had reached rock bottom.

But that season in Division Two was the start of the long road back. We might have gone out to Bolton Wanderers early on in the FA Cup, but that year saw the emergence of a 20-year-old who became

Bench press(ure) – the tension shows as Terry Neill, Bill Nicholson's unlikely successor, plus his staff (including the legendary Johnny Wallis) and players battle relegation in 1975

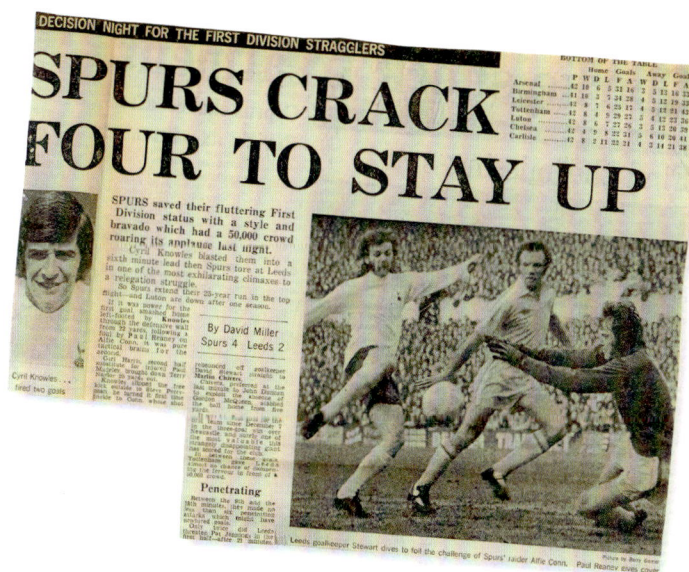

DECISION NIGHT FOR THE FIRST DIVISION STRAGGLERS

SPURS CRACK FOUR TO STAY UP

By David Miller
Spurs 4 Leeds 2

SPURS saved their fluttering First Division status with a style and bravado which had a 50,000 crowd roaring its applause last night.

one of the greatest players ever to wear the shirt in Glenn Hoddle, and we returned to Division One at the first attempt. One of the first things Keith said when he was given the manager's job was, 'I'm going to make this a team', and from the side that was promoted back at the first attempt, he had me and Glenn. The following year brought two of Tottenham's most sensational signings of all time – Ossie Ardiles and Ricky Villa, our World Cup winners. We still went out of the FA Cup that season, but this time we made it to the sixth round where Manchester United knocked us out after a replay. In 1980 we lost by one goal to Liverpool at the same stage – a fluke volley by Terry McDermott. Nobody believed he meant it. The ball came to him and it was a bumpy pitch – I don't think he lifted the ball himself, it came to him and he followed up from 30 yards out. But it was a great goal anyway. It won Goal of the Season, and they went on to win the title.

But the point is that we'd done nothing in the FA Cup for years. The desperation for a trophy had been growing by the minute, but now at last we were on the up. From 1973 the momentum had been downwards; it had it gone as low as it could get. But then it started building up again with two successive quarter-finals. So actually if you were looking for a trend, you could say that in the early 1970s Spurs were a cup team, then in the mid-1970s we weren't much of a cup team at all.

But then in the summer of 1980 Keith revamped our strike force with two more signings in Steve Archibald and Garth Crooks, and suddenly it looked like we might be a cup team once again. The key components of the side were in place now: Glenn and me from the relegation season, then Ossie and Ricky – two World Cup winners

Relegation finally came in 1977 but on the last day of the season there was a mood of defiance. Steve was consoled by fans in the West Stand (above), a sign that the captain and his team-mates would be supported in their efforts to rebuild and – as a banner marched around the pitch by two supporters promised (right) – return to the top flight

"That season in Division Two was the start of the long road back"

– whose arrival represented our 'promotion' to the next level They gave us built-in status and made our team decent enough for Archie and Garth to join us while thinking: 'I'm joining a club that might win something.'

I think I played a part in Garth coming to us, as it happens. Ray Evans – who signed pro for Tottenham the same year as me – later went on to play for Stoke, where Garth had come up through the youth team. Garth had let it be known that he was looking for a move and Ray phoned me and asked, 'Do you think your manager might be interested?'

'I don't know, but I'll put it to him,' I said.

That started the process. It doesn't mean anything comes of that sort of conversation every time, but it was the Tottenham link between Ray and me that helped Garth get to us. I think Garth was very interested in getting to London anyway because he was already doing a bit of DJ-ing and that was obviously easier to do in London than anywhere else. I'm not saying it dominated his thinking, but it was in his mind that if he was going to London he might just get involved in Capital Radio and all that sort of stuff.

It sounds disrespectful to the players who were there before Archie and Garth, but actually they weren't at that level. They didn't have the pace. Chris Jones was a very good mover. Terry Gibson was all heart and energy and everything that went with that. Colin Lee was a jumper. But none of them had the sort of cutting-edge class that Archie and Garth had. Break through, one v one, goal! They both wanted to score. That might sound stupid – why would you be on the pitch if you didn't want to score? But I think they *expected* to score, and if one couldn't score they wanted the other one to score. They were a partnership that fought for each other. And the six of us were the nucleus of the team Keith was building for the 1980s.

Before the start of the 1980/81 season we went on tour to Sweden. At every training session and every pre-match meeting we talked about what we were going to do, and what we could do better, that season. We had a plan from start to finish. The most pre-thought out idea of the lot involved Glenn being a very special midfield player and me playing alongside the centre-back, bringing the ball out and running between two players to create the hole to play Glenn in.

It was building up for us to do something special. We all knew what the FA Cup meant, and we'd gone 14 years without getting our name on it. Fourteen years and I'd been a Spurs player for every one of them. At 20, in 1972, I was made vice-captain for our UEFA Cup home tie against Lyn Oslo when Martin Peters failed a fitness test. I took over as captain when Martin left in 1975. On 30th April 1980, against Wolves, I made my 473rd league appearance for the club, breaking the record previously held by Pat Jennings. I was 28 and in my playing prime. I'd led us back from relegation. Now it was my job to lead us to glory.

Back in Division One after just one season away, Spurs strengthened by pulling off one of the most famous transfer coups ever as manager Keith Burkinshaw recruited two World Cup winners in Argentina's Ricky Villa and Ossie Ardiles

The start of something special

With a new stand being built and the team starting to click on the pitch, as the FA Cup third round draw was made there was an optimism at White Hart Lane despite the tough times

By Julie Welch

The date was 3rd January 1981. The Western world was still reeling from the shooting of John Lennon outside his apartment in New York. Margaret Thatcher was Prime Minister, the Yorkshire Ripper was still on the loose. and Prince Charles had started dating Lady Diana Spencer. Liverpool were top of the league, leading Aston Villa on goal difference. Ipswich Town were a point behind with two games in hand.

Winter at White Hart Lane was even colder than usual. The recession might have meant gates were falling all over the country. The policy at Tottenham Hotspur might have always been to spend money on the ground or the squad, but not both. Now, though, the board of directors had gone big; along with upgrading the strike force they were lashing out on a new stand, and westerly gales howled across the construction site where the old West Stand had been. Even so, the usual Spurs brand of pacy, free-flowing football was filling up its remaining three sides, not to mention contributing to the goals for and – sometimes more often than was desirable – goals against tally.

The old year had ended with recession and rising job losses. The town of Consett in County Durham boasted the highest unemployment rate in the UK after the closure of its steelworks in September 1980, and inflation was running at 18 per cent. The

> "The board of directors had gone big; along with upgrading the strike force they were lashing out on a new stand"

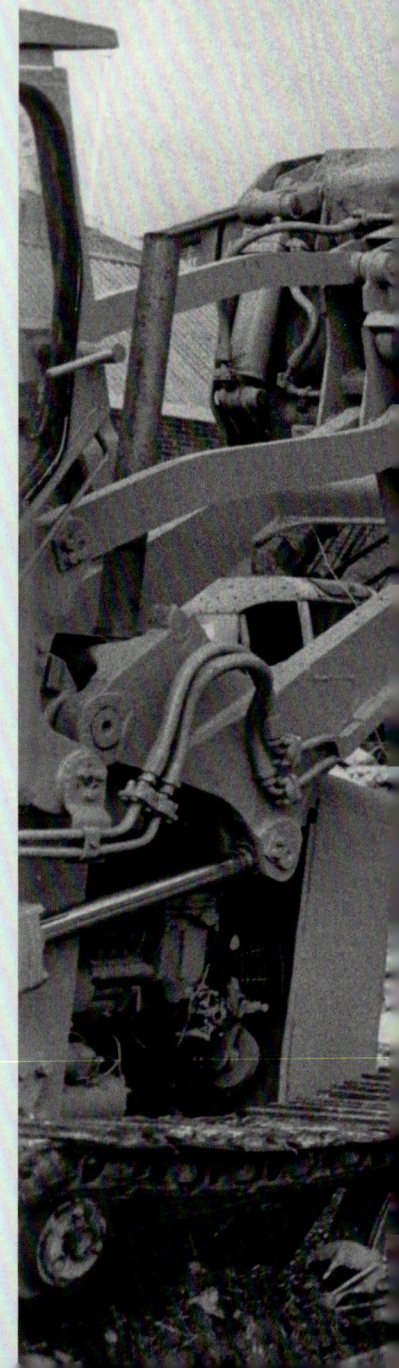

Vauxhall Viva had been superseded by the Astra, British Leyland had launched the Metro and the Ford Escort Mark III represented the wheels of choice for the nation's boy racers. Great Britain had won five gold medals at the Moscow Olympics and Bjorn Borg beat John McEnroe in the men's singles final at Wimbledon.

The 1979/80 football season had closed with Liverpool as league champions. Second Division West Ham were temporarily feted in N17, having beaten Arsenal 1-0 to get their hands on the FA Cup through a sight as commonplace as Ralph Coates with a perm: a Trevor Brooking header. The TV viewing figures for the match topped even the live broadcast of the SAS storming the Iranian Embassy to free 26 hostages held by a six-man terrorist team from the Democratic Revolutionary Front for the Liberation of Arabistan. At the end of May, Nottingham Forest won their second successive European Cup, a goal by their portly winger John Robertson enough to clinch victory in Madrid over Hamburg SV, the German league champions. But that summer Spurs fans had a reason to be cheerful, too. Keith Burkinshaw had persuaded the board to fork out for Steve Archibald and Garth Crooks.

Archibald was a taciturn Glaswegian, the Stoke-born Crooks a witty showman with a side-hustle in local radio. This pairing of temperamental opposites came good straight away. On the first day of the new season, a 43,398 crowd, plus one or

"Archibald was a taciturn Glaswegian, the Stoke-born Crooks a witty showman"

two demolition men perched on the rubble, saw Crooks score his debut goal against Nottingham Forest. In midweek the other half of Tottenham's new big-money duo provided a brace in a 4-3 defenestration of Crystal Palace, Terry Venables's so-called 'Team of the Eighties'. There followed a series of highs and lows, including the defeat in October by bottom-of-the-table Manchester City. But the message was getting through. Tottenham Hotspur was a team on the up.

While all this was going on, the early rounds of the 1980/81 FA Cup were being contested. The action had got under way that August with a preliminary round of 74 clubs featuring ding-dong battles between outfits such as Worsbrough Bridge Miners Welfare and Ottery St Mary. This was followed by four qualifying rounds where the big guns such as Billington Synthonia and Appleby Frodingham were allowed in. Finally, in November, came the first and second rounds proper where clubs from Divisions Three and Four entered the fray. Once that was done and dusted it was time for the draw for third round, in which the proles got the chance to knock out the gods of the First and Second Divisions.

The draw for each round took place at the Football Association's headquarters in Lancaster Gate, where a row of old men in blazers watched solemnly as another old man in a blazer rifled through a velvet bag of clinking steel balls. Over the next few months, kids would be hiding in the school toilets on a Monday morning to listen to the draw live on smuggled transistor radios. Fans would sidle out of work to switch on car radios and plot journeys to ramshackle football stadiums with floodlights on pylons. The FA Cup meant something. Something big. Replays, and sometimes replays of the replays (no penalty shootouts in those days), whipped up the national feeling of

anticipation. The semi-finals would be held at England's most prestigious stadiums, such as the stately home-esque Villa Park or Sheffield Wednesday's Hillsborough, with its excitingly modern cantilevered roof. To win at Wembley was to earn immortality.

This season the draw for the third round was pretty nuts, with a high number of top-tier clubs due to meet each other. Ipswich Town were pitted against Aston Villa, so one of the title contenders would be booted out straight off. Arsenal, who were fighting it out for fourth place in the table, had to go to Goodison. Even so the mood at Highbury was complacent given that Everton were struggling in the last throes of the Gordon Lee era.

Manchester United's new signing from Nottingham Forest, Garry Birtles, had forgotten where the net was and their opponents, Brighton, were managed by the pugnacious former Spurs captain, Alan Mullery, who would relish the chance of giving last season's runners-up a hammering. There was a mid-table clash between Leeds and Coventry. Most people expected Wolves to ease past Stoke.

The basket case of the First Division, Crystal Palace, had to visit Maine Road, home of Manchester City, whose early form had been similarly dire, prompting the season's first managerial sacking – the fedora-hatted, Playboy Bunny appreciator Malcolm Allison. He had been replaced by John Bond, who had brought about a slight improvement but few expected them to progress much further.

Of the other First Division clubs, all-powerful Liverpool had the jammiest tie of the lot – Altrincham. The non-leaguers had a fine history of giant-killing but for them to win at Anfield was most definitely flying-pigs territory. Lawrie McMenemy's Southampton, stocked with veteran internationals, had one of the easier draws – against Chelsea, mired in debt in the Second Division and trying to shrug off the taint of rip-roaring '70s hooliganism.

Spurs drew Second Division opposition too, but the challenge was tougher. Much tougher. QPR were now managed by Tottenham old boy Terry Venables. A member of the 1967 FA Cup-winning side, he knew what made the club tick. The season before, he had been manager of newly promoted Crystal Palace and had taken them to the top of the First Division before eventually finishing 13th, one place above Spurs. From then on it had been all downhill and, disgruntled by the Crystal Palace board's failure to spend the profits from the sale of land to Sainsbury's, the man regarded as the cleverest coach in the country left at the start of October to work his magic at Loftus Road. The tie was quickly written up by the press as 'a London derby between two of the game's most cerebral sides'.

Tottenham's form in the run-up to the QPR tie had been true to type, combining attacking brilliance and a defence with a mat in front of it saying 'Welcome'. In mid-December they had beaten Manchester City 2-1 and followed that up by giving Ipswich Town's title pretentions a hefty kick with a 5-3 thrashing featuring goals from Perryman, Ardiles, Archibald, Hoddle and Crooks. True to form, three days later they suffered a 4-1 spanking by Middlesbrough at Ayresome Park. Boxing Day brought a home 4-4 ding-dong with Southampton and on the following day Spurs went to Carrow Road to eke out a 2-2 draw against Norwich. The team was still a work in progress. Graham Roberts had only just made his debut, while Ossie Ardiles was thousands of miles away playing for Argentina in the Gold Cup in Uruguay.

Spurs weren't consistent enough to fight for the title. But this was Burkinshaw's fifth season in charge. He needed to win a trophy. The club needed to keep together a team which promised to become a force in the league again. For that to happen, they had to hold onto their key players. Tottenham's headache was that Hoddle, Ardiles and Villa could, in theory, all leave at the end of the season. With the directors committed to the rebuilding of the West Stand it was imperative that Tottenham had a good cup run to keep their star players and pacify the bank.

They had to win this tie.

Far left: Garth Crooks scores on his debut for Spurs against European Cup holders Nottingham Forest. His signing, along with Steve Archibald, was the final piece in the jigsaw that enabled Spurs to challenge for major honours again

Below left: A new direction for Spurs was also in the offing at board level, as joining Arthur Richardson (centre) and the club's directors at White Hart Lane was a new face in Douglas Alexiou (far right)

FA CUP THIRD ROUND QPR v SPURS

My neck of the woods

Drawing QPR in the first round meant a return to my old stomping ground and a match-up against my former team-mate and sharp-witted Spurs legend, Terry Venables

Steve Perryman joined Spurs in 1967, despite the best efforts of several other London clubs – including QPR – to sign him

SOCCER NEWS – by JAMES CONNOLLY

Spurs scoop London rivals for schools star

SPURS, the confirmed spenders, have just beaten all the big clubs for a player who didn't cost a penny. Yesterday, England Schoolboys inside forward **STEPHEN PERRYMAN** joined them as an apprentice professional.

Spurs chief scout Charlie Faulkner should be very happy with his coup. Manchester United and all the top London clubs were in on the greatest schoolboy chase since Terry Venables signed for Chelsea some years ago.

Q.P.R. in at the death with Spurs, made a dramatic late night effort to sign Perryman on Friday.

'BETTER FUTURE'

"Stephen trained at White Hart Lane last winter and liked the set-up," his father, Ronald Perryman told me last night. "I let him make up his own mind. He felt that he had a better future with Spurs and I am quite happy about him going there as an apprentice. Now it is entirely up to him."

Stephen, whose home is at Northolt (Middlesex), will be 16 in December.

● Young Stephen, now on Spurs books, gets in some heading practice—in his garden !

Queens Park Rangers and I went back a long way. Playing them was almost like a home match. I still lived on the west side of town and if Spurs had a fixture there I would just walk from the station and join the team at Loftus Road. Back when I was growing up you supported your local club, and for me and my brothers – Ted and Bill – it was Rangers, with some occasional visits to Brentford, so on the day we started our '81 campaign I walked much the same walk as I'd made many times before.

In those days Rangers had been one of the clubs pulling out all the stops to get me to sign apprentice forms. Two of their players, Jim Langley and Frank Sibley, would pick me up at our house and take me to training. Bill Dodgin, the manager, took me to play golf, and Rodney Marsh – their star player – was roped in to present me with his shirt. The club was run by good people, it had a reputation for developing young players, and I could walk to their training ground from where I lived. But they were in Division Three at that time, whereas West Ham, another of the clubs romancing me, were in Division One and had Bobby Moore, Martin Peters and Geoff Hurst – what role models for a young footballer.

It would have been a nightmare to travel across town to the outer reaches of East London for training, though – even worse than the two hours it took to get to Tottenham. And that indoor gym at Tottenham held a strong attraction for me – that was where I could see myself training every day. You could just feel that this was a place where you could improve and that was a major pull.

Arsenal, another of the clubs after me, didn't feel warm to me. Tottenham certainly weren't all over you, they weren't cuddlers, but it felt warm. So my heart was saying, 'Stick to what you know – QPR, home territory'. My head was probably saying 'West Ham' because of its players. In the middle ground was the common-sense choice. Bill Nicholson was a great man who had been successful. I could see he was straight and fair. The facilities were excellent. One close, one too far away and one do-able. So Tottenham it was.

Terry Venables was manager of QPR in 1981. He and I went back quite a way, too. When I joined Tottenham in 1967, they had just won the FA Cup. Terry had been part of the Spurs side that had beaten Chelsea, though his time at the club was ending just as mine was beginning. Dave Mackay always seemed to have a bit of a thing against him. They grated on each other. You can imagine why – Terry was the cheeky chappie from Dagenham with fingers in all sorts of pies outside the game and Dave was the fierce, focused Scot. We'd see them come out a number of times from the gym when they'd obviously been at each other. I don't know that Terry ever got on that well with Bill Nick and Eddie Baily, either. I'm guessing this from afar, but their characters wouldn't have aligned. He didn't work

> **"Back when I was growing up you supported your local club and for me and my brothers it was Rangers"**

THE WEMBLEY SETTING FOR THE 100th F.A. CUP SEASON

ACTION FROM SPURS' EARLIER TIES

Above — v Hull City — at home in the Fourth Round.

Top Right — v Queens Park Rangers away in the Third Round.

Bottom Right — CHRIS HUGHTON scores against Coventry City here in Round 5.

hard enough for Eddie, and he wasn't consistently good enough for Bill. The game was changing, influenced by the 1966 World Cup. Everyone was doing away with wingers. Bill probably hung on longer than most, but it was important to him how much ground you covered. It was almost as if Terry was a good footballer but couldn't do the running that is needed when you are outnumbered.

Also they knew he had eyes for opportunities elsewhere, and that wouldn't have suited them either. You had to be Tottenham-minded for Bill. Terry's sidelines were understandable – you've got to plan for when the game's over, and you use what you've got. In Bill's eyes, though, there might have been something wrong with that attitude. Even the fact that I had a sports goods shop didn't sit right with him. If I was playing poorly at some point, he'd say, 'You're standing too long in that shop. Go home and rest.'

Bill bided his time in terms of replacing him, but Terry left for QPR in 1969 and then, five years later, joined Crystal Palace where he started his coaching career as part of Malcolm Allison's firm and took over in 1976. Phil Holder, who had been my best mate since we were apprentices at Tottenham, was on Palace's books by that time and one day he spoke to me about something they were doing in training with Terry that he thought would do me a big favour in my

Bill Nicholson talks to his players prior to the 1967 FA Cup Final, and paying close attention is Terry Venables (second from the right), who would go on to become one of the best coaches of his generation

game. 'Don't run straight with the ball,' Phil said. 'Run at angles, then if you get closed down you can always turn back to where you just came from.' Phil showed me the drill they were doing and it was typical of Terry's super-clever football brain. Typical Dutch – turn left, get shut down, turn back on your right – the sort of move you'd do in basketball.

Terry was sharp, no doubt about that – a new, thinking type of coach who asked the right questions of the right people, had opinions, and was always on the lookout for developments in the game. He could turn a group of players on, especially young players, yet he knew how to handle older players as well. I couldn't really see a weakness in him, football-wise. Interestingly, he had sought me out five months back at Selhurst Park. It was our second league game of the season, when Spurs had won 4-3 and Terry was still in charge at Crystal Palace. It had been one of my best games. I was playing alongside the centre-backs and I just kept bringing the ball out like we did in the Second Division days. I didn't get this feeling many times but I did during that season in the second tier – a sense I was controlling the pace of the game. That August day at Selhurst Park I got to experience that feeling again, and it seemed Terry noticed because afterwards he approached me in the Players' Lounge. 'I want to meet you for lunch,' he said, 'and I want you to tell me what's on your mind when you're bringing the ball out.'

It was very clever of Terry to have picked up on it. He had seen something he liked and thought, 'What's behind that? What's your thinking?' But was he trying to tap me up? He was certainly trying to tap something. If nothing else he was definitely tapping my brain. The thing is, I never came home from training and thought, 'Today the doors are opened to my understanding of how to play.' There wasn't one eureka moment. It was more a sort of drip, drip, drip. But what I was doing was very new to the English game. The only other example I can think of was how Morten Olsen, the captain of Anderlecht, brought the ball forward when we beat them in the UEFA Cup Final. He was brilliant at it, but I'd not seen anyone else do it. I think this was Terry seeing something he liked, either in what I was doing or in me as a player, and of course if a player's been at a club a long time then at some point he might be thinking about leaving, mightn't he?

"Terry was sharp, no doubt about that - a new, thinking type of coach who asked the right questions of the right people"

Always an innovative student of the game, former Spurs player Terry Venables had taken the helm at QPR in 1980

Out of respect for the tip that Phil had passed on to me, I perhaps should have accepted his invitation. Who knows what that lunch might have led to? If nothing else, it might have led to me being on his staff in later days. But would I ever want to work with him? Had I got enough that he would want to work with me? The lunch would have been advantageous for us both but I probably thought Terry was a bit too clever for me at the time, and therefore he would have gained more out of it than I would have done. So I decided not to go – why would I want to give away the key to something I did to the manager of a rival club?

This was even more relevant now Terry was managing QPR. For some years Rangers had been the classic yo-yo club. They won the League Cup in 1967, finished the season as Division Three champions, achieved back-to-back promotions to Division One, and then got relegated after one season. In the mid-1970s, when Dave Sexton was their manager, they returned to the top tier and in 1975/76 missed out on the title by one point. After that they went down again. So they were too good for the Second Division and not good enough to stay in Division One, a situation that Terry had probably been brought in to rectify.

We were playing better football than the early '70s side but we were a young team still in the process of being built, and maybe that was to our detriment. Sometimes we were playing without thinking about the result. At times during the first part of the season we were like West Ham could be, opening the game up so much that when a move broke down we were wide open ourselves. A coach like Terry would be smart enough to set QPR up to exploit that.

He was very good at set-pieces and those little extra details – not just what might happen on the day, but what he could control on the day. He obviously liked talent, and would have had huge respect for Glenn, which meant that he would be looking to his players to dampen him down. They also probably wouldn't be averse to a bit of skulduggery, like blocking off or pulling people out of the wall to make a gap they could shoot through. They'd be told to get at our centre-backs, because most people thought they could. Terry was just sharp, very sharp. He worked out a lot of things beforehand. He was that sort of character. Without being completely over the top, he would do whatever was necessary. After all, his team wasn't as good as ours, and if they just lay down and died, they weren't going to win,

continues on p34

QPR 0 Spurs 0

3rd January 1981, Loftus Road. Att: 28,892

By Julie Welch

If any Spurs fans out there thought it was going to be a doddle reaching the next round of the FA Cup they were soundly disabused of that notion at Loftus Road yesterday.

It has been said of this Tottenham side that Glenn Hoddle is the leader of the orchestra and Steve Perryman the man who gets the orchestra there on time, but there was fat chance of sweet music while a substantial part of the string section was missing in the form of Ossie Ardiles, who is currently billeted in Uruguay on international duty for Argentina. QPR's own creative maestro, Tony Currie, was out injured too, and with both teams frustrated by a 50mph gale that meant controlling the ball was like trying to nail custard to the ceiling, a match that had been flagged up as a must-see clash between two of London's more entertaining sides ended in frantic stalemate.

It was less than five months ago that Terry Venables had the opportunity to observe Tottenham's strengths and weaknesses at first hand. Since October he has been tasked with leading QPR back to the sunlit uplands of the First Division, but back then he was still manager of the Crystal Palace team that received a first-day-of-the-new-season 5-3 drubbing at White Hart Lane by a swings-and-roundabouts outfit that combines two terrifyingly good new strikers with a midfield driven by Perryman's unique combination of brains and steel and a defence of the kind that has, in the last month alone, shipped 19 goals.

QPR's game plan, it followed, was to test Spurs' generosity with a non-stop onslaught on Barry Daines, but so inept was their attack that any lapses by the away side went unpunished. Tottenham's usual open, free-flowing play, meanwhile, had to be ditched much of the time in favour of stonewalling. What resulted was a fraught but tedious 90 minutes featuring only two good chances, one on either side.

Steve Archibald missed his with 11 minutes gone and Terry Fenwick fluffed his with 20 minutes left. In between all that, Terry Yorath was so busy firefighting that he hardly ventured as far as the centre circle, and after the restart Spurs had to do without their other World Cup winner when Ricky Villa limped off. From then on, the prospect of a replay at White Hart Lane on Wednesday seemed inevitable.

Afterwards, both managers were in a testy mood. 'They weren't playing their natural game,' complained Venables.

'You have to tighten up in FA Cup games,' Keith Burkinshaw grumped back. 'One slip and you could be out.'

By the night of the replay the wind might have dropped, but Ardiles will still be missing and quite possibly Villa too. Since their triumph in the 1972 UEFA Cup the only thing Spurs have won is promotion back to the First Division after being relegated in 1977. Tottenham folklore dictates that the club habitually wins something when there's a '1' in the year. On yesterday's showing, you wouldn't want to put your money on it just yet.

Steve Archibald goes on the attack at Loftus Road, but he couldn't add to his goal tally in a tense and nervous cup tie

THE 100th F.A. CUP SEASON

Action from our Third Round tie with Queens Park Rangers.

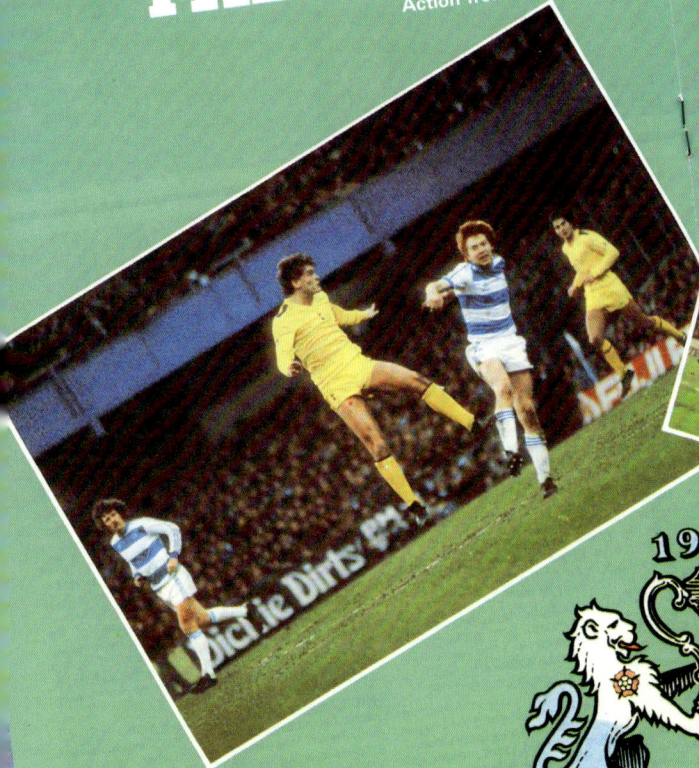

GLENN HODDLE leaps to head the ball in the goalless draw at Shepherd's Bush.

JOHN LACY supports the attack in the replay, won here 3-1 by spurs.

1981

THE FOOTBALL ASSOCIATION CHALLENGE CUP

100

ONE HUNDREDTH FOOTBALL ASSOCIATION CHALLENGE CUP COMPETITION

QPR

Manager: TERRY VENABLES
Colours: Blue and White Hoops, White Shorts

JOHN BURRIDGE
John has made appearances with five League clubs starting his career with Workington. In 1975 he signed for Crystal Palace and made 92 League appearances prior to joining us recently.

DON SHANKS
Don combines the ability to play in a defensive role at right-back with the skill to switch to an attacking midfield role when the occasion demands. He joined us from Luton for £40,000 in 1975.

IAN GILLARD
Ian is a former England under-23 and full international who first played in the Rangers' side in 1968/69. He is now the club's longest serving player.

TERRY FENWICK
Signed professional for Crystal Palace in 1976 after being a member of their successful Youth Team. He made his first team debut in 1977 and has since been selected for England's Under-21 squad.

STEVE WICKS
Steve made well over 100 League appearances for Chelsea before joining Derby for £275,000 in 1979. Within a few months he was back in London with Rangers following a £300,000 transfer.

GLENN ROEDER
Though Glenn most often plays as a central defender, he has also proved an outstandingly creative midfield player. An England "B" international, he joined the club from Orient for £250,000 in 1978.

MIKE FLANAGAN
Mike was once on Spurs' books as an apprentice but made his name as a prolific goalscorer with Charlton before moving to Crystal Palace for £650,000.

ANDY KING
Andy earned a reputation as a goalscoring midfield man at Luton and Everton before signing for us in Rangers this season for £400,000.

SIMON STAINROD
Simon has scored many goals for us for £275,000 from Oldham where he was a top scorer last season. He began his career with Sheffield United and signed for Oldham in 1979.

GARY WADDOCK
Gary made remarkable strides after gaining a place in our League eleven last season. He was picked twice for the Republic of Ireland and is very much a part of their current World Cup squad.

BARRY SILKMAN
Much travelled Barry joined us from Brentford this season. After starting his League career with Hereford, he played for Crystal Palace, Plymouth, Manchester City and Maccabi before joining the Bees this season.

DAVID McCREADIE

Referee
Mr. G. REEVES (Leicester)

Linesmen
Mr. J. ROOST — Yellow Flag
Mr. GERMEY — Red Flag

TOTTENHAM HOTSPUR

Manager: KEITH BURKINSHAW
Colours: Yellow Shirts, Yellow Shorts

1	**BARRY DAINES**
2	Barry has deservedly come into his own over the past three years, during which period has been the first-team goalkeeper for much of the time. He had previously spent more than four years as the patient deputy and he made his League bow in 1971/72.
3	**TERRY YORATH**
4	Terry, who has been capped by Wales on 56 occasions, joined Spurs from Coventry for £300,000 in 1979. He began his career with Leeds and moved on to Coventry in a £135,000 deal in 1976. Terry is now hoping to move into coaching management.
5	**CHRIS HUGHTON**
6	Though Chris can only take a place in Spurs' first-team last season, he was quickly elevated to full international level. Now he is a fixture in the Republic of Ireland team, winning his eighth cap against Cyprus in November.
7	**GRAHAM ROBERTS**
8	Tottenham paid Weymouth £35,000 – believed to be a record for a non-League player – for Graham last May and he has recently been making the occasional appearance in their First Division side.
9	**JOHN LACY**
10	John has been back at the heart of the Spurs' defence this season after missing most of last term. He began as a Fulham amateur and made his League debut for the Cottagers in 1972. Spurs paid £200,000 for him in 1978.
11	**STEVE PERRYMAN**
12	Steve has been a member of the Spurs' senior squad since making his bow in 1969. He spent his early years in midfield and was capped by the England under-23 at that position. Now he has become an outstanding centre-back.
	PAUL MILLER
	Paul developed in the reserve sides at White Hart Lane and got his initial chance in the first-team two seasons ago. He became a fairly permanent member of the first-team last season, but has appeared in midfield this term.
	STEVE ARCHIBALD
	Steve had already netted 15 goals before the Christmas games and was fully justifying the £800,000 fee Spurs paid Aberdeen for him in the summer. A Scottish full and under-21 international, Steve began his career with Clyde and moved on to Aberdeen in 1978.
	RICARDO VILLA
	Ricardo joined Spurs from Racing Club of Argentina, shortly after helping Argentina to the World Cup final in 1978. Spurs invested a joint fee of £750,000 in Ricardo and Ardiles who became the first foreigners signed on the English club after a change in the law.
	GLENN HODDLE
	Glenn now seems certain to play an important role in England's 1982 World Cup challenge, having won four caps so far. He has been in the Spurs side since 1975 and last season he was top scorer with 23 goals.
	GARTH CROOKS
	Spurs invested a £700,000 in Garth's transfer from Stoke in the summer and he is certainly doing the scoring job expected of him – he had scored 12 goals before Christmas. He was on three occasions the top scorer for Stoke.

TONY BOLWIN (Pig 9)

	QPR	0 (0)	
TOTTENHAM HOTSPUR		0 (0)	TOTTENHAM HOTSPUR

FORWARD MARCH!

Watch the goals go in next time—Venables

By REG DRURY   QPR 0 Tottenham 0

Above: Midfield mayhem as Spurs find it hard going against their Second Division rivals

Right: Glenn Hoddle in acrobatic action during the replay at White Hart Lane. He scored Tottenham's third and decisive goal in the replay to put the tie to bed

"We were actually lucky we hung on enough to get a replay"

continued from p31

were they? So if anyone was going to cause an upset, Terry seemed a likely candidate.

Even so, we only had a short team talk that day, as per normal. There's a danger of telling your team too much. It puts them on edge. Keith and Peter would brief us about the opposition, but it was never overdone. Their attitude was that an opposition player might have looked great on the day they saw him but he was actually not that good. After all, if an opponent had watched me play against AC Milan in our 1972 UEFA Cup semi-final they'd have said, 'Close that Perryman down, don't let him get a shot in.' Our route to goal back then was Martin Peters shooting from the edge of the box or Chiv running

and smashing one in from the halfway line, like he did in the final against Wolves. It certainly wasn't me...

Maybe we weren't on edge enough in that first game against QPR, because we had a very, very poor game – we could easily have lost. Anyone can beat anyone, we know that, especially in a cup tie. Bookmakers wouldn't make any money if there weren't some surprises on the way. The team wasn't at full strength. Ossie was on international duty. Chrissie Hughton had picked up a knock in our Boxing Day game and Ricky was injured in the second half and had to go off. We were actually lucky we hung on to get a replay.

But if you're going to win the FA Cup, these are the things you have to overcome. An iffy display. A big player not available. As important as Ossie was to us, one less player on a given day is not the end of the world, and the way things panned out at Loftus Road, Terry Yorath – playing in defensive midfield – stepped up to be man of the match. We took full advantage of our second chance, beating them 3-1 at home the following Wednesday, and deservedly so.

You always kept an eye on the other results. There were teams you wouldn't want to be drawn against. Ipswich Town, one of them, had knocked out Aston Villa. Everton had beaten Arsenal and Nottingham Forest had scraped through against Bolton. Liverpool were through against Altrincham. No surprises there. The draw for the next round had been made on Monday morning so we already knew who we faced next and it wasn't one of the big guns. Instead we were home to Third Division Hull City.

You're not really up there till you do something great in the league – which we weren't capable of – or a claim a cup victory. With a draw like that, maybe this was going to be our year?

Three injured, Ossie's away, but Spurs' toast is..

ABSENT FRIENDS

🏆

3RD ROUND

Archibald moves in

TOTTENHAM HOTSPUR
Football & Athletic Co. Ltd.

TOTTENHAM HOTSPUR V Q.P.R.
F.A. CUP 3RD RD REPLAY K.O. 7-30
WEDNESDAY 7TH JANUARY 1981
EAST TERRACE ENCLOSURE

PRICE
(INC. VAT)   ENTRANCE

£1.80   55301071   37-39

TO BE RETAINED

1882
AUDERE·EST·FACERE
TOTTENHAM HOTSPUR

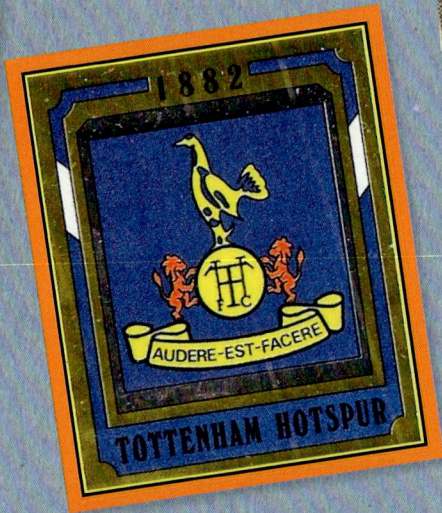

Tottenham Hotspur
3(2)
Manager: Keith Burkinshaw
(White Shirts, Blue Shorts, White Stockings)

Queens Park Rangers
1(0)
Manager: Terry Venables
(Red Shirts, Red Shorts, Red Stockings)

Tottenham Hotspur	No.	Queens Park Rangers
BARRY DAINES	1	JOHN BURRIDGE
TERRY YORATH	2	DON SHANKS
PAUL MILLER	3	IAN GILLARD
GRAHAM ROBERTS	4	TERRY FENWICK
JOHN LACY	5	STEVE WICKS
STEVE PERRYMAN	6	GLENN ROEDER
GARRY BROOKE	7	MIKE FLANAGAN
STEVE ARCHIBALD	8	ANDY KING
RICARDO VILLA	9	SIMON STAINROD
GLENN HODDLE	10	TONY CURRIE
GARTH CROOKS	11	BARRY SILKMAN
	12	

(handwritten): DON McALLISTER, TONY GALVIN, MIKE HAZARD, DAVID McCREERY)

OFFICIALS

Referee: MR. PETER REEVES
(Leicestershire)

MR. PETER REEVES of Leicester, who had charge of the first match at Rangers' ground on Saturday, is again in control this evening. He started refereeing with the Leicestershire County F.A. in 1966 and graduated through the Football Combination to the Football League. He has refereed a number of big matches and was appointed to the F.I.F.A. list in season 1978-79. Mr. Reeves is employed as a sales director for a hosiery company. He played for England schoolboys in his youth, became a professional with Leicester City and Mansfield Town. His other interests include walking, tennis, squash, cricket, gardening and crossword puzzles.

LINESMEN:

MR. R. B. BANNING
(Hampshire)
Red Flag

MR. D. J. AXCELL
(Essex)
Yellow Flag

FIRST TEAM ROLL-CALL

Football League, Division 1 appearances, with League Cup figures in brackets. Individual match line-ups are shown on the Facts and Figures page.

Archibald	
Lacy	
Villa	
Perryman	25 (7)
Crooks	25 (7)
Hughton	25 (7)
Hoddle	25 (7)
Ardiles	25 (7)
Daines	24 (6)
Yorath	24 (7)
McAllister	24 (6)
Miller	18 (6)
Roberts, G.P.	15 (5)
Taylor	11 (6)
Kendall	8 (1)
Brooke	7 (2)
O'Reilly	6 (1)
	4 (1)
	3
	2 (1)
	1

Substitutes used: LEAGUE: Armstrong 4, Roberts, Yorath and Taylor 3 each; Brooke 4 each. Galvin 2, G.P. LEAGUE CUP: Taylor 2; Roberts, G.P. 1. F.A. CUP: Ardiles 3; Villa 3...

GOALSCORERS — LEAGUE: Archibald 15; Crooks Hoddle (2 pens) 10; Ardies 3, Villa and Lacy 2 each; Taylor... LEAGUE CUP: Taylor... Ardiles 4 each; ...

Designed and Printed by...

Spurs 3 QPR 1

7th January 1981, White Hart Lane. Att: 36,294

Spurs goalscorers: Crooks, Galvin, Hoddle

By Julie Welch

Done and dusted. They might not have broken into full flair mode but Spurs had little trouble dumping their Second Division opponents, QPR, out of the FA Cup yesterday, much to the relief of fans still scarred by memories of early exits in the darkest days of the previous decade. Goals from Garth Crooks, Tony Galvin and Glenn Hoddle settled a matter they had failed to resolve at the weekend, and though Simon Stainrod pulled one back with a header just after the restart, the home side rarely had to break out of a canter. Hoddle was in great form, firing passes around with a master's sense of angle and timing. Sadly, though, the prospect of a mini-competition between him and Tony Currie, his opposite number in midfield, to decide which of them was the most superhuman went south early on. Mike Flanagan, QPR's main striker, hobbled off six minutes after kick-off to be replaced by the midfielder David McCreery, leaving Currie short of a target to pass to.

Meanwhile, Garry Brooke, brought in to fill in for the absent Ossie Ardiles, must be hopeful of a regular spot in the side after yesterday's performance. It was his cross just before the half-hour that Crooks converted with a short-range drive at the far post. The 19-year-old then provided the final touch to tee Galvin up for a smart chip that sailed over keeper John Burridge's head in the 40th minute. A late drive from Hoddle after Steve Archibald jinked his way through the QPR defence put the result beyond doubt.

Galvin's goal was a good moment for the former non-league man. His signing in the summer of 1978 went virtually unnoticed among all the hoopla surrounding the arrival of Ardiles and Ricky Villa – hardly surprising since it would have been a long stretch to find anything in common between kissing the Jules Rimet Trophy in the sun-drenched Estadio Monumental, Buenos Aires, and showering in a dribble of cold water after patrolling the mud-clogged wing for Goole Town. Then just when Galvin thought his Spurs career was reaching lift-off it was held back by an excruciating pelvic injury requiring an operation and long recovery. You could never call him a magician, but now fully fit he appears to possess one seemingly mysterious ability – whenever he is ploughing a furrow on the left, Spurs promise great things. They've got Hoddle's sublime skill, they've got Steve Perryman's drive and aggression – now here's Galvin, the extra piece that makes it all work.

Tottenham's defence continues to look something of a work in progress, mind. With Chris Hughton still absent after picking up an injury in the Boxing Day 4-4 ding-dong against Southampton, they are likely to have breathed a sigh of relief upon finding out that their next opponents in the FA Cup are Third Division Hull City. Though considering Wrexham have just delivered one of the first shocks of the competition by dispatching holders West Ham, it won't do to get excited about allegedly inferior opposition just yet.

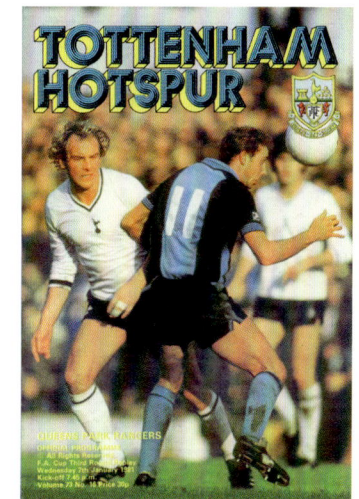

Tony Galvin put in an outstanding performance, scoring Spurs' second goal and constantly harrassing the visitors' defence

It was the evening before Tottenham's FA Cup semi-final against Wolves, and Ivan Cohen and his Sheffield-based group of friends had discovered the hotel where Spurs were staying the night before the match at Hillsborough. 'We went to the hotel hoping for autographs,' recalls Ivan, 'and some of the team were in the bar. There were about half a dozen of us, and Keith Burkinshaw pulled out a £20 note and bought us a round of drinks – £20 in those days was a fortune.'

You could look back at football in the '80s in two ways. You could remember it as a time when the game was scarred by hooliganism, excoriated by politicians and blighted irrevocably by three crowd tragedies, the logical consequence of years of neglect of stadiums. Charlton Athletic's was so dilapidated it was closed down as a death trap. You could recall the five years when English clubs were banned from playing in Europe, a time when ordinary fans were considered pariahs who had to be conveyed to away games on Football Special trains that dumped them not on the main platforms but far away from 'respectable' customers on where the goods trains came in.

Or you could remember the good side of the '80s – a decade when players weren't famous the way they are now, not in the eyes of the general public at any rate. As Steve Perryman observes about the time the squad were recording *Ossie's Dream*, 'We weren't on a level with Chas 'n' Dave. They were the ones who were known to the people out there in a way we weren't. They were more recognisable than most of us.'

It was great for us fans, of course. Not being famous made the players accessible. 'The time we used to go for a drink would be after the games,' Tony Galvin reflected in *The Boys From White Hart Lane*. 'We stayed together. We used to go to this pub when we got off the coach, the Bull's Head near the training ground, and chat about the game. The supporters used to come in, we'd chat to them. You wouldn't believe that now, would you? Playing in Leeds and getting back to Cheshunt about eight, nine o'clock and the supporters who'd been at the game coming in and having a chat about it.'

There were other joys. You could roll up and park your car in a street near the ground, then buy a ticket at the gate. It would be cheap – £1.80 at most, and 90p for juniors. With the terraces being mostly admission through the turnstiles on the day, long queues would form early for big games, especially for the under-16s' entrance. If you were lucky you'd find a turnstile operator who might be generous with his assessment of your age. Or he'd let two of you squeeze through the one turnstile.

Going to a game was a rite of passage. It was the first place you could go where you were free from parental supervision and teachers telling you what to do. You could swear and shout. There were progressions of your fanhood. At 12, you'd start with The Paxton. Then you'd graduate to the lower end of The Shelf. When you got to the upper end of The Shelf, you'd earned your spurs.

A different ball game

With the fans standing behind fences on the terraces and very few matches on television, football in the 1980s was a very different experience from the modern game

By Julie Welch

"Before every game, fans would sing a song for each player during the pre-match warm-up, 'Oh Stevie Stevie, Stevie Stevie Stevie Stevie Perryman!'"

Steve Perryman enjoys the adulation of the young Spurs supporters who could readily identify with their heroes

You could choose where you stood. To ensure a good spot, it was important to get to the ground before 1pm, or even earlier if it was a big game. The cue for for the turnstile operators to open the gates was when Willie Morgan, the stadium announcer, started up his music. He'd play the hits, low key, not blaring as it is now. At 2.45pm there would be the Memory Jerker, when he'd select a game from the corresponding week from years gone by. He would give a precis of the match then play the song that was number one in the pop charts at the time.

The Park Lane was the main home end, filled mostly by younger fans. The Shelf was always packed and popular, although things changed in the mid-'80s when it was redeveloped. 'The Cage', which was the higher terrace on the corner of Worcester Avenue, always had a reputation for being a place for the hardest and most passionate fans.

'I had a couple of friends I'd go with occasionally,' says Spurs fan Pete Haine, 'but most of the time I went on my own and met up with people in the ground – people you stood next to in the same place on the terraces for years. When I first started it used to be The Park Lane and then I slowly graduated up to The Shelf, the top tier, where all the singing was. You always used to see the same faces, the same people – it was all about being part of a crowd of like-minded people.'

In the '80s football hadn't spread into popular culture the way it has now. Children might have collected Panini stickers and swapped duplicates in the playground, but the middle classes regarded football fandom as some sort of esoteric hobby, like cultivating bonsai trees or playing the harpsichord, with a bit of violence thrown in. 'There was very little football on telly,' says another Tottenham supporter, Alan Fisher, 'and so football wasn't really talked about outside of fellow football fans. I think that was a big cultural difference. You couldn't really participate in football unless you went to games.'

That said, the '80s was a time when fewer people went to football because there were other leisure pursuits. Living standards had improved and people had more money. 'You went out with the family as an alternative to going to football,' Fisher continues. 'So although this time is fondly remembered by Spurs

Spurs fans queue in the rain for the chance of securing a precious FA Cup Final ticket. Nothing was going to dampen the excitement of supporters for Tottenham's first appearance in the final for 14 years

during the pre-match warm-up,' Alan Fisher recalls. 'Oh Stevie Stevie, Stevie Stevie Stevie Stevie Perryman! We'll take more care of you, Archibald. Hoddle Hoddle Hoddle Hoddle, born is the king of White Hart Lane.'

With the old West Stand being demolished during the 1980/81 season, Willie Morgan's studio was in the south-west corner by the directors' box, with a high window affording a limited view and not exactly high-tech facilities. 'It was Steve Perryman's job to press a button at the bottom of the staircase before the players ran out,' Morgan remembers. 'It would ring a bell in the directors' box to let me know they were on their way. I would stand outside the studio and as soon as I heard the players were in the tunnel I'd start *Glory, Glory Tottenham Hotspur* for them to run out to.'

And here's another difference between then and now. If the game was called off, fans would go and watch another team. Ivan Cohen's family lived in Hackney, and when he was growing up he went with his brothers and a group of friends, some of whom actually supported Arsenal. 'It wasn't uncommon for us to go to White Hart Lane one Saturday and Highbury the next,' he explains. 'If you told that to young people now, they'd think you were nuts. There was rivalry but no animosity. Of course, by the start of the '80s that was changing.' Nevertheless, the takeaway point is that you had to go to football to watch football. It wasn't a television programme then. You wouldn't be on the sofa but right there on the terraces, Percy Dalton's peanut shells crunching underfoot.

'In the early '80s you still had peanut sellers going round,' explains Alan Fisher. 'They bunged a quid to a gateman and jumped in with their large sacks of Percy Dalton's, crying, "Peanuts, peanuts". People expressed their surprise at how this one guy got round the whole ground so easily but in fact there were two of them – identical twins.'

You wore a uniform, of sorts. Rosettes were old school – now it was scarves all the way. Mostly you bought stuff from the pitches and stalls outside the ground – the Spurs Shop and trademarking didn't take over until later in the decade. Scarves

fans you'd have many games at White Hart Lane where crowds were 20,000 or less. I remember one game on a bank holiday – in those days you could pop out, get a beer and take it back onto the terrace – when you could actually get served because there was no queue. There was nobody there. So I think there was a determination among people who went to football to show their loyalty by being there and singing songs. It was old-fashioned terrace camaraderie.'

'The crowd, as it grew and kick-off approached, made its own atmosphere,' agrees Pete Haine. 'From two o'clock onwards most people would be in the stadium singing and making a really big noise, especially for the bigger games.'

'Before every game, fans would sing a song for each player

could be worn round the neck, tied round the wrist or hitched round your belt. Bobble hats were out of date – now headgear was floppy, with or without a pom-pom on the top. A few butcher's coats, white and hand-decorated in felt tip, added a vintage touch – they were still around from the late '70s. And now there were Argentina flags and shirts.

The players' shirts were different, too. Le Coq Sportif had produced one of the first shiny shirts in football. The name of the French brand provided a link with the Spurs cockerel and positively dripped with continental flair. This was a new team and it went along with the new image – we had cool Argentinians and cool French shirts. Glenn Hoddle's jersey was long and his shorts were short. You could barely see them – it was like he was wearing a mini-dress. Le Coq Sportif didn't last long – soon it was Hoddle in Hummel, a shirt emblazoned with the name of Holsten. The players didn't much fancy the lager, but the kit looked great.

This development of football apparel was all part of the increasing commercialisation of the game. The chairman and owners were changing. In the '70s clubs were run by the likes of Bob Lord, a diminutive Burnley pork butcher. Now it was Cap'n Bob – Robert Maxwell, who bought Oxford United because it was close to his mansion, Headington Hall, and the pitch would

make a handy landing spot for his helicopter. At the end of 1982, control of Tottenham Hotspur, which up till then had been run by local worthies, was taken over by Irving Scholar, a Monaco-based Spurs nut and property developer.

Half-time entertainment had moved on, too. Instead of police dogs chasing pretend villains on the pitch, there was the half-time draw for the lucky £1,000 Spurs Lottery ticket. Willie Morgan would emerge from his box and step onto the pitch to welcome the celebrity guest invited to pick a ticket from the drum. On one blowy afternoon, singer Eartha Kitt spun the drum too vigorously and the hatch flopped open, releasing hundreds of tickets onto the pitch to be scattered by the wind.

It's easy, of course, to look through rose-tinted spectacles. The '80s was an era when creature comforts were non-existent and safety standards low to abysmal. Even Wembley, the cathedral of the game, was a bit of a tip. It was well-known that you needed to hitch your trousers up above your ankles when visiting the gents toilets because of the, um, overflow on the floor. On the plus side, it was easy to access a better seat than you'd paid for, or even to get in free.

'The challenge,' says Pete Haine, 'was that if you had a ticket for the lower standing you could always climb up to the higher standing. There were no stewards to stop you, it was just a four-foot wall to clamber over to get to the top tier, where the view was so much better. Once I went with a mate and he didn't have a ticket, so he jumped the turnstile. Once you got close there were those graduated steps on the outside of the stadium. You could see people being hoisted on shoulders and jumping through the open windows to get in that way.'

Stadiums now are cleaner, safer and ritzier. The food might be better and the toilets cleaner, but the camaraderie of the terraces was lost forever with the installation of seats, along with the chance to hang out with the players in the Corner Pin and the Bell and Hare. This was a time when the only way to watch the game was to be there, not watching in a pub or at home but actually being part of it – and all for £1.80.

Some of us even miss the peanuts.

"You wouldn't be on the sofa but right there on the terraces, Percy Dalton's peanut shells crunching underfoot"

At a time when the game was blighted by hooliganism, clubs installed fences to keep fans off the pitch

81

MEET THE TEAM

"Before the final I had the honour and privilege of introducing my team-mates to Her Majesty the Queen Mother as they lined up on the Wembley turf.

These 11 individual characters and I carried the hopes and dreams of thousands of Spurs supporters on our shoulders. I knew them like brothers and trusted them with my football life.

I can't remember exactly what I said to the Queen Mum, but the following pages contain my reflections – with the benefit of hind-sight – on my team-mates, and the other members of the squad, who would (eventually) go on to lift the trophy and bring the glory glory days back to White Hart Lane."

Steve Perryman

Fact File

Spurs 1969-86

852* (3) Appearances (Sub)
39 Goals

1980/81 FA Cup

9 Appearances
0 Goals

Honours

League Cup 1971, 1973
FA Cup 1981, 1982
UEFA Cup 1972, 1984

Statistics comprise first-team appearances in the Football League, FA Cup, League Cup, UEFA Cup and European Cup Winners' Cup

* Including one abandoned game

MILIJA ALEKSIC

Goalkeeper

Fact File

Spurs 1979-82
32 Appearances
0 Goals

1980/81 FA Cup
4 Appearances
0 Goals

Honours
FA Cup 1981

'**A**lex' was our keeper for the last portion of the 1980/81 season after Barry Daines was injured, and he was middle of the road, reliable – I can't think of any games where he cost us. I always own up that I don't know a lot about goalkeeping, but I know what I like and as I'd played in front of Pat Jennings it was always going to be difficult for Alex to completely measure up in my eyes. No one could use their voice the way Pat did, and no one could be as decisive a reader of a through ball. I don't know that Alex had any obvious weaknesses, but I don't know what his strengths were either, in a way.

He was a good kicker of the ball, for sure, but probably when fans talk about him now it isn't for some unbelievable save of his but for what happened in the 1980 FA Cup third round against Manchester Utd, when Joe Jordan smashed into him. Alex was stretchered off with a broken jaw and Glenn put on the jersey for the rest of the game (he kept a clean sheet, too). That's the game where Ossie scored very late on to win us the tie 1-0.

Alex was a bit like Gary Lineker in looks – suave, well-dressed, skinny-ish. He came from up north, Staffordshire, but had a Serbian dad which explains his name. He started as a 17-year-old at Port Vale and there's a story about him that did the rounds that he was so meticulous he used to iron his bootlaces before he played. He was an understudy for their regular keeper and obviously it didn't work out for him that well there because he then went to play in non-league football. He did get some silverware, though – he was part of the Stafford Rangers team that beat Barnet to win the 1972 FA Trophy.

After that he moved around a bit, first to Plymouth Argyle, then a couple of loan spells at Oxford United and Ipswich Town before Harry Haslam signed him for Luton Town. He had three years there before Keith bought him for £100,000 in 1978, I suppose as back-up for Barry as Pat Jennings had gone to Arsenal. If it was hard for Barry having to make up for Pat leaving, it was hard for Alex too because for his first two seasons he was hardly ever first-choice, and sometimes not even second, because Mark Kendall made a few appearances too. If you look at Alex's record he only appeared 32 times in three seasons but then he got his big chance in March '81 when Barry got injured.

After his career-high 1981 FA Cup win, he only made two more first-team appearances for us because Ray Clemence joined us the following season and Alex lost his place. He dropped back into non-league with Barnet and eventually went on to be a golf pro in South Africa. But what a time in Spurs history for him to take over the number one spot – and he didn't let us down, did he? He sadly passed away in 2012, but his name is etched in the club's history because of that incredible cup run.

> **"What a time in Spurs history for him to take over the number one spot"**

MILIJA ALEKSIC

FULL NAME: Milija Antony Aleksic.
BIRTHPLACE: Newcastle, Staffs.
HEIGHT/WEIGHT: 6 ft. 1 in./12 st. 9 lb.
MARRIED: Yes, to Valerie.
CHILDREN: None.
CAR: BMW 320.
PREVIOUS CLUBS: Port Vale, Eastwood, Stafford Rangers, Plymouth, Luton.
TRADE BEFORE TURNING PRO: Motor mechanic.
CLUB NICKNAME: Alex.
WORST EVER INJURY: Torn knee ligaments.
FAVOURITE FOOTBALL LEAGUE PLAYER AND WHY: Glenn Hoddle — because he's unpredictable.
FAVOURITE OTHER TEAM: Ipswich.
FAVOURITE FOREIGN PLAYER AND WHY: Pele — he had everything.
BEST ALL TIME BRITISH TEAM: Banks, McGrain, Beattie, McFarland, Moore, Baxter, Charlton R., Giles, Best, Law, Hurst.
ALL TIME INTERNATIONAL XI: Banks, Vogts, Wilson, McQueen, Beckenbauer, Keegan, Cruyff, Pele, Puskas, Simonsen.
FAVOURITE AWAY GROUND: Anfield.
FAVOURITE FOREIGN STADIUM AT WHICH YOU HAVE PLAYED: Olympic Stadium, Tokyo.
BEST GOAL SEEN SCORED: Alan Mullery's goal of the season for Fulham against Leicester.
MOST DIFFICULT OPPONENT: Terry McDermott.
MOST MEMORABLE MATCH: One against Santos.
OWN MAGIC MOMENT IN FOOTBALL: Getting to the FA Cup Final with our recent semi-final win over Wolves.
BIGGEST DISAPPOINTMENT: Getting injured in FA Cup match against Manchester United last season.
FAVOURITE OTHER SPORTS: Golf, squash and badminton.
MISCELLANEOUS LIKES: Modern music and watching television.
MISCELLANEOUS DISLIKES: Shopping with the missus.
FAVOURITE TV SHOWS: Cannon and Ball and all documentaries.
TV SHOW YOU ALWAYS SWITCH OFF: Crossroads, if it's possible.
FAVOURITE READING: Unsolved mysteries.
FAVOURITE MUSICIAN/SINGER: Eagles, Christopher Cross, Alexis.
FAVOURITE FOOD: Beef Wellington.
FAVOURITE DRINK: Red wine.
BEST COUNTRY VISITED: Japan.
FAVOURITE ACTOR/ACTRESS: Clint Eastwood, Bette Midler.
BEST FILM SEEN IN PAST YEAR: Ten and Apocalypse Now.
BEST FRIENDS: Paul Barron, Paul Mariner, Paul Price, Terry Bailey — to name just a few.
BIGGEST INFLUENCE ON CAREER: Seeing close friends doing well.
WHAT DON'T YOU LIKE ABOUT FOOTBALL?: Playing in the reserves and injuries.
SUPERSTITIONS: None.
PRE-MATCH MEAL: I don't eat before a match.
PERSONAL AMBITION: To keep in the first team.
PROFESSIONAL AMBITION: To stay in the senior side for the next six years.
CAREER AT TEN PLAYING: To start a garage business in the Midlands.
A PLAYER FOR THE FUTURE: Paul Mariner — he will become better and better as an international.
WHO WOULD YOU MOST LIKE TO MEET: Spike Milligan.
ADVICE TO YOUNGSTERS: Be honest and try to work as hard as you can.

PAUL MILLER
SPURS

FULL NAME: Paul Richard Miller.
BIRTHPLACE/DATE: London/Oct 11, 1959.
HEIGHT/WEIGHT: 6ft/12st 12lbs.
MARRIED: No.
CAR: Capri 1600 GL.
PREVIOUS CLUBS: None.
TRADE BEFORE TURNING PRO: Signed straight from school.
CLUB NICKNAME: 'Max'.
WORST EVER INJURY: Thigh strain.
FAVOURITE FOOTBALL LEAGUE PLAYER AND WHY: My skipper Steve Perryman — he's a great professional.
FAVOURITE OTHER TEAM: Spurs reserves.
FAVOURITE FOREIGN PLAYER AND WHY: My Spurs team-mate Ossie Ardiles. He's so clever on and off the pitch.
BEST ALL-TIME BRITISH TEAM: Banks, Madeley, Wilson, Moore (all England), England (Wales), Ball, Charlton R., (England), Giles (Eire), Best (Northern Ireland), Greaves (England), Law (Scotland).
ALL-TIME INTERNATIONAL XI: Banks, Kaltz, Beckenbauer (West Germany), Marinho (Brazil), Moore, Cruyff (Holland), Charlton R., Greaves, Maradona (Argentina), Pele (Brazil), Best.
FAVOURITE AWAY GROUND: Highbury.
FAVOURITE FOREIGN STADIUM AT WHICH YOU HAVE PLAYED: Kuala Lumpur, Malaysia.
BEST GOAL SCORED: My first for Spurs against Bristol City, 1979.
BEST GOAL EVER SEEN: Glenn Hoddle's against Man. Utd. in the League Cup second round, 1979.
MOST DIFFICULT OPPONENT: All of them.
MOST MEMORABLE MATCH: Last season's FA Cup Final replay against Man. City.
MAGIC MOMENT IN FOOTBALL: Winning the above match.
BIGGEST DISAPPOINTMENT: Losing.
FAVOURITE OTHER SPORTS: I like watching all sports.
MISCELLANEOUS LIKES: Good food.
MISCELLANEOUS DISLIKES: Traffic jams and unpunctual people.
FAVOURITE TV SHOW: 'Benson'.
TV SHOW YOU ALWAYS SWITCH OFF: 'Crossroads'.
FAVOURITE READING: Fiction and biographies.
FAVOURITE MUSICIAN/SINGER: Stevie Wonder and Billy Joel.
FAVOURITE FOOD: Beef.
FAVOURITE DRINK: Champagne.
BEST COUNTRY VISITED: America.
FAVOURITE ACTOR/ACTRESS: Robert De Niro/Jane Fonda.
BEST FILM SEEN IN PAST YEAR: 'The Jazz Singer'.
BEST FRIEND: Jerry Murphy at Crystal Palace.
BIGGEST INFLUENCE ON CAREER: My parents.
WHAT YOU DON'T LIKE ABOUT FOOTBALL: Hooliganism.
SUPERSTITIONS: None.
PRE-MATCH MEAL: Chicken.
PERSONAL HONOURS: None.
PROFESSIONAL AMBITION: To be successful in football and business.
CAREER AFTER PLAYING: To win trophies.
A PLAYER FOR THE FUTURE: Spurs junior Kenny Dixon.
WHO WOULD YOU MOST LIKE TO MEET: The Royal Family.
ADVICE TO YOUNGSTERS: Listen and learn, but always be yourself.

Paul Miller in action against Wolves' John Richards.

PAUL MILLER

Centre-half

Paul 'Maxie' Miller was immaculate, classy-looking and fashionably turned out. But appearances can be deceptive. A lot of people you think are tough aren't tough when it comes to the street. Paul was. He wanted it every minute of every day. Deep down he was from tough stock. Not in a Terry Naylor way, not in a meat market-type way, but in an East End, stand-up-for-yourself way. Good ally, Paul Miller. Good ally.

In a way, I know what supporters think about our defence in 1981. They've always assumed Graham Roberts was the one who got after people and who forwards feared. He was the gritty, thou-shalt-not-pass hard man. Against Anderlecht in the 1984 UEFA Cup Final, Graham scored the goal and scored the penalty, and with me out injured he was captain for the night so he lifted the trophy. So fans understandably saw Graham as the 'saviour' figure. Paul was more of a saboteur. His attitude was, 'I'm going to wear you down.'

So they were different types. Graham was a non-league acquisition from Weymouth and Paul was homegrown, signed by the club as an apprentice. As a combination they clicked very quickly. 'They both played angry, didn't they? I liked to instigate that in a way, but you can't put that quality into someone – they had it already. Sometimes you'd need to make Paul more angry. I knew how to do that. I would

> **"He was loyal, he put his heart and soul into it. And it was a big, big heart. He loved the club."**

wind him up. 'You having a nice day, Maxie? Any chance you could start playing?' That always did the trick.

If you were looking for perfection, neither was the ideal centre-back but both had a hell of a lot going for them. Like Graham, Maxie had front but it was a more considered front – more a London sort of front. He was brought up in a Stepney pub with a taxi driver dad and a nice mum – a proper mum. Saying he had cunning is too strong a word because it sounds critical, but he was shrewd and streetwise, knowledgeable about how things should be done – how you should dress, how you should act. No one had more respect for that white shirt than him. If you wanted to tick boxes for the typical up-and-coming man who should play for Spurs, it was Paul Miller. He was loyal, he put his heart and soul into it. And it was a big, big heart. He loved the club.

One story sums up Paul for me. After he left Spurs he moved to Charlton Athletic, and at the end of the 1986/87 season he helped them hang on to their top-flight place in the Play-off Final against Leeds. You can imagine – it was like a war. One of you is going to go down. It's going to be nasty. Lennie Lawrence says to this day that Paul Miller won the game for Charlton. He took on four or five in the tunnel at half-time.

People underrated Paul. But if I was cornered in the tunnel I'd want him next to me every time.

Fact File
Spurs 1979-87
281 (4) Appearances (Sub)
10 Goals

1980/81 FA Cup
9 Appearances
1 Goal

Honours
FA Cup 1981, 1982
UEFA Cup 1984

GRAHAM ROBERTS

Centre-half

Fact File

Spurs 1980-86
276 (11) Appearances (Sub)
35 Goals

1980/81 FA Cup
9 Appearances
1 Goal

Honours
FA Cup 1981, 1982
UEFA Cup 1984

'Robbo' was blood and guts. He proved that many times. I don't think putting Charlie Nicholas over the advertising hoarding at Highbury, as he did in 1984, is the best example of what he was about. Instead, I remember the way he carried the flag in our 1984 UEFA Cup Final against Anderlecht, and stepped up to smash home the first penalty in the shoot-out – that's Robbo.

He was all-action. He had front – more of it than Sainsbury's. At times he would pick the ball up and just surge forward. I'd think, 'Ah – I've got to change my position because he's charged out of defence and created a hole, I can't just watch.' And then I'd be thinking, 'Do you know what, I think he's going to shoot. Don't shoot. Ah, fuck me, he's shot!'

Anyone with a more 'playing the percentages'-type brain would not shoot like he did. God, it was great what he did, to see him have the courage to surge forward no matter the opposition. It often made things happen for us. As a player, Robbo's naivety showed for both good and not so good. He took things on out of naivety and he was often successful because of that naivety. He obviously learned as he went along, though, so there was gradually less and less of it than when he first came to us.

When you're putting a team together you think about the characteristics you need to be successful. Have you got enough fight? Have you got enough pace? Have you got enough knowledge? Have you got

enough bottle? Have you got enough quality on those free-kicks and corners that are becoming more and more important? Robbo ticked some of those boxes for us that weren't being ticked well enough before – his partnership with Paul Miller meant we definitely had enough fight and bottle in us. They didn't take shit off anybody.

Military people like to say that for soldiers to do what they have to do it's best for them to be people who don't think too much, people who don't have doubts. That's Robbo – the thought of missing that penalty against Anderlecht would not have entered his brain.

The point I'm making is that when the chips are down it's folk like Robbo you need. Once at Exeter, after a legends' game, the players came up for food and a few questions, and this chap was interviewing Mark Falco. At the end he said, 'Mark, you took one of the penalties against Anderlecht – where did you put it?'

'In the net.'

It's not funny, but it is. I would immediately have responded along the lines of, 'Well, I put it left… or right… whatever… I decided this way because…' It would have been a full answer, anyway.

Mark just said, 'In the net.'

The lesson is, don't pick people who think too much to take penalties. They'd think themselves out of it. I would have been of that ilk. 'Well, which is the goalie's strongest side? What are his habits?' Stuff like that. Robbo was like Mark. He was that soldier. He would just go and put it in the net.

> **"Robbo's partnership with Paul Miller meant we definitely had enough fight and bottle in us"**

Spotlight on . . .

GRAHAM ROBERTS
Spurs

FULL NAME: Graham Paul Roberts.
BIRTHPLACE/DATE: Southampton, July 3, 1959.
HEIGHT/WEIGHT: 5ft 10in/12st 12lbs.
MARRIED: Yes, to Ann-Marie.
CAR: Datsun 120Y Coupe.
PREVIOUS CLUBS: Weymouth, Portsmouth, Bournemouth.
TRADE BEFORE TURNING PRO: Fitter's mate.
CLUB NICKNAME: 'Robbo'.
WORST EVER INJURY: Broken ankle.
FAVOURITE FOOTBALL LEAGUE PLAYER AND WHY: Glenn Hoddle — so much skill and ability.
FAVOURITE FOREIGN PLAYER AND WHY: Ossie Ardiles — skilful, close control and awareness.
BEST ALL TIME BRITISH TEAM: Banks, Moore, Cooper, Perryman, O'Leary, Brady, Hoddle, Bremner, E. Gray, Keegan, Law.
ALL-TIME INTERNATIONAL XI: Banks, Vogts, Moore, Alberto, Cooper, R. Charlton, Cruyff, Best, Pele, Law, Jairzinho.
FAVOURITE AWAY GROUND: Anfield.
BEST GOAL SCORED: In the FA Cup sixth round win over Exeter last season.
BEST GOAL SEEN SCORED: Garth Crooks' falling volley against Everton last season.
MOST DIFFICULT OPPONENT: Kenny Dalglish.
MOST MEMORABLE MATCH: The 3-0 FA Cup semi-final replay win over Wolves last season.
OWN MAGIC MOMENT: Winning the FA Cup Final last season (pictured right).
BIGGEST DISAPPOINTMENT: Not making it into League football before I was 21?
FAVOURITE OTHER SPORTS: Golf, tennis and pool.
LIKES: Eating out, and watching old movies.
DISLIKES: Smokey places and flying.
FAVOURITE TV SHOW: Sweeney.
TV SHOW YOU ALWAYS SWITCH OFF: Party Political Broadcasts.
FAVOURITE MUSICIAN/SINGER: Stevie Wonder.
FAVOURITE FOOD: Steak.
FAVOURITE DRINK: Lemonade and blackcurrant.
BEST COUNTRY VISITED: America.
FAVOURITE ACTOR/ACTRESS: John Wayne and Barbra Streisand.
BEST FILM SEEN IN PAST YEAR: The Jazz Singer.
BIGGEST INFLUENCE ON CAREER: Everyone at Tottenham.
WHAT DON'T YOU LIKE ABOUT FOOTBALL: Travelling and hooliganism.
PRE-MATCH MEAL: Steak.
PERSONAL AMBITION: To play for England.
PROFESSIONAL AMBITION: To win the League title.
CAREER AFTER PLAYING: Starting my own business or coaching.
PLAYER FOR THE FUTURE: Ian Crook (Spurs).
WHO WOULD YOU MOST LIKE TO MEET: Prince Charles and Lady Diana.
ADVICE TO YOUNGSTERS: Keep your feet on the ground.

Graham Roberts

49

match makers

CHRIS HUGHTON
Spurs and Eire

NAME: Christopher William Gerard Hughton.
BIRTHPLACE/DATE: Forest Gate, London, Dec 11, 1958.
HEIGHT/WEIGHT: 5ft 7½in, 10st 6lbs.
MARRIED: Yes, to Cheryl.
CAR: Olive green Datsun 120Y Coupé.
TRADE BEFORE TURNING PRO: Lifts engineer.
FAVOURITE FOOTBALL LEAGUE PLAYERS AND WHY: Ossie Ardiles — for a small man he has great all round ability and holds people off so well. Trevor Brooking — for big man so skilful.
FAVOURITE OTHER TEAM: West Ham.
FAVOURITE FOREIGN PLAYER AND WHY: Pele — a player who had everything.
ALL TIME BRITISH TEAM: Banks; Cohen, Moore, Watson, Cooper; Brady, Bremner, Hoddle; Best, Keegan, R. Charlton.
ALL TIME INTERNATIONAL TEAM: Banks (England), Carlos Alberto (Brazil), Krol (Holland), Passarella (Argentina), Cooper (England); Keegan (England), Ardiles, Maradona (Argentina); Pele (Brazil), Cruyff (Holland), Best (N. Ireland).
FAVOURITE AWAY GROUND: Old Trafford.
FAVOURITE FOREIGN STADIUM AT WHICH YOU HAVE PLAYED: Grasshoppers stadium, Zurich.
BEST GOAL SCORED: Took a return pass and scored in top corner against Chelsea in an FA Youth Cup final.
BEST GOAL SEEN SCORED: Glenn Hoddle's volley against Forest last season.
MOST DIFFICULT OPPONENT: John Robertson.
MOST MEMORABLE MATCH: Playing for Eire against England at Wembley this year.
OWN MAGIC MOMENT: My Spurs debut against Man United in the League Cup. Gordon Smith was injured and it was a big shock to hear I'd been picked.
BIGGEST DISAPPOINTMENT: Being knocked out of the FA Cup by Liverpool.
FAVOURITE OTHER SPORTS: Table tennis, snooker, tennis, cricket and watching golf.
FAVOURITE TV: Soap, sports programmes.
TV SHOWS YOU SWITCH OFF: Old films.
FAVOURITE MUSICIANS/SINGERS: Stevie Wonder, Marvin Gaye, Third World.
FAVOURITE FOOD: Chicken curry.
FAVOURITE DRINK: Coca-cola.
BEST COUNTRY VISITED: Switzerland.
FAVOURITE ACTOR: Dustin Hoffman.
BEST FILM SEEN IN PAST YEAR: Rocky Two.
BIGGEST INFLUENCE ON YOUR CAREER: Ron Henry and Peter Shreeves, youth and reserve team coaches at Spurs.
WHAT DON'T YOU LIKE ABOUT FOOTBALL? Dirty players.
SUPERSTITIONS: I always put my shorts on last.
PRE-MATCH MEAL: Fried chicken.
INTERNATIONAL HONOURS: Full Eire caps v England, United States, Argentina and Switzerland. Though I was born in England, I qualify for Eire because my mother was born there.
PROFESSIONAL AMBITION: To win trophies with Spurs and more Eire caps.
CAREER AFTER PLAYING: I'm too young to think about it, yet.
PLAYERS FOR THE FUTURE: Terry Gibson (Spurs), Paul Allen (West Ham).
WHO WOULD YOU MOST LIKE TO MEET: Stevie Wonder.

CHRIS HUGHTON

Left-back

I might inadvertently have played a small role in Chrissie's playing career. He came to Spurs as a left-sided midfielder, even though he was actually right-footed. Then I was injured in an important youth game and Peter Shreeve and Ron Henry balanced things by putting him in at left-back. Chrissie never looked back after that. He was just the perfect combination with Tony Galvin – they had legs, they had energy – plus he brought a bit of pace to a back four that, while it wasn't pedestrian, otherwise wasn't the swiftest by any means.

Chris was with us from schoolboy days but initially had a part-time contract because he wanted to complete his four-year apprenticeship as a lift engineer before turning pro, which shows his common-sense attitude to life. He was always totally professional and very consistent. Keith always said that one of his biggest gifts as a manager was that in me and Chrissie he had two full-backs that he could almost guarantee weren't going to get injured. Maybe that's putting too much emphasis on full-back play, but if you've got a weakness in that area, wow, can you get exposed. As a manager you're always thinking, 'Where do I have to worry about with this team?' and I think Keith was saying, 'I don't have to worry about those two.'

Chrissie never went through a football apprenticeship. When he

> **"He could stand his ground, but he was totally correct in the way he went about things, and still is"**

made his debut in 1977, in the League Cup against Liverpool, he was still playing as an amateur, training two nights a week and appearing for the reserves on Saturdays, and I think in a way that widened his outlook on life – in his early days he wrote a column for a left-wing paper, which wasn't something you'd find most footballers doing.

In his manner and in the way that he dressed he was always suave, always correct. You could call him 'Mr Smooth', except that sounds a bit negative and it's not meant to be. It was smooth in a nice way, like you'd say about a whisky. He was cleverly smooth. 'The Charmer' they used to call him. I can't remember ever falling out with him. No one did. Not on the field, not off the field. Never had a row with anyone. He wasn't afraid to make his point, but he would do it in a thought-through way and could back up his opinion without being aggressive.

When we played Coventry in the FA Cup, having scored the opening goal in our 3-1 win, he gave away a foul late on against their midfielder Steve Hunt. Chrissie apologised and they shook hands. It was a nice old-fashioned way of saying, 'If that had been done to me I'd have been a bit upset.' That was Chrissie. He could stand his ground, but he was totally correct in the way he went about things, and still is. The proof is the way he's gone on to have such a long career in the game.

Fact File

Spurs 1979-90
389 (9) Appearances (Sub)
19 Goals

1980/81 FA Cup
6 Appearances
1 Goal

Honours
FA Cup 1981, 1982
UEFA Cup 1984

81

MOMENT IN TIME

5th April 1978, White Hart Lane
Tottenham Hotspur v Hull City, Second Division

"This is mine. I'm getting this.

It's the last home game of the season and we've got 10 minutes left to do something, so I've moved up front. We need a goal. Who else is going to take responsibility if the skipper doesn't?

Chris Jones bundles into the keeper, the ball falls to me, and I'm on my backside as I slide it in.

The whole of White Hart Lane goes crazy."

Steve Perryman

THE FOURTH ROUND SPURS v HULL CITY

A tough nut to crack

We made hard work of beating Hull City, drawing on the mental strength and resilience built up when we had bounced straight back from relegation three years earlier

Thinking back, you could say that goal I scored against Hull in the last but one game of our promotion season was probably one of the most important I ever scored, if not quite the most – a couple against AC Milan might just have the edge. Hull were where we'd been the season before – right at the bottom of the table – while we were near the top, fighting it out with Southampton and Brighton for the last of the promotion spots. Most of that campaign we'd been winning week in, week out – one game after the other. It looked as though we were going to earn promotion easily, then we fell away right at the end. We'd started to get nervous. It didn't quite get to the panic stage but it would have done if we hadn't secured those two points against Hull.

I don't have too many memories of that game, perhaps because it was outshone by the one afterwards which got us promoted back to the First Division, but I do remember we'd already had one goal wrongly disallowed. All the play was in Hull's half but we couldn't get the ball over the line. There was a dispute afterwards as to whether my goal should have stood, but maybe the referee was trying to make up for his error in disallowing that earlier one.

Apparently when the ball hit the net a lot of fans ran onto the pitch. Stewards and police had to pull them off me, and Keith got hold of a microphone and politely asked the crowd to get off the pitch because we were going to need it next season. It was starting to sink in that we were on the brink of getting back to the top tier. My goal had put us in a situation where we only needed to eke out a draw in our last game, away to Southampton.

I'd done it quite often that season, moving up front if we weren't getting anywhere. You could say that Jimmy Greaves was lucky, the number of times the ball just seemed to drop to him in the box. But that was all down to his instinct for being in the right place at the right time. When he did that, he was forcing something to happen. That was his main role as a striker. It wasn't my main role in the team but if it isn't happening you've got to force it. I wouldn't have done it as a defensive midfielder but that season Keith had switched me to the centre of defence and if we needed a goal I'd push up to the front. Although I don't think my instincts as a goalscorer were that great – as proven by the records books – I definitely had the kind of mentality that spurred me on to try in any way I could to recover a bad situation, and that came to the fore when we were really stretched.

"Goalscoring wasn't my main role in the team – as proven by the records – but if it ain't happening you've got to force it"

One of Steve Perryman's most important goals – the winner against Hull City in 1978 – that took Spurs to the brink of promotion from Division Two

You've got to know when to do it, and when not to do it, obviously. You can't let ego take over the 'teamness' of it. But in cases like against Hull that season I think it's the ultimate 'teamness' to go and put yourself on offer. Of course, it's a risk because you're leaving a hole at the back and if the keeper had made a save and they'd gone down the other end and we'd conceded, people would have been saying, 'Why did you do that because now we've got a worse goal difference?' That's what putting yourself on offer means – you're doing what you believe to be the right thing even if it runs the risk of criticism. But fortune favours the brave. If there's a choice, be bold. That's part of being a leader. Be bold with a decision, with an action. Yes, you're putting yourself on offer, but if you don't, it's costing the team.

This might sound odd, but that season in the Second Division is my favourite from my time at Spurs. You might say I was only there because a First Division club hadn't come in for me. You might say that goes to prove I wasn't a top, top-level player because I did it against inferior opposition – though saying that, there wasn't such a big gulf in quality between the top and second tier then. But for me it was because I found the perfect position for my game at the time. I had the luxury of space at the back. Though I wasn't selfish enough

to tell the keeper to give me the ball every time, there were loads of occasions when I started play from the back. If you've been in centre midfield, if you're combative but can play as well, you'd be a mug not to use that space. Therefore I used it. I must have been a godsend to the midfield players to help set them free, and that was a major part of how we played. Of course, once teams know that's your style of play they're going to try and stop it, but the more confident I got the more they couldn't stop it. I think people began to look at me as a different player after that season. It was probably one of the reasons why Ossie in particular rated me, because I understood midfield players' problems and needs. I could serve him and Glenn the ball.

Our most memorable match in the 1977/78 season came in October when we beat Bristol Rovers 9-0 – it still stands as Tottenham Hotspur's record league victory. Four of the goals that day were scored by Colin Lee, who had been signed from Torquay United for £60,000 two days earlier. Ian Moores scored a hat-trick. However, three years later they had both moved on. So had a lot of the other players – Terry Naylor, Jimmy Holmes, John Pratt, Neil McNab and Peter Taylor. After promotion Keith built an almost entirely new side.

By the time we played Hull again, in the FA Cup run, the fortunes of both clubs had gone in opposite directions. While Spurs weren't going to be challenging at the top of the league because of our inconsistency, we'd taken two points off Ipswich Town – one of the main title contenders – before Christmas, and the Saturday before the cup tie we'd celebrated a win over Arsenal with two goals from Archie. We were becoming a force to be reckoned with.

In contrast, Hull had finished the 1977/78 season bottom of the table, dropped into the Third Division and had not come back. But in one way it was like nothing had changed since that night in 1978 – we couldn't get past their goalkeeper.

Garry Brooke saved the day. The press had made a lot of him being disappointed at only being named as substitute now Ossie was back in England. Garry had certainly been an effective player for us that season, but guess what? Ossie's a World Cup winner. Of course you put him in the side. But when it got late in the second half Ossie was pulled, Garry came on and his direct running and his shooting boots turned the match.

Right: Spurs needed to defend well against what turned out to be a dogged Hull side in the fourth round tie

Far right: Garry Brooke is congratulated by Terry Yorath after the youngster came on to break the deadlock late on in the game

"Garry Brooke came on and his direct running and his shooting boots turned the match"

It was the type of game when you struggle to score, but when you eventually do your opponents don't collapse necessarily but they do sort of… relax. Their mood changes to, 'It's over. We've done our best.' The tension goes and you end up scoring another one when really it's not a 2-0 game – sometimes it can even get to 4-0 or 5-0, even though for 70 minutes it was goalless. You end up really breaking them down once you know they're out.

The other results from that round favoured us again. A lot of our First Division rivals had been drawn against each other and now Manchester United were out, beaten 1-0 at the City Ground by Nottingham Forest. Everton had knocked out the reigning league champions, Liverpool. West Bromwich Albion had gone out to Middlesbrough and Manchester City had beaten their new manager John Bond's previous club, Norwich City, 6-0. Southampton, our old partner in promotion, were through with a 3-1 win over Bristol Rovers.

There had been the usual FA Cup shocks, always a big part of the competition's appeal. Leicester City, who had been held to a 0-0 draw at Filbert Street by Third Division Exeter City, were beaten 3-1 at Exeter's home ground. There was nearly a big upset at Vicarage Road where Elton John's Watford got a draw with Wolves before losing 2-1 at Molineux, while it took a replay at Portman Road for Ipswich Town to get past Shrewsbury, who had held them to a 0-0 draw at home.

We had been lucky so far, meeting lower division opponents. In the next round we would face a First Division side for the first time in the competition. It wasn't Ipswich, who now Liverpool had gone were the favourites to lift the cup. It wasn't Nottingham Forest – the champions of Europe – either. It was Coventry. A name which stirred memories of a turbulent time in Spurs' history… and in mine.

Spurs 2 Hull City 0

24th January 1981, White Hart Lane. Att: 37,532

Spurs goalscorers: Brooke, Archibald

By Julie Welch

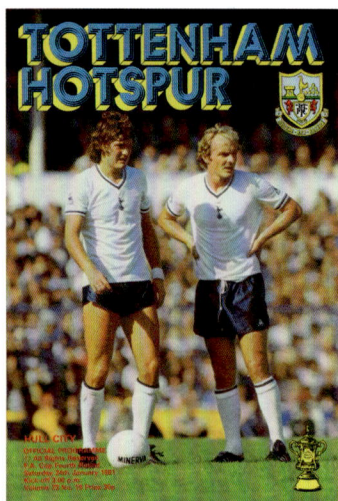

Home game, Third Division opposition – how hard could it be? Frustratingly, uninspiringly, embarrassingly hard as it turned out at White Hart Lane yesterday. All it took was for Hull City's keeper, Tony Norman, to turn into Peter Shilton for the afternoon.

With most of the game being fought out within 40 yards of Norman's goal, it seemed only a matter of time before Spurs would put the tie to bed, but a combination of Hull's beefed-up defending, Norman's temporary transmogrification into a world-beater and Tottenham's overwrought and increasingly ineffectual attack led to a barren first half. Ossie Ardiles was back in the side after his sojourn in Uruguay, but his buzzing artistry made little headway. Garth Crooks set up a string of chances for himself in the first half and missed out on each one, and even Glenn Hoddle was unable to produce one of those sublime passes that would rip the whole frantically tangled structure apart.

Things showed little improvement after the restart. There's nothing like holding out against one of the most glamorous attacking line-ups in the league to boost a lower-tier club's confidence, and as the clock went on ticking ominously towards full-time Spurs'

supporters must have been contemplating the prospect of a seven-hour round-trip to Boothferry Park for the replay, while Hull City's board of directors were no doubt turning their thoughts towards the cash injection it would bring. Then finally, with 71 minutes gone, Garry Brooke sprinted on for the flagging Ardiles and the more direct style he brought to the attack changed everything.

A couple of months back Brooke's name on the team sheet was greeted by a resounding 'Who's he?' His debut came in November in the disappointing home defeat to West Bromwich Albion, but since then the 20-year-old youth-team product has been a more than adequate stand-in for Ardiles, scoring twice in Tottenham's 4-4 Boxing Day draw with Southampton. Now here he was doing his 'hot knife through butter' act to break the deadlock seven minutes from time with a low drive from outside the box.

And so it was done. You could see Hull's collective slump of the shoulders and hear the sighs of relief from the Tottenham faithful, which turned to full-on roars of triumph when Steve Archibald added a clinching goal a minute before the end.

The question now is whether this underwhelming performance was just a stumble along the path or whether this is going to be another season when Spurs fall short. When they are on song they play some of the most exhilarating football going, their 5-3 whupping of title challengers Ipswich Town last month a case in point, but such is their maddening inconsistency that a week later they went under 4-1 to Middlesbrough, and it took them two goes to fight their way past Queens Park Rangers in the last round. The big question now is, which Tottenham Hotspur is going to turn up in the fifth round?

Garth Crooks – and fans in the packed East Stand terraces – can't believe it as another chance goes begging against Third Division Hull

Action from our Fourth Round tie with Hull City

THE 100th F.A. CUP SEASON

Action from our Fourth Round tie with Hull City

TOP LEFT — PAUL MILLER gives TONY NORMAN, the Hull goalkeeper, an awkward moment.
BOTTOM LEFT — GARTH CROOKS in a heading duel.

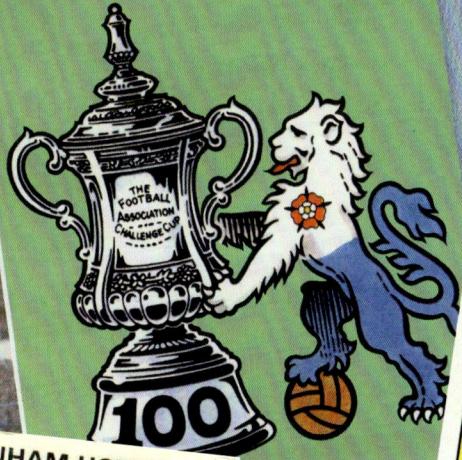

THE FOOTBALL ASSOCIATION CHALLENGE CUP

100

Tottenham Hotspur

Manager Keith Burkinshaw
(White Shirts, Blue Shorts, White Stockings)

Hull City

Manager Mike Smith
(Black & Amber Striped Shirts, Black Shorts, Black Stockings)

BARRY DAINES	1	TONY NORMAN
DON McALLISTER	2	STEVE HOOLICKIN
PAUL MILLER	3	Roger McNeil BRIAN FERGUSON
GRAHAM ROBERTS	4	STEVE RICHARDS
Terry Yorath JOHN LACY	5	Dennis Booth STUART CROFT
STEVE PERRYMAN	6	JOHN ROBERTS
OSVALDO ARDILES	7	BRIAN MARWOOD
(1) STEVE ARCHIBALD	8	STEVE McCLAREN
TONY GALVIN	9	KEITH EDWARDS
GLENN HODDLE	10	CRAIG NORRIE
GARTH CROOKS	11	NICK DEACY
(1) Gary Brooke (for 7)	12	STUART CROFT

2 (0)   0 (0)

OFFICIALS

Referee: MR. TRELFORD MILLS (Barnsley)

MR. TRELFORD MILLS of Barnsley started refereeing in the Barnsley and District League, and graduated to the Football League via Barnsley and Sheffield Leagues and the Central League.
He officiated in a U.E.F.A. Cup game in 1976 and in F.A. Challenge Trophy semi-finals both in 1977 and 1979. He also refereed a Football League Cup quarter-final in 1978 and the F.A. Youth Cup final of 1979.
He is employed as an insurance representative and his other interests include cricket and gardening.

LINESMEN:
Mr. D. J. SIMMONS (Surrey)
Red Flag

Mr. E. BURNS (Somerset)
Yellow Flag

SCORECHECK

Here are other F.A. Cup-ties being played today. Half time scores will be announced.

BARNSLEY
ENFIELD TOWN

EVERTON
LIVERPOOL

FULHAM
CHARLTON ATHLETIC

MANCHESTER CITY
NORWICH CITY

NEWCASTLE UNITED
LUTON TOWN

NOTTINGHAM FOREST
MANCHESTER UNITED

SHREWSBURY TOWN
IPSWICH TOWN

SOUTHAMPTON
BRISTOL ROVERS

WATFORD

4TH ROUND

Action Highlights

SPURS v HULL CITY
MAIN PICTURE — DON McALLISTER
tops GARTH CROOKS in putting Spurs under pressure. INSET — STEVE ARCHIBALD scored a late second goal to give Spurs a 2-0 win and a passport to today's Fifth Round.

BROOKE
Ardiles stand-in is Spurs hero

WELL DONE — Steve Archibald salutes Garry Brooke

Steve Perryman was just 20 years old when he was first handed the role of Spurs captain, leading the side in several matches during the 1972/73 season in the absence of Martin Peters

Steve Perryman remembers Bill Nicholson having a go at Martin Chivers on one occasion and Alan Mullery shouting back at him, 'Hey Bill, he's just won us the game.' Back then Steve just listened. He was barely out of his teens. It was a case of observe, learn as much as possible and meanwhile keep your mouth shut. 'I certainly wasn't going to be loud with the first-team squad when I broke into it,' he says. 'The louder you are the more ammunition you're giving people to nail you.' But watching Mullery defy his manager by defending his team-mate gave Steve his first insight into what it takes to be a captain.

'I think in the end, when they're judging you, the question has to be: Did you stand up?' he says. 'How can you be a captain without upsetting anyone? It's not a popularity contest. You can't be a 'yes' man.'

When you want to illustrate the greatness of Steve Perryman, club captain of Tottenham Hotspur from 1975 to 1986, there are many examples you can give. You can introduce him as the warrior leader who in the Second Division inspired the fans to follow Spurs to the ends of the earth, or at least to Mansfield. Or you can talk about how he was the unflinching protector of his team on and off the pitch and the captain who wasn't afraid to speak truth to power, be it manager or chairman. He once heard a team-mate described as a 'bottler'. Then and there he thought, 'They'll never say that of me.' Or you can discuss the emotionally intelligent thinker who knew how to motivate his team-mates and what made each one tick. As Graham Roberts has said, 'Steve was a fantastic influence on me. He would keep your feet on the floor; he would do everything to make sure you didn't get big-headed. Nothing was ever too much for him if it would help the team out, help his team-mates. He would bollock you, but only in the right way – it was for your benefit. That's what a captain is, a leader from the front.'

It's a sentiment echoed by Garry Brooke. 'We all knew Keith was in charge, but if anybody had a problem you went to Stevie. He would talk you through the game – "Brooksey, five yards to your right, so-and-so's on you." He could be a horrible bastard as well. He would cut you down to pieces if you weren't doing it. But you had respect for that, it was an old-fashioned thing. He played a vital part in bringing on my game. He was the last great captain we ever had.'

But maybe the best demonstration of the sort of captain he was is contained in the glowing tribute paid to him by the late John Syer, the sports psychologist brought in by Keith Burkinshaw to work with the team. 'Steve Perryman took care of us in the same way he took care of everyone,' wrote Syer. 'When we got to the hotel on away games, he'd invite us up to his room, order tea and biscuits and make sure we understood what the team needed from each of the players. He was the greatest captain of any team in any sport that I've ever been involved with. The way he built up relationships was unique.'

The phrase 'the art of captaincy' sounds pretentious,

Our captain and leader

If ever a human being was born to be the captain of Tottenham Hotspur Football Club it was Steve Perryman – a natural leader who the players from the '81 team still call 'Skip' today

By Julie Welch

"How can you be a captain without upsetting anyone? It's not a popularity contest. You can't be a 'yes' man"

but as Steve puts it: 'The captain has a very important role to play. Anyone who thinks they just toss a coin is way off the mark. I watched England play a friendly once. They made about eight substitutes and the armband got thrown around like it was a bit of confetti. That belittles the role. Even in a friendly, it's too serious for that.

'If you're a captain and you're just running around shouting, "Come on!" the message isn't landing on anyone. If the manager asks you afterwards, "What were you doing, what were you saying to them?" and you say, "Well, I told them, 'Come on!'" – what does that mean? Come on left? Come on right? My point is, the more you tell someone directly what they need to do, the more it makes you aware of what you yourself need to be doing. "Come on!" is vague and fluffy, and that makes you more vague and fluffy yourself. Why aren't you being more purposeful, the way you want your team-mate to be?'

Bill Nicholson spotted this potential very early. Steve was 20 when he first captained Spurs – and was made club vice-captian – for the 1972 home game against Lyn Oslo in the UEFA Cup after Martin Peters failed a fitness test. This was to be the last competition Spurs won before it all unravelled for Bill, and Terry Neill arrived from Arsenal via Hull City to take the manager's job. When Peters left Spurs for Norwich City in March 1975, Neill made Steve captain.

We all know what happened next. Neill decamped to Arsenal at the end of the 1975/76 season, leaving Keith Burkinshaw to

> "I wasn't the best player, but I was a better organiser, thinker and communicator and that was why I was living with that bunch of players"

take over. Steve found himself leader of a team in decline. The next two seasons of relegation and promotion provided his baptism of fire. 'That was when the bond between Keith and me was formed,' he says. 'I was a naïve captain and he was a naïve manager, and we were finding our way through together. You definitely have to grow into the job, and I think I'd truly grown up by the time I led that '81 team.'

By then Steve had been a first-team player for 12 years – he made his debut against Middlesbrough in 1969, having come through the youth team – and a spin-off from his status as a one-club man was the example it set. 'Me being captain was a good model for the young players to follow, because I'd been one of them. Terry Gibson has talked about how I was one of his favourite players growing up, and then he ended up getting in the team and couldn't believe he was getting changed in the same dressing room as Steve Perryman. Not,' he adds quickly, 'that I've ever seen myself in that kind of glowing light. I think the good thing about me was that I didn't get above myself. When you play with Jimmy Greaves and Pat Jennings, and Alan Gilzean and Mike England, you realise your limitations. Even when I was older, I couldn't pass like Glenn, or be all-action around every blade of grass like Ossie. It meant it was very easy not to fancy myself. I can do them all at a level, which was what encouraged

Steve Perryman is all smiles in 1976 with team-mates and manager Keith Burkinshaw (fourth from right) and physio Mike Varney (far left) but it was a testing time to be Spurs captain

Bill to pick me in the first place, and keep picking me, but I didn't really fancy myself as a footballer.'

That, he thinks, was what gave him license to talk to other players when there was something they could be doing better. 'I wouldn't be criticising Glenn about his passing but let's say I didn't like the way he was taking too long to get back. Because I would have got back quicker, I felt I could say something. I couldn't have done it as a 17-year old, I just did what I did and went home, no more. But by the time I was leading this team I had absolutely worked out my game, and so I was working out everyone else's game. I wasn't the best player, but I was a better organiser, thinker and communicator and that was why I was living with that bunch of players. That's why I was captain. I could have an opinion on their game.'

The opinions were rarely sugar-coated. In *The Boys From White Hart Lane*, Paul Miller claims that team meetings could be 'lively'. Steve agrees. 'They could be, yeah. That's how a team works. It doesn't do any good to sit back and moan afterwards. It's the easiest thing in the world to go quiet in the dressing room. Say it. Step up now. There's an honesty to that, and we certainly had honesty when we got back to Cheshunt after a game. We'd go to the local, The Bull's Head. Not everyone would be there but if they could be, they would be. It's easier for honesty to come out over a pint of beer at 11 o'clock at night than at five o'clock in the dressing room after a game. If something wasn't right, you'd have had time to calm down and give it more thought.'

It was in the intimacy of the dressing room, though, that important truths would be conveyed. 'There was a lot of piss-taking, a lot of putting people in their place and a lot of paying respect to what I'd call life admin,' he says. 'That would be making sure letters from fans were answered, for instance. The conversation could be about what we'd seen on telly last night, or nice restaurants we'd been out to. A lot of talk about girls. It's normal talk with a lot going on underneath the surface.

'I'm not a bawler or a screamer or a shouter as such. But don't be a captain if you want to be everybody's friend. I was from the Bill Nicholson school of giving praise. In other words, if you'd

Use your head: Perryman makes sure the message gets across in the 1981 FA Cup clash against Coventry

the promotion season but with the arrival of Ardiles and Villa found himself edged out of the first team. 'It was during an 11 v 11 at Cheshunt, the so-called first team against the reserves,' recalls Steve, 'and the reserves were smashing the life out of us. I was in centre midfield and I was treating it like a cup final, but there were certain players on that pitch who weren't that bothered about us being 4-0 down, so I think the other team got a bit above themselves. I caught Neil and he said something and a fight developed. It ended – we were fine. But we both took one. That's how it is. He was standing up for his team and I was standing up for mine.'

And in the end, that determination to stand up for his team is what characterised Steve as a captain, as an old friend once reminded him. 'He said that if Glenn or Ossie or one of the other players got hurt by an opponent – intentionally hurt – someone in the crowd would say, "Steve, five minutes."

'"What do you mean?" I asked him.

'He said, "It meant Steve will do him in five minutes. You couldn't help yourself. It wouldn't be one minute, because that would have been too obvious. But it was like a stopwatch in your head. Before five minutes was up that player would get repayment for what he had just done."

'That's how it had to be. In a way, I was protector of the talent in our team. That was a way of me playing my game, putting extra into what I had. You could ask, "Why are you motivated by your opponent doing something bad against your team? Why stoop down to their level?" Well… I was never taught to be nasty. I was never taught to run the ball to the corner flag or bend the rules. But if someone nailed one of our players, even though you didn't always come off best, it needed doing. And that isn't about me being proud of it, it was me standing up for our team. Which is my club.'

And it always would be. When Steve left Tottenham in 1986 to play for Oxford United, it wasn't long before he was asked to be captain. He turned the offer down, respectfully, with the words, 'I don't understand you. I don't know what makes you tick.'

Steve Perryman, you will always be our captain.

done all right you didn't get any, but you'd certainly hear about it if you hadn't done all right. I also learned from the Eddie Baily school of delivering it by taking the mick. When I had to be hard and tough it would be with a bit of love, a bit of humour, a bit of ramming home the point, with a large helping of the truth. I would always try to be respectful with it, so if it happened to be criticism hopefully it was taken in the right way. That was my place in the dressing room.'

The success of his approach is underlined by the respect and affection in which he is still held by those who played under his captaincy. It was rare for him to fall out irrevocably with a team-mate. 'I preferred to fall out with a group,' he says. That said, someone who wasn't a fan was Neil McNab. This was a talented player who had been a big part of the midfield during

MEET THE TEAM
OSSIE ARDILES
Midfield

OSVALDO
ARDILES
TOTTENHAM HOTSPUR

Fact File

Spurs 1978-88
293 (18) Appearances (Sub)
25 Goals

1980/81 FA Cup
7 Appearances
1 Goal

Honours
FA Cup 1981
UEFA Cup 1984

Introduced by Steve Perryman

I always look upon one of the goals Ossie scored for us against Manchester United as a feather in my cap. It was in the FA Cup in the 1979/80 season. I took a free-kick and found his head in the box. I said to him afterwards, 'If I can find your head in the box I must be a good player...'

Because Ossie was no giant, was he? The first time I set eyes on him, I was surprised by how thin he was – and how short. I remember thinking, 'What on earth are he and Ricky going to think about our training kit?' The shorts must have been about three times too big for him. They stuck out by at least six inches either side. And we wore cricket shirts, made of thick cotton with long sleeves. Which was great when it was cold but evil when it was hot in pre-season, when they joined.

Of course, my attitude towards Ossie was already influenced by what I'd seen of him playing those games for Argentina in the 1978 World Cup. If he wasn't a giant physically he was a giant in ability. So I may have been influenced by that and imagined him bigger than he actually was. But he did look steely. That probably made me warm to Ricky's face a bit more than Ossie's at first – I had the feeling that Ossie was making the decisions for the pair of them.

"If he wasn't a giant physically he was a giant in ability"

Ossie was obviously very intelligent – he'd trained to be a lawyer before football overtook that side of things. He didn't have to be able to speak the language in order to know what was going on. There was always a lot of piss-taking going on in the team and later on I said, 'How did you read all that before you could understand English?'

He said, 'Steebie, look at the eyes. It tells you everything.'

I think he followed my judgment about certain things he didn't know already – about people, for instance. But he was his own man, and would challenge me if he thought I was wrong, along the lines of, 'I think he's better than you think he is.'

Ossie was exceptional at linking it all up. He wasn't a paid captain but he was a paid 'joiner-upper' of people. He had this wonderful way of letting you know that he appreciated your game. He would do that by talking to you about your play. During our first pre-season, he said to me, 'You. When I see you I see Passarella.' All I could say was, 'Really?' I'd never have put myself in the company of Argentina's World Cup-winning captain. Maybe he was just planting a thought in my head.

If you had a good word from Ossie, it was worth more than just a good word. This was a World Cup winner saying he liked you. He liked your game. Good man. Good man, Ossie.

TONY GALVIN

Midfield

I've heard many times that Tony Galvin was the player our opponents wanted to try and stop. He wasn't particularly fast, but he could run and run. If the full-back took the ball off him, Tony would be at him, and at him again. Just think about a forward taking on a full-back. If your average for getting past a full-back is 50-50, that's not a great average for the defender but it is for the forward, and I don't think I saw Tony ever finish less than 50-50. It wasn't so much about his skill, it was more his ability to keep taking that man on. He wore down his opponent's legs. He was difficult to get past, too. All knees and elbows, but talented as well. He was just straightforward. No nonsense. It was like a young Keith or a young Bill Nick being out on the pitch up and at 'em. No one was going to outwork him.

He may have had a university degree, in Russian Studies, but he was down to earth. He was educated but he had a real sort of coal miner's attitude to life – 'Hard work is repaid.' In its own way his intelligence showed on the field. He just brought something different to our group of players. We were rated as a very classy team, and Chrissie was the smooth one – a smooth mover and dresser – and Tony was the perfect balance to that.

He and Chrissie made our left side rock solid. If one made a mistake, the other made up for it. The fact that they both played for the Republic of Ireland was helpful, although neither of them was noticeably Irish. They were quick enough, urgent enough, and they cared enough, so the left was a formidable side for people to take us on. You've always got to be asking, 'Where do the goals come from?' and a lot came from Glenn looking for Tony, who would already be on his way to meet the pass and get the ball into the box.

It was difficult for Tony at Spurs at first because he was from Huddersfield and there was a lot of mickey-taking about the way he dressed and how people couldn't understand his accent. He took a while to come good because, although he signed at the same time as Ossie and Ricky, Keith advised him to finish his teacher training course in case he didn't make it. That was typical Keith, blunt and full of common sense – 'There's your offer, take it or leave it.'

That was Tony, too, as per the common sense. The team had a problem on the left. Ricky didn't like to play there, and nobody else was up for it, but Tony had learnt to kick with his left foot when he was a kid and he seized his chance. He made himself selectable. He was unspoiled by the game of football where you can get carried away with yourself. He was just very normal. Sometimes straightforward wins.

> **"In its own way his intelligence showed on the field. He just brought something different to our group"**

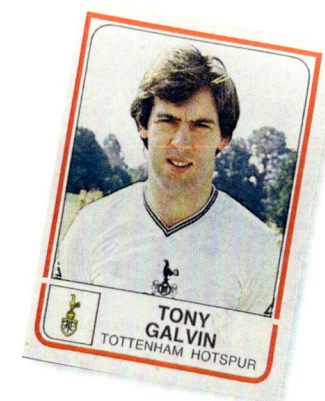

Fact File

Spurs 1979-87
262 (11) Appearances (Sub)
31 Goals

1980/81 FA Cup
8 (1) Appearances (Sub)
1 Goal

Honours
FA Cup 1981, 1982
UEFA Cup 1984

GLENN HODDLE

Midfield

TOTTENHAM **GLENN HODDLE**

Fact File

Spurs 1975-87

478 (12) Appearances (Sub)
110 Goals

1980/81 FA Cup

9 Appearances
2 Goals

Honours

FA Cup 1981, 1982

The bond between Glenn and I was that we were the two who had been through that promotion season of 1977/78. It was part of his development from a youngster to a world-class talent, although I don't know if development is the right word. Certain people do it from day one and Glenn was one of those people. At 20, he was already recognised as a midfield sensation. I'm not sure he ended up a better player at the end of his career than he was at the start.

Any forward who played with Glenn and didn't run forward when he got the ball was stupid, because Glenn was talented enough to pick any run out. He played to feet into the box, in behind, whatever was needed. Plenty of people picked up on what I once said about him, that he played as though he had a set of golf clubs where his feet should be. He could hit a two-iron, or a five-iron, or a nine-iron depending on what was required. He also had those long legs. If ladies ever mentioned Glenn to me, they'd always go on about 'those thighs!'

He was elegant, sort of languid in his way, and a great foil for Ossie's 'choo-choo-choo-choo' approach. Glenn was more 'mmm-mmm-mmm-mmm'. He was also a music freak. When it came to recording *Ossie's Dream* for the FA Cup Final, I think he was the only one of us who could actually sing – as he proved when he and Chris Waddle recorded *Diamond Lights* later on. He was always listening to something. It was never my thing, but once when we were on tour somewhere he caught me with earphones on and said, 'Steve Perryman's listening to music. The game is truly gone.'

Glenn was sometimes criticised as a luxury player who didn't put in the hard graft, but if you look at all our big wins no one is doing more work than him. The more times he had the ball, the better team we were. Just keep him moving. Because if it went from me to Glenn, that was a trigger for the front two to go *whoosh!* That was a hell of a weapon, and I made it my number one job to give Glenn the ball.

He was a star player but he didn't really want to be treated like a star player, he wanted to be treated fairly. Ossie was magnificent for him, because he was a World Cup winner. He didn't kowtow to Glenn, it's just he understood what he had to do to make Glenn shine even more. If you praise some people they end up getting above themselves, but that wasn't the case with Glenn. If you praised him it would just add to his quiet confidence. And that was part of what made him special. He had absolute confidence and faith in his own ability – 'Give me the ball'!

> **"The more times he had the ball, the better team we were"**

match makers

GLENN HODDLE
Spurs

FULL NAME: Glenn Hoddle
BIRTHPLACE/DATE: Hayes, Middlesex, October 27, 1957
HEIGHT/WEIGHT: 6ft ½in, 12st 4lb
MARRIED: To Anne
CHILDREN: None
CAR: Volkswagen Scirocco
PREVIOUS CLUBS: None
TRADE BEFORE TURNING PRO: Schoolboy
CLUB NICKNAME: 'Hod'
WORST EVER INJURY: I once missed five weeks when I damaged the cartilage in my right knee
FAVOURITE BRITISH PLAYER AND WHY: George Best — for his superb all-round ability
FAVOURITE OTHER TEAM: West Ham
FAVOURITE FOREIGN PLAYER AND WHY: The Dutchman Van Hanegem and Wolfgang Overath of West Germany. They were so skilful and terrific passers of the ball
BEST ALL TIME BRITISH TEAM: Jennings, McGrain, McFarland, Moore, Cooper, Ball, Currie, Brooking, R. Charlton, Keegan, Best
ALL TIME INTERNATIONAL XI: Jennings (N. Ireland), Vogts (W. Germany), Beckenbauer (W. Germany), Moore (England), F. Marinho (Brazil), Cruyff (Holland), R. Charlton (England), Van Hanegem (Holland), Kempes (Argentina), Pele (Brazil), Best (N. Ireland)
FAVOURITE AWAY GROUND: Stoke — I made my debut there and scored
FAVOURITE STADIUM AT WHICH YOU HAVE PLAYED: Athletico Madrid
BEST GOAL SCORED: My volley against Manchester United in last season's League Cup
BEST GOAL SEEN SCORED: George Best's goal against Sheffield United when he beat about five players
MOST MEMORABLE MATCH: My debut for England against Bulgaria at Wembley in November 1979
OWN MAGIC MOMENT IN FOOTBALL: Scoring against Bulgaria in the above match
BIGGEST DISAPPOINTMENT: Getting relegated with Spurs to the Second Division
FAVOURITE OTHER SPORTS: Tennis and golf
MISCELLANEOUS LIKES: Listening to my LP's and going to pop concerts
MISCELLANEOUS DISLIKES: Smoking and getting injured
FAVOURITE TV SHOW: All sports programmes, Two Ronnies and Fawlty Towers
TV SHOW YOU ALWAYS SWITCH OFF: Panorama and any political programme
FAVOURITE READING: Soccer magazines
FAVOURITE MUSICIAN/SINGER: Elton John, Bad Company, Eagles and Foreigner
FAVOURITE FOOD: Steak and chips
FAVOURITE DRINK: Lager
BEST COUNTRY VISITED: Bermuda
FAVOURITE ACTORS/ACTRESS: Peter Sellers, Clint Eastwood, Barbra Streisand
BEST FILM SEEN RECENTLY: China Syndrome
BIGGEST INFLUENCE ON CAREER: My family and the coaching staff at Spurs
WHAT DON'T YOU LIKE ABOUT FOOTBALL: Losing
PRE-MATCH MEAL: Chicken
INTERNATIONAL HONOURS: England Youth, Under-21, B team and full international caps
PERSONAL AMBITION: To be happy and successful
PROFESSIONAL AMBITION: To win the League Championship
CAREER AFTER PLAYING: Too early to say — I might stay in the game or I might get a sports business of some kind
A PLAYER FOR THE EIGHTIES: Vince Hilaire of Crystal Palace and two young Spurs lads, Stuart Beavon and Mark Hazard
ADVICE TO YOUNGSTERS: To work hard, be dedicated and have the willingness to go all the way

Glenn Hoddle

67

The trappings of football stardom, 1980s style: Glenn Hoddle outside his home in Bishop's Stortford in 1981 (far left) and picking up endorsements and sponsorship deals (above)

Glenn Hoddle

Superstar in the making

Glenn at home with his then-wife, Christine Ann. By now Glenn was one of the best and most coveted players in the game. He had made his debut for England, and with his contract at Spurs in its final year he was linked with clubs at home and abroad

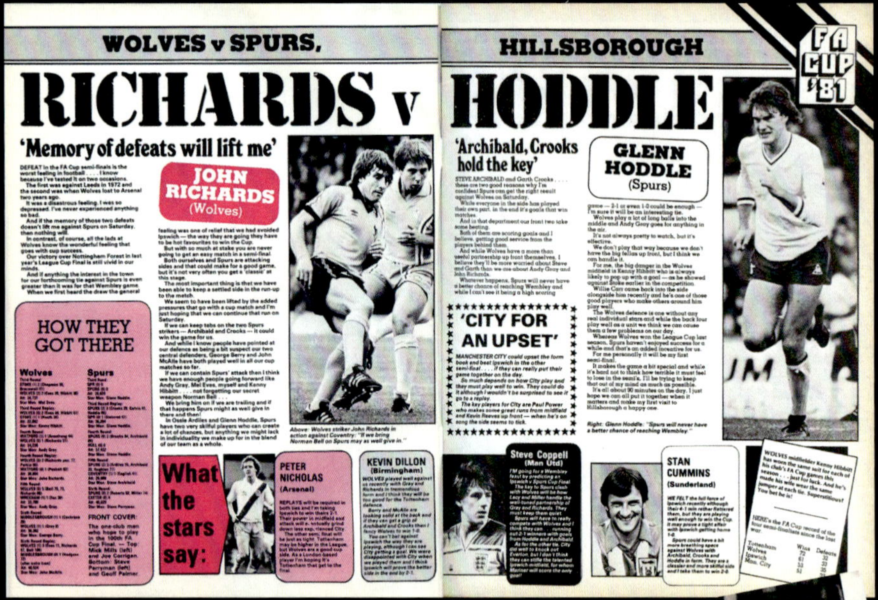

Cover star: Hoddle's column in *Match* magazine (above and right) featured his thoughts on each game in the cup run, while *Shoot!* put Glenn on the front page of its 1981 FA Cup Final special

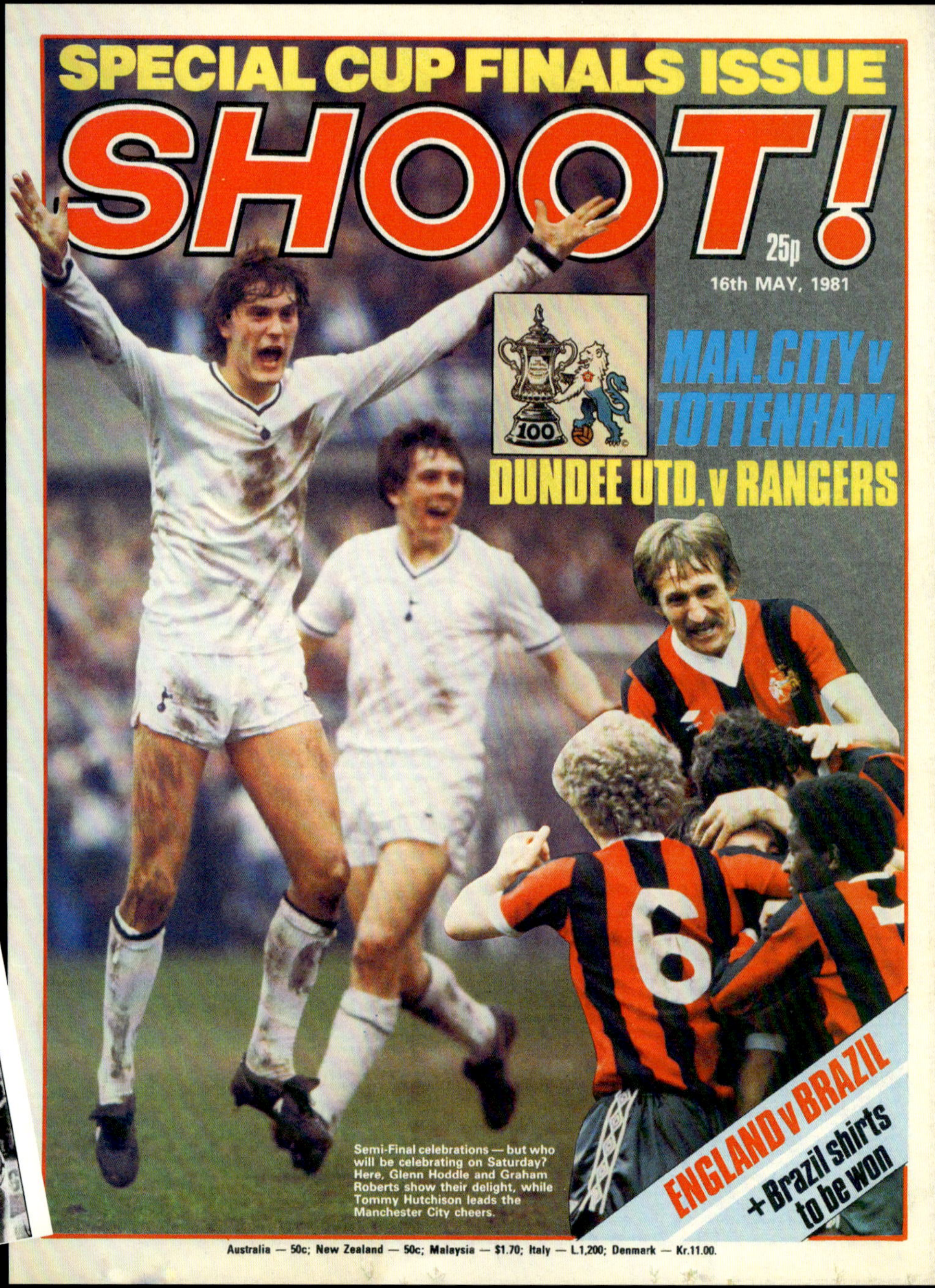

WOLVES v SPURS,

RICHARDS v

'Memory of defeats will lift me'

JOHN RICHARDS (Wolves)

HOW THEY GOT THERE

Wolves | Spurs

What the stars say:

PETER NICHOLAS (Arsenal)

FRONT COVER:

HILLSBOROUGH

HODDLE

'Archibald, Crooks hold the key'

GLENN HODDLE (Spurs)

'CITY FOR AN UPSET'

Steve Coppell (Man Utd)

KEVIN DILLON (Birmingham)

STAN CUMMINS (Sunderland)

FA CUP '81

SHOOT!

SPECIAL CUP FINALS ISSUE

25p

16th MAY, 1981

MAN. CITY v TOTTENHAM

DUNDEE UTD. v RANGERS

Semi-Final celebrations — but who will be celebrating on Saturday? Here, Glenn Hoddle and Graham Roberts show their delight, while Tommy Hutchison leads the Manchester City cheers.

ENGLAND v BRAZIL + Brazil shirts to be won

Australia — 50c; New Zealand — 50c; Malaysia — $1.70; Italy — L.1,200; Denmark — Kr.11.00.

The Spurs star gives you an exclusive insight into the Wembley feeling

'The happiest moment of my career' BY GLENN HODDLE

GLENN HODDLE

CUP FINAL '81

ON THE EVE of the big Wembley game, Match brings you pictures of the Spurs and England midfield star as you've never seen him before.
Photographer DUNCAN CUBITT visited Glenn's Hertfordshire home to give you a glimpse of his private world — away from the hustle and bustle of FA Cup soccer.

BELOW (left): Glenn poses with some of his most prized soccer possessions — the 'Young Player of the Year' award he won in 1979, the England cap he was awarded against Wales last year and the match ball from Spurs' League game against Coventry at White Hart Lane last season when Glenn scored a hat-trick as his side won 4-3.

RIGHT: Glenn swings into action with the little ball. I like many of the top stars of our game he enjoys a relaxing game of golf.

TOP (right): Steve Davis watch out! Glenn's right on cue as he puts in some snooker practice in the spare room.

BOTTOM (right): A little less energetic, but just as enjoyable as Glenn wages a tactical battle on the chess board with his wife Anne.

MY PROUD MOMENT BY GLENN HODDLE

CUP FINAL '81

IT'S the year of the Cockerel and I think it will be crowing after our FA Cup Final replay with Manchester City tonight (Thursday).

We know we can play a lot better than we did at Wembley on Saturday.

We won't be changing our tactics, but we will want to make a better start.

City were magnificent in the first half on Saturday whereas we only really started to play after half-time.

Extra-time was just cruel to both sides.

I think 1-1 was a fair result although once we got the equaliser I felt we had a good chance of winning the game.

Having said that, at the end of the day I was happy enough . . . .

The journey to Wembley was great. When our coach reached the top of Wembley Way we gave it a chorus of our song and that got all the boys going.

Most of the fans walking to the stadium were Spurs supporters and it was at that moment it really hit me that we were in the Cup Final.

I didn't feel that nervous though — even when we got out on to the pitch. I just felt proud.

And it has to be one of the best feelings in football when you walk out of that tunnel and hear the roar of the crowd.

City certainly had the best of the first 45 minutes, but in the dressing room at half-time we weren't too worried because we hadn't really played and we were still only one down.

We did leave it a bit late though . . . .

It was in my mind that Spurs had never lost an FA Cup Final and I couldn't help thinking how terrible it would be if we lost.

That's why there was such a great feeling of relief when our goal went in.

The free kick was something we had practised in training before.

My shot was heading for the top corner, but I think Joe Corrigan may have saved it if the ball hadn't hit Tommy Hutchison's shoulder.

Maybe we had a bit of luck there, but it didn't matter about that because the pressure was getting to us.

Once we got the equaliser we went all out to win it in the remaining ten minutes and I think that's why we blew up a little in the second period of extra time.

We were going down like nine-pins, but City's players were feeling it too and they couldn't really capitalise on it.

I was absolutely shattered at the end of the match . . . but we'll be rarin' to go again by the time kick-off time comes round tonight.

Right: The expression on Glenn Hoddle's face shows mixed feelings as he salutes the Spurs fans after the final whistle . . . complete with supporter's cap.

I COULDN'T HELP CRYING BY GLENN HODDLE

CUP FINAL '81 Replay

THE tears just rolled down my cheeks as the final whistle blew on our FA Cup Final replay with Manchester City.

Spurs had won the Cup and it was the happiest moment of my football career, but at the same time I realised it might be my last game for the club.

When I looked up at all the fans they were so pleased it just choked me up and I cried for a couple of minutes.

Whether I will finally decide to stay at Spurs or join another club I still don't know. All I will say is that I hope the current side doesn't break up.

I'm sure victory in the FA Cup can be a stepping stone to even more success.

But at present I'm keeping an open mind regarding my own future. I just want to see what comes up.

England have a couple of World Cup qualifiers coming up and obviously I'm hoping to be part of the international set-up.

I'll be going on tour with Spurs next month and then I'm off on holiday to America for a couple of weeks. When I get back I hope to sort out my future.

Whatever happens I'll never forget the night Spurs won the 100th FA Cup Final.

It was terrific . . . fantastic . . . too good to put into words.

Going up those steps at Wembley to collect a winner's medal is every player's dream.

But it was far from plain sailing. When Kevin Reeves put City 2-1 ahead from the penalty spot in the second half there was a moment when I thought it wasn't going to be our day.

We lost it for a while after that setback, but we managed to get back into our rhythm.

I've been told it was a great game to watch and overall it was a lovely game to play in because we were playing so well.

To be fair I think City played as well as they could on the Saturday before, whereas we knew we still had something up our sleeves.

I was as pleased for Ricky Villa as much as anyone. His winning goal was the best I have ever seen in a Cup Final.

It was specially pleasing when you consider that he was taken off in the first game.

I'm sure no-one would argue now that Spurs manager Keith Burkinshaw was wrong to play Ricky at the start of the replay!

He had something to prove and the first ten minutes or so were vital to him. His first goal couldn't have come at a better time.

Once we got 3-2 up we knew the Cup was there for the taking, but I had a few heart attacks in the last few minutes — especially when that shot from Dennis Tueart whistle just past the post.

I think that you must look at it over the two games though and when you consider what Milija Aleksic had to do in our goal, compared to the saves Joe Corrigan made for City, it tells its own story.

Naturally enough the scenes in our dressing room at Wembley after the replay were incredible.

They almost had to throw us out in the end. We were in the bath celebrating for almost an hour!

At the same time I felt for the Spurs lads who didn't get a place in the team, although they joined in the celebrations afterwards.

And you couldn't help but feel sorry for the City players. They battled really hard for two games and when I looked at their faces at the end of the replay I couldn't help thinking how we would have felt in their shoes.

An emotional moment as Glenn hugs Spurs substitute Garry Brooke at the end of the match. The man with the base of the FA Cup. Tottenham hat and scarf is Spurs goalkeeper Milija Aleksic.

MATCH WEEKLY

Match magazine visited Glenn at home prior to the final and watched him relax playing golf, snooker and chess in jumpers that could be politely described as 'the fashion of the time' (far left), while Glenn's column (left and below) after the final and the replay reflected on a week of unprecedented high emotions

RICKY VILLA

Midfield

RICARDO VILLA
TOTTENHAM HOTSPUR

Fact File

Spurs 1978-83
168 (11) Appearances (Sub)
25 Goals

1980/81 FA Cup
5 Appearances
3 Goals

Honours
FA Cup 1981

We didn't know much about Ricky when he arrived because we'd only seen him once in the World Cup, coming on as a substitute against Brazil, when he mullered somebody. That certainly wasn't Ricky. That was someone with a Ricky mask on. That was *so* not Ricky.

The real Ricky brought us panache and style. He was so likeable and so charming. He came over as smooth and confident, and we were quickly saying, 'Phwoar, what have we got here?' But we weren't quite sure what he was on the pitch. At first glance you'd say he was a defensive midfield player, or even a centre-back, or maybe a big lump of a centre-forward. Not a mover with the ball; not a fluid, moving thoroughbred.

Most dribblers I'd come across were wiry. George Best, Charlie Cooke, Cliff Jones, Alfie Conn – they were wiry in-and-outers. In later years, though, there was Gazza, and he was strong, wasn't he? Ricky was more like that, in that he was a *runner* – a strong, purposeful runner with the ball. A thoroughbred. If you watch a re-run of the FA Cup first round replay against Manchester United from January 1980, the one with Ossie's last-minute goal, you will see the pressure we were under, but you'll also notice Ricky was getting hold of the ball and dribbling over big distances – every time he did that, even though nothing came of it because he had no support, he was giving us a break, letting us catch our breath.

> **"Ricky brought us panache and style. He was so likeable and so charming"**

It took Ricky a lot longer to adapt to England than it took Ossie. Because he couldn't speak the language at first, Ricky's face would say a thousand words his brain couldn't communicate – 'We're here! We're here!' It generally wore a big smile, but he must have been thinking, 'What on earth have we done? How am I going to get out of this one?' Imagine being brought up on a ranch, as he was, then living in rented accommodation in Broxbourne. Not that Broxbourne has anything wrong with it – but it's not a ranch, is it? Thank goodness he had Ossie to look after him.

It was obvious Ricky was a nice man with lovely ethics and manners. But he could get so low, so disappointed. I think the difference between his highs and lows was unusually wide. The difference between mine, in comparison, was narrower because of the consistency of my game compared to his. But my playing style dictated my consistency, whereas Ricky was a player who tried to do special things. If you want to do special things on the pitch you're not going to pull them off every time, otherwise they wouldn't be special, would they?

Ricky wasn't the kind of player I'd typically appreciate because he was a maverick. But he was a nice maverick, and an effective one. When we do talks together now, whatever the first question he's asked is, he will always reply with, 'Thank you so much. Thank you for this welcome. I can't believe you still remember me.' And he's won everyone over. No matter what he says after that, he's won.

match makers

RICARDO VILLA
Spurs and Argentina

Full Name: Ricardo Julio Villa.
Birthplace/Date: Roque Perez, about 70 miles from Buenos Aires. August 18, 1952.
Height/Weight: 6ft. 13st 3lbs.
Married: Yes, to Cristena.
Children: None.
Car: Rover 2600.
Previous Clubs: Racing Club.
Trade Before Turning Pro: Schoolboy!
Club Nickname: Ricky.
Worst Ever Injury: Last year I strained ligaments in my right knee and was out for two months.
Favourite British Player And Why: Kenny Dalglish – he is so talented on the ball and scores goals.
Favourite Other Team: Liverpool.
Favourite Foreign Player And Why: My favourite player playing abroad is Kevin Keegan. My favourite foreign player is Argentinian team-mate Daniel Passarella. I chose them for the same reason – they are great players and great people.
Best British Team: Shilton, Anderson, Thompson, Lloyd, Mills, Wilkins, Kennedy, Brady, Coppell, Dalglish, Robertson.
All Time International XI: Yashin (Russia), Alberto (Brazil), Perfumo (Argentina), Passarella (Argentina), Marcolini (Argentina), Gerson (Brazil), Cecchini (Brazil), Cruyff (Holland), Keegan (England), Pele (Brazil), Best (N. Ireland).
Favourite Away Ground: Aston Villa.
Favourite Stadium At Which You Have Played: Bernabeu Stadium, Real Madrid.
Best Goal Scored: My first for Spurs last season in the opening game against Nottingham Forest. It was only from close range, but it was memorable.
Best Goal Seen Scored: Mario Kempes first goal for Argentina in the '78 World Cup Final.
Most Difficult Opponent: Phil Thompson (Liverpool).
Most Memorable Match: My first game for Tottenham against Nottingham Forest.
Magic Moment In Football: Being part of the World Cup winning squad.
Biggest Disappointment: My first three years as a professional. I was not happy with my game then.
Favourite Other Sports: Tennis, motor racing.
Miscellaneous Likes: Shooting and fishing.
Miscellaneous Dislikes: Getting up in the mornings.
Favourite TV: Any film.
TV Show You Always Switch Off: Political broadcasts.
Favourite Reading: Any magazine.
Favourite Singer: Tom Jones.
Favourite Food: Roast beef.
Favourite Drink: White wine.
Best Country Visited: France.
Favourite Actor/Actress: Clint Eastwood, Sophia Loren.
Best Friend: 'Ossie' Ardiles.
Biggest Influence On Career: Carlos Menotti, the Argentinian manager. He gave me so much confidence.
What Don't You Like About Football: Close marking.
Superstitions: I always make sure my right leg is the first to touch the pitch as I run out.
Pre-Match Meal: Coffee and toast.
International Honours: Argentinian full caps, Under-21's and Youth honours.
Personal Ambition: To be happy with my family and friends.
Professional Ambition: To win the league with Tottenham and play in Europe.
Career After Playing: I shall probably go and work on my ranch in Argentina.
A Player For The Eighties: Diego Maradona of Argentina.
Who Would You Must Like To Meet: Muhammad Ali.
Advice To Youngsters: To work hard all the time and not to get big-headed.

81

MOMENT IN TIME

August 1974, White Hart Lane, Bill Nicholson's office

"Bill's office was functional, not flashy, just like the man himself. Very clean, tidy and organised, and if more than three players were in it with him it was tight.

That day, it was just him and me.

'Do you know what you're saying, Steve? Do you realise what you've just said?

'Bill, you've asked me what I think. I've told you what I think.'

Of course I realised what I'd said. I'd just told him I was willing to leave Tottenham Hotspur."

Steve Perryman

THE FIFTH ROUND SPURS v COVENTRY

Nearly sent to Coventry

Meeting Coventry City in the fifth round was a reminder that I could have been playing for the opposition and how the course of history – both mine and Spurs – would have been so different

It was the start of the 1974/75 season. We'd lost 1-0 to Ipswich at home and 1-0 to Manchester City away. Three days later we went up to newly promoted Carlisle United and lost 1-0 there. The team was floundering, and I was part of the flounder.

In healthier times, when the football was flowing, I was prepared to step back and let the star players have the stage. But it wasn't flowing, and so I was having to take too many steps forward, putting myself on offer. We didn't have the team to cope with it and therefore I wasn't looking that good.

The balance of a team can mean a lot, particularly for a defensive midfielder, as I was at the time. A defensive midfield player with Glenn around, or Alan Mullery, or Martin Peters, can thrive on their confidence and ability. But Glenn hadn't yet come through, Mullery had left, Martin was halfway out of the door and I was toiling. It sounds a bit disrespectful but I didn't really have the type of player that I needed around me to pull me out of it.

I was brought up to 'see it, play it', and the better the team you're in the more options you have as to how and where you play it once you've seen it. Then it comes down to your decision-making – which is the best option? When you're in a poor team there just aren't those options, there's no one – and then you end up looking crap. I wasn't the skilful, twisty-turny, Micky Hazard type who could get himself out of trouble. My game was straightforward, and all of a sudden it wasn't there to be seen.

Bill Nicholson was struggling too. When you're struggling, it's coming at you from all directions. Even the great Bill Nick would have felt the extra pressure around the club at the time. People were questioning his judgment and decision-making. When you're near the bottom of the league no one's saying, 'Yeah, but he won the Double.'

So one evening I received a phone call from Charlie Faulkner, the chief scout at Tottenham who had done the groundwork to recruit me when I was a schoolboy.

'Steve, there's something you need to know. Tomorrow you're going to get called into Bill's office and be told he's been in contact with Coventry about two of their players. They've asked for you in return. So Bill's going to ask you what you think about moving.'

Charlie, Bill and Eddie had been discussing the issue in the office. Eddie, who was a bit black and white about these things, said that my

Legendary Spurs manager Bill Nicholson in his office where, in 1974, a tense meeting with Steve Perryman very nearly saw the player leave White Hart Lane

> **"My game was straightforward see-it-play-it, and all of a sudden it wasn't there to be seen"**

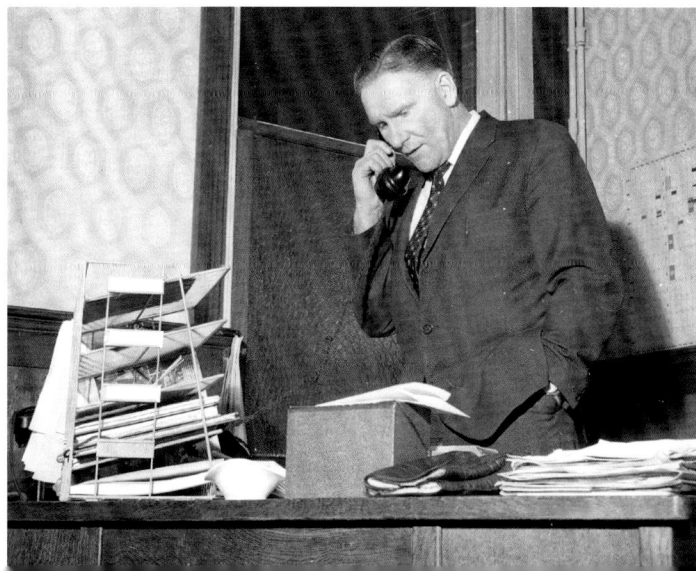

legs had gone. They'd thought I was this, they'd thought I was that, and it turns out I wasn't. Charlie was so outraged he threw a cup. Which was a nice gesture, and I appreciated the loyalty, but I also appreciated the situation was serious enough for Charlie to put his job on the line for me by warning me in advance about the meeting.

It happened just the way Charlie had predicted. The next morning I was called into Bill's office, but because I had been tipped off I went in on the front foot.

'I've never thought about letting you go,' Bill said. 'But what do you think?'

'Where is it, Bill?' I said, knowing full well it was Coventry.

'I'm not prepared to say. I'm just asking you whether you'd consider a move.'

'Okay. Well, if it's somewhere like Newcastle, no. If it's somewhere within driving distance – bearing in mind it takes me more than an hour to get here anyway – yeah. Let's talk about it.'

So, Bill told me to train as normal, not tell anyone that was going on, and go home to think about it.

So I went home to think about it.

This wasn't the straightforward, authoritative Bill I knew. With Bill, if there was a discussion it was all one-sided. That had always been part of his manner. He wasn't bolshy in any way, it was more, 'This is how it is.' There was a strength in that. You weren't asked for your opinion. You were told what to do, and you did it. You lived by his words. It was tough love, but it taught me to become a battle-hardened warrior. From him and his staff I'd learnt how honoured I

Steve Perryman in FA Cup action against Coventry. But for a quirk of history – the shock resignation of Bill Nicholson – he might have been playing for the Sky Blues at White Hart Lane in this fifth-round tie

should be to wear the white shirt. The fact that he was sounding me out showed what a state he was in. How bad things had got.

I thought about Coventry. Tottenham then was the established club doing things in the traditional way. Coventry were sort of part of the 'new wave'. Their chairman was Jimmy Hill, who was a big figure on TV as he'd come up with the idea of the 'pundits panel'. Back when I was a kid and he was a player with Fulham he had led a successful strike to get the minimum wage scrapped, so he was someone who was looking to improve the lot of footballers, whether at his club or in general. It felt like he was ahead of his time.

I went back in the next day and told Bill I was ready to leave. 'Yeah, go on then, I'll have that.'

I'm not suggesting that it was a case of my being the rat who wanted to leave the sinking ship. It wasn't like that at all. I'd been at Tottenham since I was 15, and I was sort of rooted there, I was dug in, I belonged there. But I was coming up to 24. Married, with a new baby. I had to think about what was best for everybody. I was struggling, and because I was in a bad run of form, I saw it as an escape route. It demonstrated what a cloud I was under at the time for me to even consider it. But it was instigated by others. I certainly wouldn't have instigated it myself. I didn't rate myself enough to think someone would want me.

That Saturday we lost 2-1 at home to Manchester City. Bill resigned that weekend. I doubt whether my situation was part of it, although maybe my response had shocked him into thinking, 'If Steve's prepared to leave, that's the sort of state we're in.' Bill had a big heart – that's what being a man entails, you've got to have heart to go with everything else – but he was struggling. I probably disappointed him with my reaction. He may have thought, 'We're crumbling.' We probably were.

But what if Bill had stayed and I had been transferred to Coventry? Would I have been part of the side that met Tottenham Hotspur in the 1981 FA Cup? I doubt it. If I'd gone to Coventry, I would probably have had five more moves after that. Once you have the first one, you don't belong anywhere.

Coventry in 1981 were more or less what they had been in 1974 – a mid-table side, but one with ambitions. Their ground, Highfield

Ossie Ardiles deftly dribbles around Coventry goalkeeper Les Sealey to open the scoring

"Sometimes you need a catalyst, and you'd have to say it was Ossie who had his foot on the pedal when it came to tempo that day"

Road, was about to become the first all-seater stadium in England, so they were certainly doing things in a new way. The week before they came to White Hart Lane they were flying high. They had the second leg of a League Cup semi-final against West Ham, having won the first leg at home 3-2, and the Saturday after they would have their chance to earn a place in the quarter-finals of the FA Cup.

So they'd had all this going on, they'd had that going on – lots of positives. And then they lost the second leg against West Ham 2-0. Suddenly it was different situation. Their confidence maybe took a knock, maybe they were thinking, 'We've got to come back to London again and face Tottenham Hotspur, face Glenn Hoddle and Ossie Ardiles, deal with Steve Archibald and Garth Crooks.'

It was Ossie's day. I've watched some clips of that Coventry game on YouTube and what strikes me every time is the urgency that he brought to that performance. He was the game-changer. Sometimes you need a catalyst, and you'd have to say it was Ossie who had his foot on the pedal when it came to tempo that day.

You can see his legs move urgently, and he obviously read the bad back pass that led to his goal. Talk about anticipation. And then he had enough speed of thought to beat the goalkeeper and enough space to get it on the angle. Which shows he was more than an 'urgent legs' man. He could read what you were going to do before you knew what you were going to do. He could deliver, he could pass – he could do everything. But it was built on tempo. If you have a catalyst in your team who can provide that – even out of possession when you can use it to press – then it makes a huge difference.

I had it with the ball in my Second Division days – bringing it out sharp, going for holes and then playing other people in. And that was Ossie's game. He was a specialist at that. When you've got special players in your team, one of them will come to the front, even on not such a good day. I'm not saying we had a bad day against Coventry – it felt easy for us, even though they did get one back – but we had the players who could get us out of trouble.

At the start of the year, the *Guardian*'s tips for the last eight in the FA Cup had been Liverpool, West Bromwich Albion, Arsenal, Ipswich Town, Birmingham City, Southampton and Swansea. They got that a bit wrong, didn't they? Liverpool, Arsenal, West Brom and Swansea were long gone. Southampton had been knocked out by Everton after a replay. Of the sides that were still left, the ones you didn't want to get were either league leaders Ipswich or European champions Nottingham Forest, but even if you didn't get them every other team except one was in the First Division.

And that was the one we got: Exeter City of the Third Division.

I thought, 'All home games, never having to move out of London. It's all turning out easy for us.'

Too easy?

5TH ROUND

TOTTENHAM HOTSPUR
Football & Athletic Co. Ltd.

TOTTENHAM HOTSPUR V COVENTRY

F.A. CUP 5TH ROUND K.O. 3-00 P.M

SATURDAY 14TH FEBRUARY 1981

EAST TERRACE ENCLOSURE

PRICE
(INC. VAT)

£1·80   58 30 13 44   37-39

ENTRANCE

TO BE RETAINED

Dyson boobs —and Ossie is closer to Wembley

Brooke fires a Final warning

By BRIAN MADLEY
Spurs 3
Coventry 1

Tottenham Hotspur   Coventry City

Manager Keith Burkinshaw
(White Shirts, Blue Shorts, White Stockings)

Manager Gordon Milne
(Sky Blue Shirts, Sky Blue Shorts. Sky Blue Stockings)

3 (2)   Tottenham Hotspur   Coventry City 1 (1)

BARRY DAINES	1	LES SEALEY
(1) Chris Houghton / DON McALLISTER	2	DANNY THOMAS
PAUL MILLER	3	BRIAN ROBERTS
GRAHAM ROBERTS	4	ANDY BLAIR
JOHN LACY	5	PAUL DYSON
STEVE PERRYMAN	6	GARY GILLESPIE
(1) OSVALDO ARDILES	7	John Dyless / PETER BODAK
(1) STEVE ARCHIBALD	8	GERRY DALY
TONY GALVIN	9	GARRY THOMPSON Tom English (1)
GLENN HODDLE	10	MARK HATELEY
GARTH CROOKS	11	STEVE HUNT
Garry Brooke (P 7)	12	Mark Hatfley

OFFICIALS
Referee: MR. JOSEPH WORRALL (Warrington)

MR. JOSEPH WORRALL of Warrington started as a referee at 19 and graduated to the Football League via the Warrington and District and Cheshire Leagues. He has officiated in a number of top matches.
A works accountant by occupation, Mr. Worrall is interested in all sports and keeping fit.

SCORECHECK

Here are the other F.A. Cup-ties and First Division matches being played today. Half-time scores will be announced.

IPSWICH TOWN
CHARLTON ATHLETIC
MIDDLESBROUGH
BARNSLEY
NEWCASTLE UNITED
EXETER CITY
NOTTINGHAM FOREST
BRISTOL CITY
PETERBOROUGH UNITED
MANCHESTER CITY
SOUTHAMPTON
EVERTON
WOLVERHAMPTON WANDERERS

Spurs 3 Coventry 1

14th February 1981, White Hart Lane. Att: 36,688

Spurs goalscorers: Ardiles, Archibald, Hughton

By Julie Welch

Glenn Hoddle at his breathtaking best, the crowd singing *Glory Glory Hallelujah*, and Spurs a delight – when they were going forward, that is. Two up in 20 minutes with goals from Ossie Ardiles and Steve Archibald, wobbling slightly just before the break when their defending left not so much a gap as a chasm for Coventry to exploit, they sealed their place in the quarter-final thanks to a classic piece of Ardiles goal-nabbing and a superbly precise piece of passing from Hoddle that let Chris Hughton chalk up his first goal for more than a year.

As ever, of course, the big talking point was why Hoddle is not an automatic pick for the national side. It's not only the North London faithful that regard it as a mystery. He has always had a delicate touch on the ball and a superb way with a pass, and lately he has revealed a deep-down granite-hard seam of determination that must surely clinch his place. This was a display so effortless that some were alleging that the calf injury he is said to have suffered in midweek was a bluff to lull Coventry into a false sense of security.

As for Ardiles, his return to the Spurs side after a spell on international duty has made all the difference to the way they tick. His 16th-minute goal was a prime example of the Argentinian's sharpness and urgency – it's hard to think of another player currently plying his trade in England who could combine the alertness to seize on a sloppy back pass from Paul Dyson with the quick accuracy to see it home. Dyson, poor soul, was having such a torrid time of it all-round that it probably came as a relief to him when he was hooked at the end of the first half. Only Hoddle, meanwhile, could have come up with the overhead kick to Steve Archibald that supplied Tottenham's second.

With Hughton and Tony Galvin developing a good thing between them on the left, and Steve Perryman's drive and unshowy delivery to Hoddle on the right, yesterday's performance, even without the injured Ricky Villa, suggests that Tottenham have now got the personnel they need to transmogrify from a highly watchable but inconsistent team to one capable of going for the big prizes. That's if they aren't undone by a seemingly ineradicable instinct to go forward. Yesterday that allowed Coventry to peg one back four minutes from the half-time break, when Tommy English found himself unsupervised in the wide open spaces of their defence.

Despatched from the League Cup by West Ham only four days back, this defeat closed a disappointing week for Coventry, who now, as they say, are free to concentrate on the league. Afterwards, their manager, Gordon Milne, put a brave face on it – 'We've enjoyed the ride.' Not half as much as Spurs. If tomorrow morning's draw keeps them away from Ipswich Town, there is every chance they could reach an FA Cup Final for the first time in 14 years.

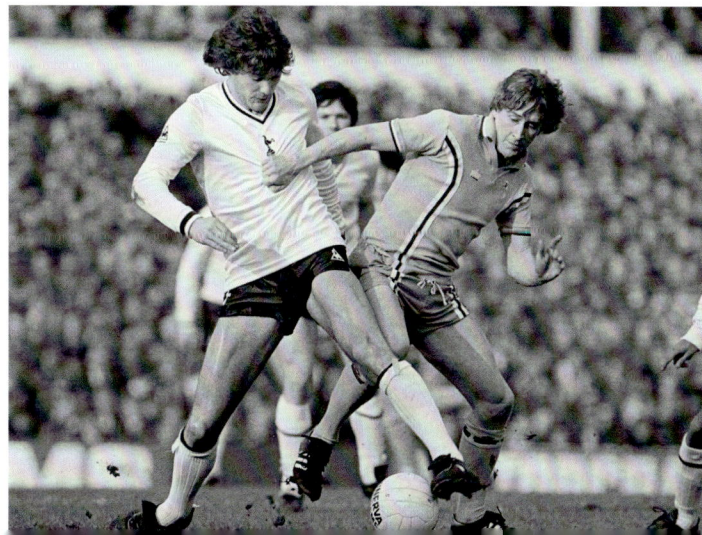

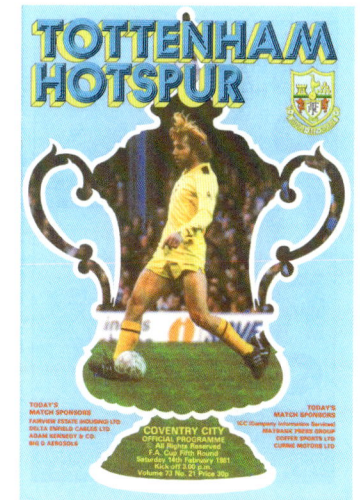

Glenn Hoddle produced another eye-catching performance in what was eventually a comfortable win over Coventry

The unsung hero

Despite relegation to the Second Division in his first season as manager, Keith Burkinshaw kept his job and was given time to build a winning team in the Spurs mould

By Julie Welch

'I loved it,' said Keith Burkinshaw, referring to the club he managed between 1976 and 1982. That was when he had a chairman who allowed him to run the club as he wanted to run it, not the place he walked out of in 1984, in frustrated disgust, with the immortal parting shot – 'There used to be a football club over there.'

It was the summer of 1976 when Burkinshaw took over a Spurs side already coming apart. Terry Neill had brought him down from Newcastle United to be his coach and they barely had time to say 'Hello' before Neill said, 'Goodbye, I'm off to Arsenal.' Burkinshaw was one of the last people to find out. After the club's end-of-season tour he had taken his family on holiday to Croatia and the first he heard of Neill's exit was when he picked up a newspaper.

'I'd only been at Tottenham for 12 months,' said Burkinshaw. 'I thought to myself, "Christ, another manager's going to come in here – what's going to happen to me? The least I can do is apply for the job".'

Fortunately, the Spurs chairman, Sidney Wale, thought Burkinshaw was a good bet to take over, though Tottenham were falling giants by then and he couldn't stop their descent. The team was relegated at the end of the season. Promotion back to the First Division at the first attempt was essential and, to their credit, the board had seen enough to give their inexperienced manager the chance to get the club back on the rails. So there it was. One season to save his job. To help him keep it, he had Steve Perryman as the lynchpin of the side, and one youngster who he knew was capable of great things the moment he saw him.

'Glenn Hoddle was only a kid when I went to Tottenham,' Burkinshaw recalled, 'and I remember him playing his first game, which was at Stoke, and I could see then, immediately, what a player he was going to be.

'He was a shy sort of kid at that stage, and no problem at all, but I could see he was out of the ordinary because if I wanted something done in training, I would ask him to do it and he'd do it perfectly from the word go. I don't think there's any other player who could have done that. And that's how he was. I never treated him differently – he didn't have any ego in that respect. The one thing I was disappointed about with Glenn was that I thought England should have had him as their top player, but in those days they were looking at the physical side of things rather than the technical side, and he played 50-odd games when he should have played a hundred-and-bloody-fifty.'

Burkinshaw also had Bill Nicholson.

'I knew Bill was at West Ham and I thought, if I can get him back to Tottenham I can give him the job of bringing in the players that we needed, which is what he wanted to do. He still lived near the ground and I called in at his house after most home matches – I don't think people realise how it was then.'

Neither did many realise, then or even now, that it was Nicholson who oversaw the legendary game against Bristol Rovers during the Second Division campaign on 22nd October 1977.

"It was the summer of 1976 when Burkinshaw took over a Spurs side already coming apart"

Straight-talking Yorkshireman Keith Burkinshaw was given time to build his Spurs team

'On the Friday morning I said to him, "Bill, I've just found out my mother's died and I've got to go up north. I want you to take over the team." And that was it. We didn't discuss a gameplan. He just said, "Ah. Fine. There you go." We won 9-0. I don't think he said a lot to me when I got back either, to be fair!

'In the league, we did really, really well up until my mum's death and then we had a couple of games where we had to get points or else we weren't going to be up again, and then we managed to get a draw against Southampton in the last match of the season, which was essential. So yes, things worked out pretty well, I think, for us. Of course, if we hadn't gone up that season I wouldn't have been there any longer.'

Instead of collecting his P45 in the summer of 1978, Burkinshaw flew to Argentina and signed two world-class footballers who had no idea what they were walking into.

'I'd watched the 1978 World Cup and Ossie was voted player of the tournament, and Ricky came in on the odd occasion. I spoke to Harry Haslam, who said, "If you go off to Argentina this weekend I'm pretty sure you'll be able to sign them." So off I went – and the fella who made everything right for me when I got there was the guy that had been sent off against England in the 1966 World Cup, Antonio Rattin. And he was the nicest guy you could ever come across. So that started things off well for me, and Ossie and I seemed to get on. Signing the two of them was pretty simple, and I think Ossie's wife really, really wanted to come to England and that helped a lot. I was a bit worried about how they'd adapt to living in England so I rented a house that was big enough to take both of their families, and the wives brought over their mothers and fathers so everyone would know it was nice to live there.'

Things didn't click immediately, however. Spurs went down 4-1 to Aston Villa in their first home fixture and were then thrashed 7-0 at Liverpool. Ossie and Ricky were discombobulated in the English game at that stage. All along, though, Burkinshaw was pretty confident that they could be up near the top rather than down at the bottom, playing football the fans wanted to see.

'Because I always felt there was something about Tottenham that was a little bit different to every other club. The football was terrific under Bill Nicholson, and that was how I wanted to play. I also think that because I wanted the football to be that good, I didn't think about what we'd have to do to win the league. It was the football that we played that was the biggest thing, really.'

Along the way, Burkinshaw was putting together the kind of team that would play his, and Tottenham Hotspur's, entertaining brand of football.

'I knew Graham Roberts and Paul Miller would never let us down. Miller loved the big stage – the bigger the game the better, as far as he was concerned; he was hugely influential.'

He also liked Chris Hughton.

'Chris was a lift engineer when I first met him, but he really came on as a footballer and played in all the successful cup sides. But I think my best bit of business has to be Tony Galvin. He was a solid player – the best value-for-money deal I ever did. He was spotted playing for Goole Town on Humberside by a friend of mine from Scunthorpe and Bill Nicholson went up there to have a look. Bill came back and said, "Sign him," and I did, even though I still hadn't seen him myself. He only cost £30,000 – it was an absolute bargain.'

The team was growing up together. For two seasons they were nearly there, but not quite. Then he added the two that were the final pieces of the jigsaw.

'Garth Crooks and Steve Archibald were exactly the types of strikers I'd been looking for. We had a great midfield and we needed forwards with good movement and good brains to make the right runs and get the best out of Ardiles and Hoddle. Archibald and Crooks did that. I knew the team needed more goals and that's what they gave us.

'In those days the FA Cup was as big as the league really. Everybody wanted to talk about every game, and the '81 FA Cup

Right: Burkinshaw's trailblazing signing of Ardiles and Villa put newly-promoted Spurs right back under the spotlight

Centre: The manager gets his message over to his skipper, Steve Perryman, during the break before extra-time in the 1981 cup final

Far right: A casual Burkinshaw appears on the back cover of the 1982 Spurs Annual with the FA Cup trophy at his feet

PIONEER BURKINSHAW PLANS ANOTHER REVOLUTION

"Instead of collecting his P45 in the summer of 1978, Burkinshaw flew to Argentina and signed two world-class footballers"

was the first thing I won with the club. Lifting the trophy was a huge achievement.'

The side that Burkinshaw built went on to win the FA Cup for the second year running in 1982, and his stint at the club finished with its crowning achievement – victory in the 1984 UEFA Cup Final. But by then a change at the top had tainted everything for him. The new regime usurped his power.

'For me, football was the main thing at the place, whereas I knew for a fact that these people were all dreaming about how much money they were going to make. So, I knew things weren't going to be quite the same. I didn't get on with the new chairman at all, and to be fair to me, the club went downhill to a certain extent after I left so I was right. It was ridiculous what happened in 1984 because if they'd left me there I'm pretty sure we would have won more trophies.

'The league was the thing that I failed on, because of the football I wanted them to play. A midfield containing Hoddle, Villa and Ardiles wasn't the best in terms of getting the tackles in, but I didn't want to sign a Graeme Souness-type player because I didn't think that type of player would bring in the quality I wanted. If we'd played really, really good football and they'd lost 1-0 I wasn't too unhappy. Which was wrong, really.

'We should have been right at the top. But the supporters loved it. We were not the best defensive team but, by Christ, we were wonderful going forward. I lived with the defensive problems. I could not sacrifice what I had in the other half of the field. It was the "Spurs Way".'

The luck of the draw

Spurs supporters of a certain vintage recall their memories of the early rounds of the 1981 cup run, including the part played by a 'lucky' coin

By the time their FA Cup campaign kicked off in January 1981, Tottenham's patchy form in the league meant that even with their new supercharged forward line there was already no hope of figuring in the title race, and 1980 had ended with the disappointment of losing to West Ham in the League Cup. Now the FA Cup was their only chance of silverware. There was a '1' in the year, it was the Chinese Year of the Cockerel – any extra supernatural help would come in handy.

'On the weekend of the 0-0 draw with QPR at Loftus Road I found an American one cent piece in my loose change,' says Pete Haine, 'and for some reason I kept it and took it with me to the replay, and all the following home ties.

'I was 26 and I'd been going to Tottenham for 12 years, from '67 then all through the '70s. I'd seen them in the good years in the early '70s and the doldrums of the relegation season. I was living in Stevenage and was married, although that marriage was falling to pieces. It's often said that football is an escape from real life, and that's what I found in the FA Cup run. It took my mind off it, at least on the days of the games. I didn't have to travel far, which helped reduce arguments at home, as all our games up to the semi-final were in London.'

Kev Clark was part of a group of four who decided Spurs were going to win the cup after the season-opening league win against Nottingham Forest. 'We thought we might as well go to every home game because then we might have a chance of getting tickets for the final,' he says. 'We went to Loftus Road, where nothing much happened. It was a nondescript game that we'd expected to win. But of course we headed down to the Lane to watch the replay, thinking, "We should do this one, we're at home now. Let's go for it," and we won comfortably.'

Ivan Cohen grew up in Hackney and was completing his PhD at Sheffield. 'I went with my brothers, Neil and Alan, and my friend Harry, who was at Leeds University, so he'd come along with

> "We thought we might as well go to every home game because then we might have a chance of getting tickets for the final"

the 'Sheffield Spurs'. We went to all the early games. You just bundled into the car, three or four of you, come down to London, stay with your parents, go to the game, then drive back the next day to Sheffield. But the teams we played in the early rounds were relatively straightforward, or should have been, and because of that you don't have these deep emotional memories that you have of the later games.'

That's pretty much the consensus among the fans – that in retrospect the first three ties were straightforward, run-of-the-mill. Almost. 'Hull was a game we thought we ought to win easily,' says Kev Clark, 'but it wasn't like that. It still wasn't the team that emerged as we got nearer the final and we were struggling.'

'I remember the Hull match being very nervous,' concurs Pete Haine. 'The expectation was that being a lower league side we'd steamroller them.'

'We had the majority of the game,' adds Clark, 'and it was frustrating because we just couldn't get past the keeper. We always used to stand in the Lower Shelf and we were getting more and more frustrated and then all of a sudden Garry Brooke came on and turned the game. Finally. He set up the second as well, and there was an atmosphere of, "Thank Gawd for that".

"And then we got Exeter and everyone thought, 'Blimey, this really is our year'"

smoothly by. It was routine, easy. I don't think we were under any pressure at all. We were all thinking "We're definitely going to win this now, we're playing against teams we ought to beat, bring on the next round, nice easy home draw and we'll be fine. Great." And then we got Exeter and everyone thought, "Blimey, this really is our year".'

'My grandfather was the classic Jewish immigrant from Poland,' says Jill Lewis. 'He probably came over in the early 1890s and lived near Tottenham as a little boy, and I suppose that's where the family connection started. My dad had been a season-ticket holder since the war, and he had six pairs of standing-order tickets that he used for friends. I began going in the 1964/65 season. My brother, who was nine years older than me, went with my dad, and then he started playing rugby for his school so it was, "Take me! Take me!" and I just loved it from the first.

'I went to all the early rounds in a group with my dad, my sister Helen, her friend Neil, and a friend of mine, Claud . She never really understood the offside rule. It was totally beyond her. But she really got into it. The only thing I remember from those first games is thinking, "We're getting a good run at this" and then we got Exeter and I thought, "Yes, that's fantastic! That's the draw we want!"

'I was 14 and I went to all the games,' says Mike Leigh. 'At that age you're so obsessed by football you

take whatever you can get. I started going when I was five with my dad. The FA Cup was such a big thing then. I was born in 1967, so I'd never seen Tottenham lift the cup and at one point we had such a wretched record of getting knocked out in the third round. In the playground it was obviously Arsenal, Liverpool and United and all that, and you had West Ham who'd won it the year before so you're thinking, "Is this ever going to happen?" Three out of those first four games were lower-division clubs and the standout memory was obviously Exeter in the sixth round. I remember their goalie played an absolute blinder and it was a very, very tough game. Roberts and Miller didn't score many so it was quite bizarre that they did it.'

'Exeter was anything but a comfortable game,' says Kev Clark, 'even though we were at home against a lower-league side. But everyone was saying, '81, the year ends in a '1', it's the Year of the Cockerel. It's not going to be a problem. We're going to win this, we know we were going to win, it's just we're making hard work of it.'

Simon Lipson went with a friend from his teens who, like him, was a trainee solicitor. 'There was something going on with Spurs at the time,' he says. 'We had good players – albeit with some weaknesses here and there – but it felt right. And once we got past Exeter there was an odd feeling that this was our year.'

'Our name,' confirms Mike Leigh, 'was on the cup.'

'By the time we drew Coventry, we had a routine for the cup games and we weren't going to change it. One of the guys lived in Edmonton, by the side of the North Circular, so we used to drive to his house, park up and walk from the A10 and over the North Circular and into the Three Crowns pub for a pre-match pint. It was a bit cold on the day of the Hull game so we had whisky chasers to keep us warm while we queued up to get into the Lower Shelf. We got settled in and the game just seemed to go

MEET THE TEAM
GARTH CROOKS
Forward

Introduced by Steve Perryman

Fact File

Spurs 1980-85
176 (6) Appearances (Sub)
75 Goals

1980/81 FA Cup
9 Appearances
4 Goals

Honours
FA Cup 1981, 1982
UEFA Cup 1984

Garth was born and raised in Stoke, so he had nothing to do with London at all, but when he came to London he came home. He was in the place where he was comfortable. That's not being disrespectful to Stoke by the way. It's simply that Garth was what you'd call a chap – he was fun – and the capital suited him down to the ground.

I think if he hadn't been a player he might have gone on to take a university degree because he had a lot of O-Levels, which wasn't the usual thing for a footballer – Tony Galvin and John Lacy were the exceptions that proved the rule. But he was like a modern version of Danny Blanchflower, who had a sideline as a Fleet Street journalist while he was at Spurs. Garth combined his football with media work – and I think it led to him leaving the hotel on a certain Friday night before Wembley to go and do his show on Capital Radio, which maybe wasn't quite right! He was guest presenter when we made our appearance on *Top of the Pops* in 1982, so it wasn't a surprise when he went on to work for the BBC after he'd retired from the game. He also showed his serious side as an active member of the Professional Footballers' Association, which he was chairman of for a while.

Garth proved he was an inspired signing straight away, scoring on his debut against Nottingham Forest and twice in our 4-3 defeat of Crystal Palace four days later. He wasn't that tall, but he had a leap in him and he was quick, which asks a lot of defenders. Pace is one of the main requirements in a striker, or at least in a strike partnership. Gilly, for example, wasn't quick, but he would flick it on and Jimmy would be gone. Garth in comparison had all the pace you could ask for, and one of our main routes to goal was for Glenn to find him with a pass.

But for all his flair and extrovert personality I had the impression it took Garth a while to believe he had all the goals in him that he did, whereas Archie was more sure of himself right from the start and always fancied himself to score. I think it's because having come from Stoke City, Garth realised he had to survive at a glamour club in the company of players who had won trophies – Ossie and Ricky, Archie and me – and he desperately wanted to be in that bracket.

It's impossible to talk about Garth without bringing Archie in, because together they were such a strong unit, and Archie would have picked him up if he was down – they joined together and they supported each other, not only in play but lots of other ways. And Garth won three trophies during his time at the club, so he's definitely put himself in the same bracket as Ossie and Ricky, Archie and me, hasn't he?

> **"He proved he was an inspired signing straight away, scoring on his debut against Nottingham Forest"**

GARTH CROOKS

TOTTENHAM

FULL NAME: Garth Anthony Crooks
BIRTHPLACE: Stoke-on-Trent
BIRTHDATE: March 10, 1958
HEIGHT: 5ft 8ins
WEIGHT: 11st 9lbs
PREVIOUS CLUB: Stoke City
MARRIED: No
CAR: Datsun 260Z Sports
FAVOURITE NEWSPAPER: Sunday Express
FAVOURITE PLAYER: Diego Maradona
MOST PROMISING TEAM-MATES: Chris Hughton and Mark Falco
FAVOURITE OTHER TEAM: Tottenham Reserves
FOOTBALL HERO OF CHILDHOOD: Pele
FAVOURITE OTHER SPORT: Tennis
MOST DIFFICULT OPPONENT: All difficult
MOST MEMORABLE MATCH: Debut for England U-21 v Bulgaria
BIGGEST DISAPPOINTMENT: Being relegated with Stoke
FRIENDLIEST AWAY FANS: Everton and Liverpool
FAVOURITE FOOD + DRINK: Steak Diane — lager shandy with lime
MISCELLANEOUS LIKES AND DISLIKES: Meeting people, talking to older professionals and listening to their stories/Bad manners and smoking
FAVOURITE HOLIDAY RESORT: South of France
FAVOURITE T.V. STAR, MALE AND FEMALE: John Cleese and Penelope Keith
FAVOURITE ACTIVITY ON DAY OFF: Sleeping
FAVOURITE SINGERS: Earth, Wind & Fire, Shirley Bassey
AFTER-MATCH ROUTINE: Having a drink with players
BEST FRIEND: Zac Harazi (my solicitor)
INTERNATIONAL HONOURS: England Under-21 caps
PERSONAL AMBITIONS: To win the F.A. Cup with Spurs and play for England
IF NOT A PLAYER, WHAT JOB WOULD YOU DO? Help deprived children of any colour or creed
WHICH PERSON IN THE WORLD WOULD YOU MOST LIKE TO MEET? The Queen

FOCUS ON
STEVE ARCHIBALD
TOTTENHAM

FULL NAME: Steven Archibald
BIRTHPLACE: Glasgow
BIRTHDATE: September 27, 1956
HEIGHT: 5ft 10½ins
WEIGHT: 11 stone
PREVIOUS CLUBS: Clyde, Aberdeen
MARRIED: To Maureen
CHILDREN: Emma, six months
CAR: Ford Cortina 2 litre coupe
FAVOURITE NEWSPAPER: Scottish Daily Record
FAVOURITE PLAYER: Diego Maradona
MOST PROMISING TEAM-MATE: At Aberdeen, Alex McLeish
FAVOURITE OTHER TEAM: Aberdeen
FOOTBALL HERO OF CHILDHOOD: Pele, Denis Law
FAVOURITE OTHER SPORT: River fishing
MOST DIFFICULT OPPONENT: All difficult
MOST MEMORABLE MATCH: My full international debut when I came on as sub against Portugal at Hampden and scored
BIGGEST DISAPPOINTMENT: Not being selected for the England game in the British Championship
FRIENDLIEST AWAY FANS: None
FAVOURITE FOOD & DRINK: Fillet steak, cointreau
MISCELLANEOUS LIKES AND DISLIKES: Winning, scoring, sleeping/losing, smoking
FAVOURITE HOLIDAY RESORT: Ibiza
FAVOURITE TV STAR, MALE AND FEMALE: John Cleese, Leonard Rossiter, the cast of 'Soap'
FAVOURITE ACTIVITY ON DAY OFF: Relaxing at home with my wife and daughter
FAVOURITE SINGERS: Genesis, Peter Gabriel
AFTER-MATCH ROUTINE: Going out for a meal with friends
BEST FRIEND: My former Aberdeen team-mate Ian Scanlon, and Gordon Thow, a former neighbour in Scotland
BIGGEST INFLUENCE ON CAREER: My grandfather Alex Hutchison and Aberdeen boss Alex Ferguson
INTERNATIONAL HONOURS: Scotland Under 21 and full caps
PERSONAL AMBITION: To be happy
IF NOT A PLAYER, WHAT JOB WOULD YOU DO? Mechanic
WHICH PERSON IN THE WORLD WOULD YOU MOST LIKE TO MEET? The Queen

Steve Archibald

SHOOT!

STEVE ARCHIBALD

Forward

The two players I fell out with at Tottenham were both Scots – Alfie Conn and Neil McNab – and when Archie and I first met I got a feeling he didn't trust me. I shook his hand like you would with any new player, and I just remember thinking, 'Hmm. Not really returning that welcome. No, "Oh, I'm pleased to be here."'

Neil had been a hell of a player for us in the Second Division and felt hard done by when he lost his first-team place after Ricky arrived. I think it resulted in a rumour that 'Steve Perryman doesn't get on with Scotsmen,' whereas the truth is two of my favourite people in the world were Alan Gilzean and Dave Mackay, so that wasn't the case at all. But by moving Neil on to Bolton Wanderers, Keith didn't give him the chance to prove that Ricky wasn't as good as him. Neil had his nose put out of joint, and probably a bit of that hard-done-by attitude got conveyed to Archie somehow, who was then a bit wary of me and Keith.

The beauty of having your own game worked out is that you can then start working out other people's. You have flashes of inspiration. During my playing days, I was always observing how other players went about their games and sometimes I'd lie in bed thinking about a player's game in terms of defending against them. I once said to Archie, 'Say if you're on a break – you always talk about how a striker

> **"He and Garth were very different personalities. One was exuberant, one was moody"**

shouldn't stand still. When the break is on and the cross is coming in, your aim is to get somewhere the defender isn't. Burst across him or drift into space. Your job when there is a cross coming in is to get somewhere a defender isn't.' It wasn't a criticism – it was me putting into words how I saw his role. That was me working out a striker's game. But Archie said, 'What, do you think I don't do that?' He got the hump. He could often be like that.

John Syer, our sports psychologist, tried suggesting to Archie that being a nicer man off the field needn't change how he was on the field – that if he wanted this angry head on the field you could approach it like you were two different people. But I think it just suited Archie's personality to be difficult. It was kind of, 'If I'm expected to act this way in this situation, I'm not going to give you it.'

He and Garth were very different personalities. One was exuberant, one was moody. They were both quick but Garth could leap, he could jump, whereas Archie was more of a feeder of flick-ons. But I think they were probably on the same wavelength – 'We're the strikers, no one really understands us. We'll get stick if we don't score, so we'd better score.' They had a common aim, and they understood each other. If one had gone five games without a goal, the other wouldn't be critical. They cared about each other.

Fact File

Spurs 1980-84
185 (4) Appearances (Sub)
77 Goals

1980/81 FA Cup
9 Appearances
3 Goals

Honours
FA Cup 1981, 1982
UEFA Cup 1984

A match made in heaven

Having struggled for goals since their promotion back to Division One, Spurs took an expensive plunge into the transfer market to buy two strikers. It proved to be the final piece in the jigsaw

Adapted from an interview by Mike Leigh and Theo Delaney for 'Archie and Garth Reunited: The Spurs Show Live' in January 2020

It seemed like a miracle, almost. From 1978, when Ossie Ardiles and Ricky Villa arrived to complement Glenn Hoddle in midfield, Spurs were frustratingly close to being a big side again but were falling short up front. Then along came Steve Archibald and Garth Crooks.

Glasgow-born 'Archie', as he rapidly became known, had only been a pro for two years. He started his career in midfield with Clyde before signing for Alex Ferguson's Aberdeen, and was part of the side that won the Scottish title.

Crooks' journey began as a youth-team player with his local club, Stoke City, and he came to first-team prominence when he replaced Ian Moores, who had got a big move to Spurs. Four years later, Crooks himself was on his way to North London.

Joining in the summer transfer window of 1980, they were two of the hottest properties available, their reputations reflected in the size of their transfer fees – £800,000 for Archibald and £650,000 for Crooks – which now would be the equivalent of signing £50 million and £40 million strikers at the same time. They would go on to be not only the final pieces in the jigsaw that made up Keith Burkinshaw's great '80s Spurs side, but one of the outstanding striking partnerships in football history.

And yet Hoddle and Ardiles actually had to be forced to see it…

When you first joined people were asking, would you click as a partnership? How long did it take?

Garth We struggled. I'd come across Steve before because we'd played against each other at Under-21 international level…

Archie I scored, he didn't!

Garth I knew he could play and when I came to Spurs to sign, the first thing I said to Keith Burkinshaw was, 'How much is Archibald on?' And he said, 'Too much. And you won't be earning that. So – we had a difficult few pre-season games. We sort of tried to get an understanding but I thought, 'We're hardly getting a touch of the ball here.' Every game was being dominated by midfield. Ardiles and Hoddle were passing the ball between themselves because they were so good. I remember Archie saying to me, on at least two occasions, 'This can't go on. We're not getting any service.'

Archie was then, and still is, the senior partner here, and I thought, 'He's brave'. I mean, there's two World Cup winners in Ardiles and Villa. There's Glenn Hoddle, the most gifted player in the country. I'm not gonna tell them they're hogging the ball. And Archie said, 'Why?' And I said, 'Well, hang on a second, we've just arrived. Just give it a few more games.'

But it got to a stage where people were saying, 'They're not scoring goals.' Archie was getting very frustrated. I remember we'd drawn another pre-season game at Cheshunt in thick mud. We hadn't scored, he was getting angry and I thought, 'This is going to end badly.'

We hadn't played a first-team game yet. So I said, 'Don't worry, I just want to try something. Stay right up as far as you can on the back man, and the next time the ball comes from Glenn or

> "We'd had strikers who weren't scoring goals and now we had two strikers who looked like they were going to score lots of goals"
>
> **Garth Crooks**

from Ossie I'm not going to play it back to them, I'm going to put it round the corner for you, I'm going to turn, and we'll play on from there.' So he said, 'All right.' So it comes in from Glenn. Normally I just give it back but this time I popped it round the corner. Archie gets it, I join on, we play a one-two and he's in on goal. Then it happened a second time. And the second time, Glenn turns to Burkinshaw and says, 'What's going on?' So I look at Burkinshaw. And Burkinshaw, to his eternal credit, says, 'Let 'em play on. Keep it going.' And that was the beginning of the partnership.

But when did Hoddle and Ardiles buy into it?
Garth It took a couple of games, but I scored in the opening league match against Nottingham Forest and then we both scored in the next game against Palace. We'd had strikers who weren't scoring and now we had two who looked like they were going to get lots of goals. I had to change my game quite dramatically. Because Steve was a real finisher in every sense of the word. He was the Harry Kane of the side, if you like. He would always be up top, and really my job became getting in and around the box for him to finish.
Archie It's true we started scoring goals but Crooksy shouldn't put himself down like that. He was a massive part of any success we had – not just on the pitch, but also on the training pitch. Him and me talking, thrashing it out and sorting the midfield players out. He was a massive part of all that – and he could finish, and he was pacy.

Do you think you two had this sort of camaraderie because you were both new boys?

Archie Well, you talk of the relationship we had – we had a fantastic relationship on and off the pitch – but it didn't happen by magic. It was hard work every single day. We'd play little 'overs' where I was going first or he was going first – the first man would step over the ball, the second man would play him through again – but we worked at it day in, day out until it became an instinctive thing. So what you saw on the pitch that seemed natural wasn't natural, it was really hard work.

We knew what we had to do. We knew we had to score goals for this club to be a success. You can have the best midfield player in the world but there's no way he's going to score all the goals. A midfield player doesn't dictate to me as a striker to make a run – I dictate to the midfield player. It's great to have a midfield player that can deliver it, but it's the striker that makes the difference. That's a fact of life.

Garth I remember that occasionally I tended to overplay a little bit, and I'd sort of go deeper and deeper. We hadn't been there that long and Archie said to me, 'Hey, hey, you! You! What are you doing? Get back up here!'

Occasionally we'd have a lot of fun before kick-off – if Steve was two goals ahead of me, I'd say, 'Yeah, it's my day today,' or something silly like that, and we'd fire each other up. I've also got to say – this fella, he had a lot of balls. I remember Burkinshaw saying in the dressing room before one game, 'Right, we're defending this corner, Crooksy, I want you here and Archie, I want you back in the box defending,' and Archie went, 'You what? No, I'm not doing that. I fucking score goals.' I couldn't

believe it. I'd never ever come across that in all my life, and I'd played with some big names.

How important was it for you both to have a good run in the FA Cup in that first season?

Archie The FA Cup was massive back then, it was on TV and the press made it big so we all bought into it. We loved it, it was a fantastic competition. The league was something different, it was a long process and a different mentality. We certainly thought we could win a cup. So we were really into it in a big way.

And then came the notorious semi-final against Wolves at Hillsborough…

Garth Back then you'd go out onto the pitch suited and booted an hour before kick-off. All the Spurs fans were there, the atmosphere was amazing, and I remember saying to Steve Perryman, 'How did they get all those fans in there?' It was like a sea of people. The atmosphere was electric, and I sometimes think that fans don't understand the impact they have on players. I remember walking out there and thinking, 'We can't lose this semi-final. Not with that lot.' Ok, Clive Thomas robbed us in the end, but I remember going into the dressing room and feeling like a million dollars because you could feel that energy coming from the fans.

Archie Absolutely, it was an amazing day and to get a goal was fantastic. Like Crooksy said, the atmosphere was incredible and for me personally I never doubted that we'd go on and win through to the next stage. It was just written, I just believed it. I knew my team. I knew the partner I had beside me. I knew I could score goals, so if we could be a bit more solid at the back then we'd go through. I never doubted it.

You proved your point in the replay at Highbury, and no one will ever forget Garth's second goal with that classic assist by Glenn Hoddle…

Garth Glenn was this extraordinary talent. Sometimes he'd say, 'Crooksy, you need to be ready because the ball could come at

> "We had a fantastic relationship on and off the pitch – but it didn't happen by magic. It's hard work every single day"
>
> **Steve Archibald**

point Hutchison was quite rightly irritated and he said, 'What's the problem? What's the big deal? If your name's on the cup, it's on the cup. If it's yours, it's yours.'

It looks like there is something to that because from the first minute of the replay it looked like the whole team was up for it...
Archie I think we were, as it turns out, especially Ricky. In the team that season we had a pretty strong mentality, a pretty strong belief in ourselves. It's a cup final, we've made an arse of the first game, the second game comes along and you're that little bit more focused. We've got all the fans here, we've got the strength, we feel the force, we just go at it and put everything we have into the final. And that's what we did – and we got the rewards.

Typical Spurs, we still found ourselves 2-1 down. Steve Mackenzie's goal could have been the greatest goal in any FA Cup Final...
Garth That's mine!

The second greatest then! The ball Glenn played over – if you watch it again, you both made a run for it...
Archie It was mine. I controlled it. And he just came in and took my glory.
Garth You miscontrolled it.
Archie: I was ready to go again, and he just steams in and hits it like Billy Big Bollocks and takes my goal!
Garth I get the goal, right, so the game's 2-2, we got the equaliser...
Archie ...and he's off to God knows where!
Garth We go back to the centre circle, and in those days at Wembley they had these big electronic scoreboards, and it's saying '2-2 CROOKS'. And for some reason I turned to Archie and I said, 'My name's in lights.' For a mad moment in the replay of the FA Cup Final I'm saying, 'Look at the lights. Told you. Told you!'
Archie I've just got to say, I'm really happy it happened. After all these years, I'll say it now.

"I never doubted we'd go on and win... I just believed it. I knew my team. I knew the partner I had beside me"
Steve Archibald

any stage.' You always had to be ready. If he got the ball, he could spin, turn on a sixpence either side and play a forward pass, and you'd be in. And if you weren't ready, you'd get scolded. He was always, 'You've got to be ready for that ball', and on that occasion fortunately I was.

But the final at Wembley on the Saturday didn't turn out as everyone hoped, did it?
Garth We started badly but fortunately luck was on our side. There was one quirky moment, before the Hutchison own goal, when it was obvious the game was going away from us. We were struggling, and we were trying to dig in, and I remember I caught Hutchison a couple of times. Deliberately. It was a bit naughty but I was just desperately trying to change the game. At one

The team behind the team

They might not have grabbed the headlines or basked in the glory, but the coaches and support team behind the scenes played a crucial role in the success of 1981

By Julie Welch

'It was winter and we were away to Ipswich. Bear in mind Ossie and Ricky hadn't seen snow, let alone played in it, before they came to England, and at half-time Peter parks his backside on the table in the middle of the dressing room, checks his look in the mirror and says, "Ossie, Ricky, love ya, love ya to bits – 85 degrees in Buenos Aires, you'll do for me. Unfortunately, six inches of snow at Portman Road, you're not going to do it for us. You're going to have to come off." What a delivery. He had so much style, Peter.'

If you want a story that completely sums up Peter Shreeve, that's the one Steve Perryman tells. The main man at Tottenham Hotspur might have been Keith Burkinshaw but behind the scenes Shreeve was most definitely a crucial part of 1980s Tottenham. The journos liked to take the mickey out of Spurs having a qualified taxi driver as assistant manager, but the players loved him.

Shreeve showed up at Tottenham in 1974 to take the job of youth-team coach. He was born in Wales but grew up in Islington and with his North London background he was particularly right for the homegrowns as he had risen through the ranks to manage the A-team and then the reserves. When Burkinshaw made him assistant manager in 1980, some of the young players he had nurtured had made their debuts or were on the brink of it. He brought on Paul Miller, Micky Hazard, Terry Gibson and Mark Falco, and smoothed the rough edges off Graham Roberts and Tony Galvin when they arrived from non-league. 'He was a lovely chap,' says Steve. 'We all had someone like Peter in our families and he wasn't much older than us, so he was clued up about what was going on.'

No matter that his playing record was undistinguished – with six years in an inside-forward role at Third Division Reading being as good as it got – he was smart, likeable and fun. And immaculate. Shreeve had a look too – the jacket buttoned over an Aquascutum tie, the Jean-Paul Belmondo trench coat in pale leather. 'He was very well dressed,' Steve confirms. 'His appearance was very important to him. He looked the part of assistant manager of Tottenham Hotspur.'

There was a yin and yang quality about him and Keith Burkinshaw. The Spurs manager preferred to play it by the

> "The main man at Tottenham Hotspur might have been Keith Burkinshaw but Shreeve was a crucial part of 1980s Tottenham"

rules. Shreeve had a more relaxed take on things. 'On an end-of-season tour Bill Nicholson's attitude would be that you can't turn the screw tight all the time,' says Steve. 'If he knew we were staying out, he wouldn't want to see it. He'd know it was going on but he'd look the other way. Keith was a bit less laid back, which is why Peter was good for him. Keith might be saying, "Pete, Pete, they're going out! They were out last night and they're going out again!" and Peter would say, "Keith, they're young men. What do you think they're going to do, sit in the hotel?"'

As it happened, Bill Nicholson was a crucial part of the set-up behind the scenes too. After the club waved him off into the sunset in 1974 he had taken on the role of scout at West Ham. But Burkinshaw had seen enough of Nicholson's legacy at Tottenham to know that getting the man back where he belonged would be a sound idea, and Bill returned to White Hart Lane as head scout. While Burkinshaw provided the big-ticket signings, coming back from Argentina with Ardiles and Villa, Nicholson was driving in apocalyptic weather to the Peak District to assess Goole Town's Tony Galvin, playing on a pitch covered with an inch of snow. Two years later, after a trip to Swindon to run his eyes over a player who turned out to be a dud, he was about to take the train back home when he got into conversation with a man on the platform who told him about a young midfielder at Weymouth who was definitely worth looking at. That was Graham Roberts. 'It was all part of Bill's way of

Left: Keeping in step – Keith Burkinshaw and his trusted assistant Peter Shreeve

Right: Steve Perryman rated Shreeve highly as a coach, believing he provided an effective balance to Burkinshaw's management style

The appointment of sports psychologist John Syer (second left) was at the time a highly innovative move. Benefitting from Syer's insights are (left to right) Chris Hughton, Steve Perryman, (with Syer's colleague Christopher Connolly offering his opinion), Steve Archibald, and physio Mike Varney

doing things,' says Steve. 'Keith would trust him to get it right.'

Nicholson wasn't the only old-stager behind the scenes. Johnny Wallis had been a fixture at the club since before the war. He had been pretty much Tottenham all the way through, except for a spell playing for Brighton. He joined the Spurs ground staff when he left school, played as a defender in the juniors and A-team and made a few first-team appearances before injury brought about early retirement. From the mid-'60s onwards the roles he occupied included youth-team coach, physio to the first team, kit man and trainer. He was the guy who ran onto the pitch with his bucket and magic sponge when a player went down.

'He was a good man,' says Steve, 'but everything was a game to him and as a kit man he was an absolute nightmare. If you came in from training and your hands were so cold that you had to kick your boots off when they were still done up, the next day the laces would have one million knots in them. I felt like saying to him at times, "John, that training kit's too big for Ossie." It was

like you could get 10 Ossies in that shirt. But I know if I'd said that he'd have found an even bigger shirt.'

The physio's role now belonged to a younger man. Johnny Wallis and the chief physio, Cecil Poynton, were old Tottenham but Mike Varney was the future. He came from a forces background and was a runner, cyclist and county-standard squash player. Here was someone who understoof the value of being fit. That earned automatic respect. 'He brought discipline and authority,' said Steve. 'He modernised the set-up and made it more professional. Mike was between eras – the ultra-new one of today's game and the old school where it was arnica on your bruises. This is not to diminish Cecil, but his favourite treatment was hot and cold. Your fat ankle would go into a bucket of ice and then it would go under a heat lamp. Then it would go back to the ice, and back under the lamp again, and so on. It was probably the best treatment at the time, whereas Mike brought with him the experience and techniques of working with military

"The players had never come across mental training in sport but the majority accepted that it had an important place"

casualties. He was used to dealing with worse injuries than a pulled hamstring. That didn't belittle your problem, but it put it in perspective. And if you had doubts about your treatment – if you weren't recovering from your injury as quickly as hoped, for instance – there would be an explanation for it. Whereas you would never ask for an explanation in my younger days – they'd take your head off.'

Something Varney was aware of was that when a player was on the treatment table his guard would be down. It was often a time for confidences. 'That's a good opportunity for a manager to find out something he might not be told in person,' Steve points out. 'The player's not going to own up to the manager that he's left home, but he might with Mike.' It was one of the reasons Varney suggested to Burkinshaw that he brought in two sports psychologists.

Mental training had yet to take off in the conservative world of English football. 'Spurs call in the shrinks' was the facetious headline in one tabloid paper when John Syer arrived at Tottenham with his colleague Christopher Connolly. Tottenham in the late 1970s was a team of talented individuals, and Syer and Connolly were tasked with turning it into a motivated and communicating force. They encouraged players to confront and explore feelings as well as tactics. They learned, for example, that it was normal to have fears and the way to overcome them was to accept that, not deny it. The players had never come across mental training in sport but the majority accepted that it had an important place.

'I'd hate to think I was a sort of grass,' says Steve, 'but I'd give them my opinion about what a player needed to work on that couldn't be worked out on the training field. I regarded it as improving the team.'

Did it help him? 'Well, the fact that they were interested in my opinion massaged my ego! And I'd learn things back from them, too. I'd say that so-and-so has got a mental block about this or that. They'd say, "We don't quite see that the way you see it, Steve." So then you go at it from a football perspective a little bit differently. If you'd said to me, go to night school and learn about psychology – no, that's not going to happen. So I was best off listening to people who were trying to improve my players, in a way I didn't quite understand, but I could help and by helping I was getting an education in return.'

So this was Tottenham Hotspur behind the scenes in 1981. The psychologists had provided the last piece of the jigsaw, turning a team of talented individuals into a motivated and communicating force.

All it needed now was for the players to prove it all worked.

A proud moment for Steve and his former youth-team manager Johnny Wallis, a long-standing Spurs servant

81

MOMENT IN TIME

**7th March 1981, 2.45pm, White Hart Lane, Home dressing room
Spurs v Exeter City, FA Cup sixth round**

"So we've got Exeter of the Third Division in the quarter-final. Exeter City. Although they have had some fantastic results to get where they are, we've got the least fancied team.'

Bill Nicholson gives us the team talk. He'd gone up to Exeter's tie against Second Division Newcastle United to scout them for us. Exeter had already disposed of Leicester City, so this was their second feat of giant-killing. Bill paints a very detailed picture of Exeter and, in not wanting to be disrespectful to them, maybe he overdoes it.

'Bloody hell,' says Ossie afterwards. 'I thought he was talking about Real Madrid.'"

Steve Perryman

THE SIXTH ROUND SPURS v EXETER CITY
Back to my future

Exeter City would go on to pay a huge part in my life, but it all started with drawing the Third Division minnows in the sixth round in 1981 and avoiding the big guns

Twenty-four years on from that team talk before our quarter-final in 1981, I got a first-hand lesson in how hard lower-tier teams are prepared to fight in the FA Cup – and as it happened it was Exeter City that delivered it. It was 2005 and I was their director of football, having acted as an unpaid advisor for some years. A lot of people were doing stuff for them unpaid because the club was in dire financial straits and facing extinction. We had lost our Football League status in 2003 when we were relegated to the Conference, not to mention we were millions of pounds in debt, with two of the directors in charge during the relegation season about to be convicted of fraudulent trading at the club.

Our Supporters Trust took the club over and for the next two years kept it going through fund-raising activities, but we were fighting to survive and desperate for a cup run. So when in the second round our 19-year-old academy graduate Dean Moxey saw the Doncaster Rovers keeper off his line and scored what turned out to be the winner from 50 yards out – and then when a Doncaster player had an open goal in front of him and headed the ball against the bar – it felt like our prayers might have been answered.

The fella who did the third round-draw was that tall long streak of an old Millwall centre-forward Tony Cascarino. He had played for the Republic of Ireland even though it turned out he wasn't really Irish at all. He pulled Manchester United out of the hat, and then us. Obviously everyone realises that the take for such a game is going to be quite something, so straight away there's people down in Exeter

saying he's the saviour of the club – as opposed to all the people who've been working for nothing behind the scenes.

I used all my experience of playing at the top level to warn our players. 'Should you manage to beat them,' I told them, 'the press are going to be on to you to give Manchester United stick. For instance, if you say, "Oh, I don't think they tried very hard," and it's the wrong type of newspaper, they could twist it into a negative story about United and it will only devalue what you've just achieved.'

Did I think we had any chance of beating them, really? It was an FA Cup tie – it could happen. It wasn't beyond belief.

Actually, no, I never thought we would beat them. I never even thought we could get a draw. I thought we were going to get battered. We were going up there, Conference League Exeter, wondering what the take was going to be because the club's survival depended on it. We were told it was going to be a sell out – 69,000. It wouldn't be

> **"You had to realise that Exeter wanted to beat us more than anything in their whole lives"**

Steve Perryman experiences the role of FA Cup underdog as Exeter City's director of football ahead of their dream cup tie against Manchester United in 2005

the usual fans: the season-ticket holders and what have you who go to watch United v City and so on. These were Manchester United supporters from outside the city who could never get tickets for regular games. They'd be coming from all around Britain. To see us get battered.

I did what I did on a typical morning of a game – get up, have breakfast, go back to my room, try to relax. I had a shower and got ready. Buttoned my shirt, tied my tie. Then I joined the pre-match meal.

'Steve,' said someone, 'you've done all the buttons of your shirt up wrong.'

'Yeah. Sorry, yeah.'

Perhaps it was because the papers had made me the focus of their coverage of the tie, talking about me using my experience, but that wasn't the only thing I did that betrayed me. One of my jobs was to fill out the team sheet. I took it very seriously, using big letters that could be understood and all that. Again, using all my experience, I go with the captain into the referee's room. About 10 minutes after we get back from the referee's meeting, there's a knock on the door. It's a member of the Manchester United staff.

'Steve, Steve,' he says, 'You haven't got a goalkeeper.'

'Ah.'

All this simply was nerves. I was the one that had been here before. I'd played there so many times. It's been mentioned in every bit of the build-up the papers have been giving it – Exeter are going to use Steve Perryman's experience of the big time and all that. But this was different. If you go up there with Tottenham Hotspur, you're going to have a fighting chance, and we had some really good days at Old Trafford. But going up there with Conference League Exeter, that was another matter. I felt vulnerable.

But United fielded a weakened side, and after Dean Moxey shot narrowly wide three minutes before half-time it started to cross my mind that we might not get battered. They weren't in a good flow, partly because Sir Alex had picked a weakened side, and I was thinking, 'What if we hang on? What if we get a replay? Think of the take. All our financial problems will be over.'

As I'm thinking this, Sir Alex decides to put on Paul Scholes and Cristiano Ronaldo.

'Well, that's it,' I thought. 'You're done. This is all over.'

But even with those two United couldn't change the flow, and we got it: our famous 0-0 draw at Old Trafford. They reckoned there were Exeter people in Manchester, still celebrating, a week after the final whistle.

Before the replay, which we eventually lost 2-0, Sir Alex told me how fit our team was. Their trackers didn't only pick up what their players were doing, they picked up ours as well, and he said Exeter had run further than any other away team at Old Trafford in the last seven years. That was because our players were chasing the ball, of course, but they *never* gave up chasing it.

So now I go back 24 years again, to Tottenham Hotspur v Exeter City in the sixth round of the FA Cup. You have to realise that Exeter wanted to beat us more than anything in their whole lives. They weren't Real Madrid by any means, but this was still their chance to take another big scalp. And of course we knew the history of the FA Cup and what the FA Cup has inspired teams to do in the past – there were no certainties in that competition. Even so, deep down I think we believed we were already into the next round; that mentally we were into the semi-final from the moment the draw was made. That

Steve Perryman gives chase against Exeter's Peter Rogers in what was a tough encounter with the Third Division 'minnows'

"Whichever way you want to look at it, it was Tottenham Hotspur who got through to the semi-final"

It took a Graham Roberts goal, an hour into the game at White Hart Lane, to break Exeter's brave resistance. Note the West Stand in the background, in the process of being rebuilt

was a very dangerous thing to think. We couldn't say we played well that game and it took a set-piece goal apiece from Graham Roberts and Paul Miller to win it.

Graham and 'Maxie' were two of a kind, in that they put their bodies on the line when they played – they went the extra inch over it at times. I'm not saying they would have been able to receive the ball in midfield like Glenn, which required a different sort of nerve. They operated more in terms of, 'It's me against you, and if you think your team's going to beat mine then piss off, that's not going to happen.' They once told me that David Pleat got rid of them because both of them gave away too many fouls – he wanted something more stylish. Which would not have been hard to achieve. Style was not their forte. But these are the players you want when the chips are down.

One time, much later when I was at Exeter, I invited Keith and Maxie to come and help me with a fundraiser for its youth set-up. Years had gone by, but some Exeter folk were still very upset because of the London Weekend Television and media coverage of the 1981 match, which they felt had suggested that we were always going to win and that we deserved to win on the day. The Exeter fans felt really hard done by, that they had been treated as though they were just nobodies. So they asked me if, for this fundraiser, they could put together some highlights showing the match from their point of view. No problem. But nothing can detract from the fact that we scored two goals and they didn't. You can have the bad luck story, you can have the biased referee, but whichever way you want to look at it, it was Tottenham Hotspur who got through to the semi-final.

Being Spurs we would have liked to have done it in more style but if on the day you haven't got style something else has got to get you through. And that something else was the tenacity and ruthlessness of the Roberts and Miller type that just turns the screw a bit tighter on the opponent.

We were the only team to get an outright win in that sixth round. Everyone else had to go to a replay. At the second attempt Manchester City got through against Everton, Wolves beat Middlesbrough and Ipswich knocked out Nottingham Forest. Ipswich were still on track for the Double, so we wanted to avoid a semi-final against them if we could. But every opponent was going to be hard to beat now.

In my early days at Tottenham, we trained around the Cheshunt roads. We would walk round and jog back, with Eddie Baily on his bike and Bill striding out in front. Then as it got further into pre-season, we would jog round and run back, and by the end of pre-season we'd just run. Anyway, early on I was walking with Pat Jennings and he said to me, 'Hey, son. When you're marching you're not fighting.' What he meant was: it's not war yet, that's to come.

Our first four cup ties had been more like marching. Now, for Spurs, it was time to fight. We'd drawn Wolves and we'd be playing them at Hillsborough. The war was about to start.

Spurs 2 Exeter City 0

7th March 1981, White Hart Lane. Att: 40,629

Spurs goalscorers: Roberts, Miller

By Julie Welch

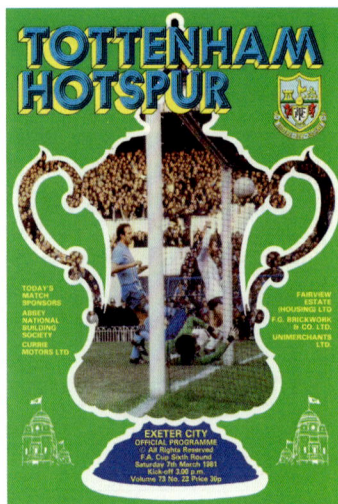

Tony Galvin is foiled again by the stubborn Exeter defence as Spurs struggle to break down their lower-division opposition

If you had a pound for every time a lower-league side was described as 'gallant' you'd be in the highest tax bracket by now. The fact that Exeter City held out as long as they did in their third clash with First Division opposition in this season's FA Cup was a tribute to the never-say-die spirit that had turned them into giant-slayers against Leicester City and Newcastle United.

Even so, that doesn't detract from Tottenham's performance. This was an exhibition of their own new-found tenacity and grit in the form of two young Rottweilers, Paul Miller and Graham Roberts. Their blood-and-guts approach to the beautiful game has transformed the North London side from flawed entertainers into a side that can win in a style that you could euphemistically describe as 'rugged'. Tottenham have not yet completely found their mojo, but without playing consistently well they are now poised on the edge of a return to the bygone era of the early 1970s when they seemed to be at Wembley every week.

Having held out all through the first half, Exeter nearly caused a sensation just after the restart when Miller botched a through ball and Exeter's Tony Kellow, an electrician in a former life, was given the chance to score his 29th goal of the season. Sadly for the visitors, Kellow's effort was straight at Barry Daines, and after that miss the 'oof' started to go out of the West Country side. Ian Pearson (inevitably a milkman in his day job) was stretchered off concussed. Spurs took over, with Ossie Ardiles at his most busily magisterial and Glenn Hoddle delivering a succession of the kind of passes of which only he is capable. Leonard Bond, Exeter's keeper – who in spite of some painful injuries had stayed strong up till then – was finally undone in the 62nd minute when Ardiles took a short corner, Hoddle curved the ball to the far post and Roberts sprang to head down and in. It was the one-time non-leaguer's first goal for Spurs since making his debut last December, and not long after that his defensive partner Miller made it two.

It was Hoddle, again, who set up the *coup de grace* with a free-kick. Bond failed to keep hold of a ball that had suddenly turned into a squirming puppy in his hands and Miller, who until he gets on the pitch looks more like top pick for a menswear catalogue, bashed it home.

The verdict? With Spurs missing a key player in Ricky Villa and still looking like a team in progress, they have nevertheless made it through to the semi-final stage. In Ardiles and Hoddle they boast two inarguably world-class midfielders. Tony Galvin is showing himself to be the essential component that makes everything else tick along. Now they have Miller and Roberts adding never-say-die spirit to Steve Perryman's reliability, intelligence and drive. They are about to come up against stronger opposition than they have met so far, but you don't have to be a Spurs fan to hope that after all these years they are back on the glory trail.

Tottenham Hotspur 2(0)

Manager Keith Burkinshaw
(White Shirts, Blue Shorts, White Stockings)

Exeter City 0(0)

Manager Brian Godfrey
(Red Shirts, White Shorts, Black Stockings)

BARRY DAINES	1	LEN BOND
CHRIS HUGHTON	2	MARTYN ROGERS
(1) PAUL MILLER	3	JOHN SPARROW
(1) GRAHAM ROBERTS	4	RICHARD FORBES
GEORGE HAZON JOHN LACY	5	LEE ROBERTS (8)
STEVE PERRYMAN	6	PHIL ROBERTS
OSVALDO ARDILES	7	IAN PEARSON
STEVE ARCHIBALD	8	PETER ROGERS
TONY GALVIN	9	TONY KELLOW
GLENN HODDLE	10	JOHN DELVE
GARTH CROOKS	11	PETER HATCH
GARY BROOKE	12	ROY PRATT

OFFICIALS

Referee: MR. NEIL MIDGLEY
(Salford)

MR. NEIL MIDGLEY of Salford started refereeing in the Eccles and District League before graduating through the Manchester and Cheshire Leagues to the Football League. He has since officiated in a number of important matches.

An engineer by occupation, he plays cricket and squash, and also enjoys gardening. A former amateur soccer player, he had trials with Preston North End.

An F.A. coach and referee instructor, he is Chairman of the Eccles and District Referees' Association and is on the F.A. panel of speakers.

LINESMEN:
Mr. P. K. HELSBY
(Hants.)
Red Flag

Mr. M. L. JAMES

SCORECHECK

Here are the other F.A. Cup-ties and First Division matches being played today. Half-time scores will be announced.

EVERTON
MANCHESTER CITY

MIDDLESBROUGH
WOLVERHAMPTON WANDERERS

NOTTINGHAM FOREST
IPSWICH TOWN

BRIGHTON & HOVE ALBION
COVENTRY CITY

LEICESTER CITY
ARSENAL

SOUTHAMPTON
MANCHESTER UNITED

SUNDERLAND
ASTON VILLA

WEST BROMWICH ALBION
CRYSTAL PALACE

TOTTENHAM HOTSPUR
Football & Athletic Co. Ltd.

TOTTENHAM HOTSPUR V EXETER CITY

F.A. CUP 6TH ROUND K.O 3-00 P.M

SATURDAY 7TH MARCH 1981

EAST TERRACE ENCLOSURE

PRICE
(INC. VAT)
£1·80

ENTRANCE
37-39

TO BE RETAINED

Spurs snuff out fairytale Exeter

ROBERTS ROCKET

Action Highlights

SPURS v EXETER CITY

MAIN PICTURE — The camera catches STEVE ARCHIBALD in mid-air as he shoots for goal in the 6th Round F.A. Cup-tie. INSET — LEN BOND, the Exeter goalkeeper, thwarts the on rushing GARTH CROOKS.

The Ossie and Ricky story

The sensational signing of World Cup winners Ossie Ardiles and Ricky Villa in 1978 was a masterstroke, and by 1981 they were national treasures in England as well as Argentina

By Julie Welch

'Keith didn't appear to have any front,' says Steve Perryman, 'but to go to Argentina and take away the best player in the World Cup…'

But the audacious swoop nearly didn't happen. A few days before Keith Burkinshaw was due to fly out to Buenos Aires he learnt that Arsenal manager Terry Neill would be on the same plane because he was interested too. 'I wasn't at all happy with Arsenal getting involved in things,' said Burkinshaw later, 'and I was beginning to have doubts. But a day before the flight, Terry pulled out and I had a clear run.'

It was the second week in July 1978. Argentina had just defeated The Netherlands to win the World Cup, and rumours were already flying around that some of the winning side would be up for grabs. That February, the EU had ruled that a player's nationality should not be an issue when deciding whether or not they were allowed to play in any given country, and it was widely predicted that Argentinian players would be arriving in England en masse. Not to join Tottenham Hotspur, though. The fancied destinations had been Arsenal and Man Utd, rather than a club that had spent the previous season playing the likes of Leyton Orient and Oldham Athletic. Yet here was their manager bringing in Ossie Ardiles and Ricky Villa virtually before they'd had time to shower and change after lifting the trophy.

The tip-off had come from Bill Nicholson's crony and fellow Yorkshireman, Harry Haslam of Sheffield United. Haslam, always on the lookout for undiscovered talent, had established a scouting network at Bramall Lane with his Uruguayan coach Oscar Arce that trawled the largely unexplored territory of South America. Not that long back Arce had been offered a useful-sounding youngster called Diego Maradona but United had been unwilling to stump up the £200,000 asking price for a 17-year-old unknown.

'I had seen Ardiles on television and had been impressed,' Nicholson wrote in his autobiography. 'He was obviously a player who would improve our side.' Bill Nick wasn't the only one who thought that. By the summer of 1978 the whole of football was talking about Osvaldo Ardiles. They were transfixed by this small, steely-eyed midfielder who played all over the pitch – attacking one minute and defending the next, even helping out the full-backs if necessary. Maradona called him 'everybody's friend'. He was unique, unclassifiable. His manager at Huracán once told him, 'You know what number you should be wearing? You should be wearing a question mark on your back!'

Ardiles had grown up in a wealthy family and alongside his development as a footballer he had been training to become a lawyer, but once he joined the national squad he never found the time to study again. Footballer or lawyer? It was no contest. He had been particularly keen to come to Europe, where the financial heft of the top clubs far outweighed what Argentina's had to offer. Plus, he was married to the daughter of a colonel connected to Argentina's ruling regime in a troubled and violent time in the country. They were living through violent times and at one stage he came under gunfire during an attack on his father-in-law's house.

"By the summer of 1978 the whole of football was talking about Osvaldo Ardiles. They were transfixed by this small, steely-eyed midfielder who played all over the pitch"

Ricky Villa and Ossie Ardiles bring a dash of exotic South American flair to North London just before the start of the 1978/79 season

DAILY EXPRESS Tuesday July 11 1978

SPURS SCOOP THE WORLD

EXPRESS EXCLUSIVE

Ardiles and Villa sign in £750,000 double deal

By Malcolm Folley

TOTTENHAM manager Keith Burkinshaw yesterday signed two of Argentina's all-conquering national side — Osvaldo Ardiles and Ricardo Villa — in a £750,000 deal.

Ardiles masterminded Argentina's World Cup triumph in Buenos Aires last month.

But while the Italians drooled over his skills and the Spaniards awaited developments, Burkinshaw caught a plane to the Argentine capital.

By last night Tottenham's £1,500 investment in his airline ticket had reaped rewards which will make the North London club the focal point of British football.

Here on Sunday

Ardiles and Villa, both 25 and midfield players, had signed three-year contracts and begun to organise their travel arrangements to arrive in London on Sunday.

The whole transaction, which breaks shattering new ground in the British game, had taken just 24 hours to complete.

Burkinshaw only arrived in Buenos Aires on Saturday. His first appointment was with Ardiles and after brief negotiations he went ahead and clinched the £400,000 transfer with his club Huracan.

Next, he saw Villa — "considered by MANY to be the best player in Argentina," and was given the encouragement to clinch the double-deal with Racing Club.

Burkinshaw's ambition was shared by the directors that one of the two plans and their wives were firm friends.

The Tottenham manager, whose club reclaimed their First Division status last season, conducted negotiations through an interpreter.

Intelligent

"Both men are extremely intelligent and want to have English lessons as soon as they arrive," Burkinshaw told me.

"Little Ardiles can read English and already makes himself understood with me.

Burkinshaw does not envisage having any difficulty getting work permits. "When I left The Department, employment, the last week that there wouldn't be any problem," explained Burkinshaw had spent

monthly combing the country for suitable players to make Tottenham a great side again. All his imagination drew a blank.

Then he watched Argentina win the World Cup. "My board gave me the go-ahead to try to get Ardiles," he said.

"I knew Harry Haslam (manager of Sheffield United) had done a bit of work with Argentinian players. He has an Argentinian coach, Oscar Arditto, and was looking for players in a cheaper bracket.

"He helped me a great deal and arranged for Tony Haslam.

Burkinshaw buys Argentine stars

land at Wembley in 1966, to act for me.

"I never expected to get the pair of them. It proves that Tottenham think big and want to be the best club in the game."

"Both by their standards the signings must be one of the biggest things in the club's history.

Now Burkinshaw hopes to fly home to complete the signing of Fulham defender John Lacy.

Argentinian expects to sign two Argentinian players before the weekend, but they will be strictly small fry.

Scotland blacklist Masson, Macari

By John Mann

DON MASSON (Derby County) and Lou Macari (Manchester United) were added to Scotland's World Cup blacklist yesterday.

The S.F.A. sentences came largely as a result of comments made by the players about their stay in Argentina.

Now three of Scotland's strong World Cup men have been banned. Willie Johnston was sent home from Argentina for a failed drug test.

Yesterday's decision came after a disciplinary selection committee reviewed inquiry in Glasgow following last Friday's session at which Ally MacLeod was asked to quit as manager.

The S.F.A.'s decision was taken.

Complaints

On Macari, they said: "The team giving false information to the Association's manager and refused to return, is recommended that no further element of the complaints against the Association and its important issue be arrangements by the players.

"In consideration of all the circumstances on Macari, the player also has not reported to the Association.

Don Masson, having admitted giving false information to the Association's manager and having refused to return, it is recommended that he would prefer not to play for Scotland, could be recommended in his desire."

"They added that their decision to send Willie Johnston home and for him to play no further part in the World Cup, had been added to by weekend, but there will be international and club commitments in Europe till June 17, 1979.

Scotland's next match is a Nations Cup-tie with Austria in September.

OPEN GOLF—TURN TO PAGES 29 AND 31

Printed and published by Express Newspapers Ltd., London, Fleet Street, E.C.4. Registered as a newspaper at the Post Office.

Ardiles had been envisaging a move to Spain or Italy. Instead, a phone call from his manager told him to go to the Sheraton Hotel to meet an Englishman he had never heard of. There was, though, an immediate connection between the pair. Ardiles found himself impressed by the fact that the man had flown out there in person. As for Burkinshaw, he knew very quickly that here was someone he could work with, a player who would raise his side to the next level. 'He came back the next day with his wife and signed,' said Burkinshaw. 'It really was that simple. It was then that Ossie asked me if I'd be interested in signing Ricky too.'

Ricardo Villa was more of an unknown quantity – a big, laidback Zapata-moustached midfielder who grew up on a ranch miles away from anywhere. He would turn out to be a spontaneous, instinctive player who could be either extraordinary or hopeless. Burkinshaw had seen him come on as a substitute against Brazil in the World Cup and could tell he had something, but what he was really thinking was that it would be nice for Ardiles to have a friend to help him settle in England.

The asking price for the pair was £750,000, an unprecedented and mind-bogglingly expensive deal at the time. Burkinshaw had to make a long-distance call to his chairman, Sidney Wale, to see if there was enough money in the bank. Twenty minutes later he was given the green light. 'I think,' he said, 'it took all of 10 more minutes to get Ricky to sign.'

The papers went crazy. 'Spurs Scoop The World' screamed *The Express*. Nothing like this had happened in English football before. The pair arrived at Heathrow to be met by a jumbo-sized press pack who immediately dubbed them 'Ossie and Ricky'. 'It proves that Tottenham think big and want to be the best club in the country,' Burkinshaw was quoted as saying.

Comparing them to the midfield he had previously been part of, Glenn Hoddle was in dreamland. 'It was special,' he said later. 'Ossie was certainly the most astute player I've ever played with. He read the game better than anyone.' Here was a player he could learn from, someone on his exalted level. For a creative, technical player like Hoddle, it was an exciting time. He really did feel it would work straightaway. During a pre-season

> "Villa struggled on and off the pitch. He was a natural number 10, a role that didn't exist in English football at the time"

friendly against Royal Antwerp, he and Villa played a series of one-twos through the middle of the pitch and he thought, 'This is wonderful. This is someone who is on the same wavelength as me. We just gelled, the three of us.'

Not everyone was smitten. 'If the trickle of foreign players becomes a flow it would be detrimental to our members,' gloomed Gordon Taylor of the Professional Footballers' Association. 'There could already be two English players put of a job at Tottenham because of the arrival of the Argentinians.' And Tommy Smith, the former boo-hiss hard man at Liverpool, promised, 'They can expect some rough treatment in the English game.'

On the opening day of the 1978/79 season, Villa and Ardiles had their introduction to English football at the City Ground. Villa swerved past Peter Shilton to flick the ball into the net and earn a 1-1 draw against the First Division champions Nottingham Forest. That had the press tipping them for the title. A week later, thousands turned up at White Hart Lane with torn strips of paper to see the Argentinians make their home debut against Aston Villa. The tickertape welcome – which had become a feature of the 1978 World Cup – emphasised the optimistic mood, barely diminished by the ensuing 4-1 defeat. Then Spurs went to Anfield, where they were thrashed 7-0.

By now the press were speculating how the pair would fare on a wet winter's afternoon in Manchester, rain running off them, and forecasting a swift return to Division Two for Spurs.

'Ossie and Ricky were all at sea in the English game at that stage,' said Burkinshaw, 'and I was beginning to think, "What the hell have I done?"'

Villa, too, was starting to wonder. Ardiles, the more cosmopolitan of the pair, spoke a smattering of English and quickly picked up the swear words he needed to know. Villa struggled on and off the pitch. He was a natural number 10, a role that didn't exist in English football at the time. At Racing Club in Buenos Aries he had been revered as their best player, celebrated for his trademark long runs and as a scorer of special goals. 'Every time I got the ball I wanted to run, so I started running, but I wasn't thinking about the finish,' he admitted.

Communication problems hampered them both, of course. The only people they could talk to outside their families were each other. In the dressing room nobody else spoke their language. They couldn't follow when the team were talking tactics or sharing a joke. 'It was a very difficult time,' said Villa, a sociable personality who felt his isolation acutely. 'If one of us had come alone it would have been hard to stay for long. With us coming together, we were stronger. We were two young people who wanted to fight to stay in England.'

There were cultural differences to be adjusted to as well. They were aghast (or their wives were, more like) to find that if they

Far left: Villa and Ardiles (right) arrive at Gatwick Airport after signing for Spurs. On the left is Ricky's wife, Cristina

Above: Laughter all round as manager and players get to know each other. As the team strove to readjust to life back in the top flight, it wasn't all smiles, however

Below: Ossie and Ricky are visited at home by Shoot! magazine as they settle into life in England

Far right: Ossie's dream destination – the pair make a pilgrimage to the twin towers of Wembley

ran out of basic stuff like bread and milk on a Saturday they'd have to go without it until Monday because the shops were closed on Sunday. They were used to croissants and coffee for breakfast and the first time they were served up a full English they wondered what the hell it was. The club worked hard to help them acclimatise and they had a translator but at training they had to watch what the others were doing and copy them. Invited to a party at one of the big London hotels, they turned up in normal clothes to discover Princess Anne was the star guest and everyone was in evening dress. In Argentina, Villa had always just sloped around in jeans. Then he turned up to training in them. 'What are you going to do at training today?' asked Burkinshaw. 'The gardening?'

It was an up-and-down season. Spurs finished 11th in the league, with the goals coming mainly from Hoddle, including a hat-trick at Coventry. They had the classiest midfield in England but no one up front to supply the end product and, as Burkinshaw said, 'A midfield containing Hoddle and Villa wasn't the best in terms of getting tackles in. But I didn't really want to sign a Souness-type player.'

'It was hard at first,' recalled Ardiles. 'You never seemed to get the space in English football. There was always someone on you from the start.' That said, Ardiles could play between defence and attack. He moved around the pitch. He didn't have to change his game a lot in England. 'I expected people to kick me, because the English game is very tough.'

Villa was philosophical. 'If you are a good player, everybody kicks you. We were good players, so we were expecting the kicks.' But he himself admitted he could be lazy sometimes and would wait for the ball to come to him

> "'I sometimes said to Ossie, 'We are very good players,' remembered Villa. 'We must play at Wembley at least once when we are here'"

so he could do something special. That didn't work in English football. You had to go looking for it and fight to win it back.

The following year was even more underwhelming. Spurs finished 14th. Burkinshaw, though, was still convinced they were heading in the right direction. The team were growing up together. Peter Shreeve's young army of homegrowns was emerging. They were playing the right kind of football. The Tottenham Hotspur kind. And then came the summer of 1980, and with it the arrival of Archibald and Crooks.

'I sometimes said to Ossie, "We are very good players," remembered Villa. "We must play at Wembley at least once when we are here."'

And then Villa tore the lateral ligaments in his knee during the first round against QPR. It was a serious injury. People were telling him to take the insurance money and retire from the game. When the plaster came off his knee was swollen like a balloon and his muscles had withered away. He was having to go to hospital every day for rehab. It was there that the desolation of his injury began to diminish. What inspired his recovery was the sight of the accident victims who couldn't even walk. He could do that. He could even run. He made his return at Everton, a few weeks before the semi-final.

The goal against Wolves at Highbury convinced him he was good to go. It was from 25 yards out and struck left-footed. He'd been cutting onto his left foot a few times during the game because he was worried that his right leg was still weak. 'I never usually scored with long shots but I collected the ball and thought there's not many people here in front of me, I should just have a go.'

That was when he knew he was ready. They all were.

'The year ended in '1', which was when Spurs were always meant to win something,' said Ardiles. 'We were also starting to become a very good team. I would say it was our destiny to win the FA Cup that year.'

MEET THE TEAM

Steve Perryman introduces the players outside the cup final starting eleven who very much played their part in the 1981 journey

Terry Yorath brought experience and professionalism when he donned the Spurs shirt

Terry Yorath

Terry was the hub player, and a good footballer. When I'd played against him in the past my verdict was he was only a bit better than average, but when you played alongside him you realised he was more than that. He had an eye for a pass, and he certainly competed. I remember watching him and Graeme Souness in a Scotland v Wales international. My God, some of the things they did to each other. Keith was still in the process of building the team and we had a lot of new young players coming in, and Terry was the experienced head that was required to balance everything. You need as many of those players in the team as you can get without it costing you legs – if you've got too much knowledge and not enough legs that doesn't work either. But Terry did a good job for us and brought us extra professionalism and a bit more thought.

Don McAllister

Don was a centre-back – hard to play against, competitive, very fierce and strong in the challenge. He joined Spurs from Bolton Wanderers, and as part of the promotion side he scored a very valuable goal for us to beat them when they were running away with the Division Two title. I suppose you could say he had 'film star good looks', that old cliché, but they were maybe a bit misleading – he was a tough, straight-talking northerner without looking like one, and a bit different from the rest of us. He always insisted he wasn't going to get tied down with domestic life and kids, although he did later on. His pride and joy was his 260Z Datsun, which was a two-seater coupé and his dream car – to be fair it was a nice car. He loved it.

John Lacy

John was a central defender signed under the radar – a bit like Tony Galvin was – around the time we signed Ossie and Ricky. He was a Scouser with a degree from UCL who came to us from Fulham and was a better player than many people give him credit for. An extremely nice man, very well educated – he didn't cause any fuss, didn't make trouble, didn't moan when he was left out or not retained in the team. I might have got this wrong but it appeared that he was happy not to be on the front line in the starting eleven, but a bit-part player when he was needed. That was good for the group because you can't have 16 hungry for the first team. You've got to have some who accept they're not going to always be part of the side. Perhaps in private he didn't accept it but he didn't show signs of being unhappy. I think he was delighted to be at a club like Tottenham and he was sensible about it.

Garry Brooke

Brookesy was one of Peter Shreeve's homegrowns, and had power in his feet, left and right. He definitely had 'shooting boots', which he showed on his full debut against Southampton on Boxing Day 1980 when he scored twice in a 4-4 draw. He was a cheeky little chappie who came from Bethnal Green and was a typical Londoner, with a very sharp wit and an opinion on everyone and everything. He and Mark Falco, for instance, if you listened to their banter without seeing people's reactions you'd think, 'Whoa, steady, whoa.' They knew Ossie appreciated their humour so they'd target Ossie, and he just loved it. As a regular sub, he was a very important part of the 1980/81 FA Cup run – he fulfilled the role, didn't he? He came on and did his bit and scored some important goals for us.

Barry Daines

Barry was very mild-mannered, very calm, and a big part of the 'going up' team. He didn't have an ounce of flashness about him. He was genuine, he was sensible – if your daughter had come home with him you'd have been delighted. We were quite close because we played in the FA Youth Cup together, but although he joined Spurs at the same time as me he didn't become a first-team regular until he was 27 because Pat Jennings had the goalkeeper's jersey. He certainly had one to take on in Pat, didn't he? Having an experienced pro like Pat in front of you meant there would be a long time when you're not even going to be on the bench. So whereas I learned my trade on the main stage, in front of 45,000 people, he was playing in front of 2,000 in the reserves, and didn't get the necessary experience of the big time. Then Pat left, and all of a sudden he was the man. He was first-choice all the way through the 1980/81 FA Cup run until he got injured in March, just before the semi-final. So he didn't have the best of luck, but to me his career is the very definition of loyalty.

Giorgio Mazzon

'George' was a central defender who played in just one of our FA Cup games, the tie against Exeter City. He was a sort of wild card – a public schoolboy from a well-do-do family who came out of nowhere. Actuwone of those wine-growing valleys in Italy, except it produced a lot of good youth players, not grapes. He'd played as an amateur with non-league Hertford Town before he joined us. He was a trier, a runner. You could rely on his workrate, for sure. He was with us for three years until he transferred to Aldershot, but a bad car crash ended his career too soon.

The Spurs squad proudly sport their smart FA Cup Final jumpers

81

MOMENT IN TIME

11th April 1981, 2.55pm, Hillsborough
Wolverhampton Wanderers v Tottenham Hotspur,
FA Cup semi-final

"I'm waiting to lead the team out onto the pitch and I'm thinking this is one of the biggest games of my life. The problem when you've been through the good times and then the not-so-great times – and you're captain and therefore responsible – is you really do know how important this game is for you. If you are the sort who can think, 'It's just another game' then you wouldn't be worried, but I've got to tell you, at this exact moment I'm *nervous*. This isn't just another game, this is a mission. It's the expectancy. We're that close. But it's no good just being close.

You've got to do it. *You've got to do it*."

Steve Perryman

SEMI-FINAL SPURS v WOLVES

So near and yet so far

With just a few seconds left on the clock we thought we'd done enough against Wolves to get to Wembley, but referee Clive Thomas had other ideas

"I wanted to give our fans a feeling of pride in our club again"

Spurs defend a Wolves attack at the Leppings Lane end early in the game. Intensely focused on the game, the players were unaware the terrace was dangerously overcrowded

The last big game we had played against Wolves was in 1972, when we met them in the second leg of the final of the UEFA Cup. It was White Hart Lane under the lights, we were wearing all-white, which I always liked, and it was Alan Mullery's last game for Spurs. I wore the number eight shirt back then, the one that had been worn by Jimmy Greaves. I couldn't do what Jimmy did, but I gave a typical performance. I worked hard. Recovered to goal. Did my job. I was sort of... reliable. Of course I made mistakes but they were for the right reasons. I was 20 years old and part of the machine. The Tottenham Hotspur machine. I was just doing my bit. I wasn't doing anything extra because in that team I wasn't good enough. It was going to be a while before I had the captaincy role to go with what I could do on the ball and without it. But I don't think anyone would have looked at me at that time and thought, 'He shouldn't be in that team.' I held up my end. No matter how good your team is, if you get outrun you can suffer, and I was part of the reason we weren't going to get outrun.

Mullery was our captain then, and it was his goal that won the UEFA Cup for us. He knocked himself out scoring it. That just reflected our team performance. It had everything you associate with a team winning a big trophy. Desire, courage, pride in wearing the Spurs shirt. The season after that we won the League Cup. Since then: nothing but frustration.

That afternoon against Wolves in that FA Cup semi-final at Hillsborough I wanted to give our fans a feeling of pride in our club again.

I felt we were about to add to our club's proud history. The supporters hadn't had that feeling for a long time. As for the younger players in our side, they'd never got to know that feeling at all. I wanted them to experience what it was like to be part of such a big occasion. Ossie obviously knew because he had played in a World Cup Final and won it, Archie had won a Scottish Premier League title with Aberdeen, but the others were new to this environment. Robbo had only been in the first team for four months. So yeah, I was nervous.

By now I was a main character in the team, in that I was part of the reason why we had any consistency at all. A lot of that was down to me. Not the flair and surprise element. I knew I couldn't do those things as well as Glenn or Ossie; I knew I wasn't as fast as Garth or a dribbler like Ricky, but I obviously had something going for me that made me able to live with those players. I was a better organiser, thinker and communicator, and that was why I was living with that bunch of players. That's why I was captain.

Bill Nicholson would have said I played within my ability, and he was right. I knew my game inside out. I had turned 29 just before Christmas. I was set as a player. I stuck to the script. Now I had got the shackles off me because I was moving through the middle part of my career. Bill had dictated how I played. In contrast, Keith and I agreed between ourselves how I played. And that's the difference between being young and being experienced.

I suppose being responsible for team morale is a massive part of the skipper's job. It was Bill Nicholson's ethic, 'Just do it right.' I helped the club do it right. That's what a leader has to do. You have to put yourself on offer to live by Bill Nick's standards. If you don't do that then you're not going to get to lift that trophy.

Up to the semi-finals it had been sort of a breeze. No football game is easy, that's for sure, but it didn't feel like we'd done anything special yet. To get to a quarter-final is not that special, is it? For instance, a poor Spurs team under Terry Neill had even got to a semi-final – the 1976 League Cup one we lost to Newcastle over two legs. In other words, you could get to a quarter-final or even a semi-final just by riding a wave. That is what it felt like we'd been doing up to the point we were drawn to meet Wolves at Hillsborough.

I remember thinking we'd got through a bit easy. All home games, apart from the QPR match. Now it was more challenging. We were out of London for the first time. But then we had Ricky back. It was a risk because since damaging his knee at Loftus Road he hadn't played, except for 45 minutes in the league against Everton at White Hart Lane, a match which finished 2-2. It was an indication of Keith's faith in Ricky's talent that he brought him back.

We did all the normal things pre-match. We stayed in a nice hotel, and had all the team meetings that were necessary. Hillsborough was

a lovely stadium, very spacious, with a really good area outside the dressing room. That kind of thing always impressed me for some reason. But something that wasn't normal was the spillage of fans onto the pitch from the Leppings Lane end. Of course that didn't approach the scale of what happened a few years later at the same stadium, but it might have been a pointer to it – why wasn't it taken on board? It started happening during the warm-up, so that was something else that made it feel out of the ordinary.

Wolves wore dark shorts along with their usual gold shirts, so we were playing in all-white because, apparently, our usual navy shorts would have clashed. I think that played to our advantage, intensifying the feeling of being on a bigger stage because of Tottenham's European history of playing in all-white. For me and our defence, the

It looked like Glenn Hoddle's goal would clinch a priceless place in the FA Cup Final, but controversy lay in store

"When you feel aggrieved, you feel an extra purpose. There would be a revenge element to the replay"

Above: Andy Gray was singled out as Wolves' danger man, and was the subject of close attention from the Tottenham defenders

Right: Willie Carr celebrates scoring Wolves' late penalty, awarded by referee Clive Thomas after what looked like a clear dive by Kenny Hibbitt. Chris Hughton (No.2) and Steve Perryman (No.6) feel the pain of victory being cruelly snatched away – but the injustice motivated the Spurs players in the replay

main threat was going to be Andy Gray, a former Golden Boot winner who had been the club's record signing from Aston Villa two seasons back, when he had been described by the journalist Hugh McIlvanney as 'the kind of player who puts his head where others are afraid to put their boots'. What sort of battle did I want to have with him? A heading battle? No – I was useless in the air. Did I want it to be a pace battle? No. Did I want it to be a physical battle? Yes. All day long. Did I want it to be a thinking battle? Absolutely. It's like anything else. You think it through. This is how you want to play in this situation against this player.

But there are obviously things you can't dictate. Like a stupid refereeing decision in the final seconds of a semi-final.

When Kenny Hibbitt set out on his run and Glenn chased back to deal with him, Hibbitt threw himself to the ground. Straight away you could tell he was faking, but the ref stood there thinking about it and then he blew his whistle and pointed to the spot.

I had a go at looking at it from the referee's point of view. Maybe the angle of his line of vision misled him Maybe it was easier to spot from where I was than where he was. But having done all I could to be fair to him, I came to the conclusion that this very experienced referee bought it. I think it suited him to buy it.

Thankfully it wasn't a goal that lost us the game. If we'd lost the game on that decision, my God how would that have felt? Everything changes. Instead, the game went into extra-time. They were on an up because they'd saved the tie. We had to shake off our disappointment. We had to regroup and dig in. The team was dead on its feet, hanging on. In the end the ploy was to get the ball to Tony Galvin so he could run it to the corner flag because we were on our last legs. But Paul Miller had been our best player on the day, particularly in that last 30 minutes, and that would have been out of sheer bravado – 'I'm here. This is why I'm here. This is us.' I knew that feeling. The 20-year-old Steve Perryman had felt it back in 1972. 'Just go out and do it.'

I can clearly remember the coach ride home. Even if it had been Glenn's fault, which it wasn't, why would you have a go at him? We are a team. *A team*. Why would you even think about hurting that togetherness, that teamwork, that team spirit? That last-minute goal for Wolves could have been a big psychological blow, but the fact that we'd held it together in extra-time gave us strength. We were *convinced* we were going to beat them in the replay. Everyone had the same feeling. The chance hadn't gone. It took a real dodgy goal to undo us. We are good enough.

When you feel aggrieved, you feel an extra sense of purpose. Well, I certainly do. There was going to be a revenge element to the replay, though not the normal one of, 'You just kicked my mate, so now you're having it', which is a football ethics thing. It was *so* not a penalty. We were within a whisker of winning it, and then it was taken away from us.

Now we were going to take it back.

Spurs 2 Wolves 2 aet

11th April 1981, Hillsborough. Att: 50,174
Spurs goalscorers: Archibald, Hoddle

By Julie Welch

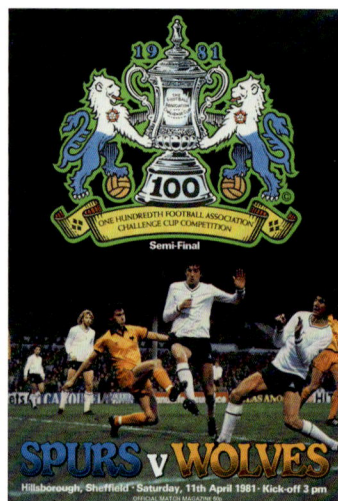

Steve Archibald stretches to score and put Spurs in front early in the game at Hillsborough

Fourteen years after they last laid their hands on the coveted trophy, Tottenham had their vision of a place at Wembley dramatically and cruelly obliterated by Willie Carr's equaliser from the penalty spot in the 91st minute of normal time.

Wolves were desperately plunging and lunging in time added on when Andy Gray slipped a pass to Kenny Hibbitt who, surging forward for an opening, felt Glenn Hoddle's breath upon his neck and seized the opportunity to go splat.

Did he fall or was he pushed? 'Clive Thomas was the only referee in the country who would have given that decision at that time,' said Keith Burkinshaw, although according to Wolves manager John Barnwell, 'You get punished if you make untidy tackles in important areas and Hoddle's was an untidy tackle.' But to slightly misquote Mandy Rice Davies, he's the Wolves manager, he would say that, wouldn't he?

The true extent of the injustice to Spurs only emerged later when Hibbitt said candidly, 'It was not a foul – I had to go down because it was our last chance,' an admission that must surely bring both the player and the game into disrepute.

The bizarre aspect of the incident was Thomas' lengthy, attention-grabbing pause before awarding the penalty in spite of his clear view of the players involved. Carr's theatrical equaliser now enters Thomas' canon of eccentric interventions, along with the disallowed goal by Everton's Bryan Hamilton in their 1977 FA Cup semi-final against Liverpool, Brazil's disallowed effort in the 1978 World Cup, and – most recently – Alan Kennedy's hotly contested extra-time goal for Liverpool in this season's League Cup Final.

A surreal and more disturbing element was added to this sensational tie by the spillage of supporters onto the pitch perimeter within the opening 10 minutes. While first impressions were that this was standard crowd disorder, it was quickly made apparent that these were escapees from a horrifying-looking crush in the Leppings Lane end of the ground – a review of crowd safety must surely follow.

These two aspects bookended an absorbing contest. Even the uncommitted must have had adrenaline coming out of their ears at the end of extra-time in a tie enriched by a stark contrast in footballing styles. Spurs brought class and youth; Wolves brought muscle and grizzled experience. Spurs deployed the fluent midfield skills of Ossie Ardiles and Hoddle to achieve an impressive percentage of accurate

Glenn Hoddle's mastery of free-kicks enabled him to place his shot to perfection and restore Tottenham's advantage just before half-time

passing and shooting, while Wolves relied heavily on long balls to Gray and the veteran John Richards in an approach reminiscent of the club's glory years of the 1950s when it was they, not Tottenham, who seemed nailed on to achieve the first Double in football history.

Spurs first went ahead with only four minutes gone, when Chris Hughton's pass from the left found Tony Galvin who reached the byline before pulling back a cross for the excellent Steve Archibald to tap in. It seemed like bad news for Wolves, whose attacking resources, apart from the threat relentlessly imposed on Steve Perryman by Gray, could surely not match those of their opponents. Yet they were able to draw level within another seven minutes. The risk of fielding the rookie Wayne Clarke paid off when he took possession on the left and dispatched a veering shot towards goal. Perryman and Gray rose for it, with Gray triumphant on this occasion; he headed the ball back into the danger area and Hibbitt's first-time shot went home just inside the post.

If it had not been for Paul Bradshaw in the Wolves goal, Spurs could have taken the lead again soon after the half-hour was up. That was when Archibald set up Crooks for a superb shot that produced a notable save. Two minutes later, however, Bradshaw was picking the ball out of the back of his net after George Berry appeared to foul Ardiles on the edge of the box. The resultant free-kick was coolly chipped by Hoddle over the Wolves wall to put Tottenham ahead again on the brink of the half-time break.

As the second half got under way, Spurs appeared to be energetically in command, and it was not until the 79th minute, when Norman Bell came on for Clarke, that the Wolves attack began to look as if it still had a pulse. The sub had barely warmed up when, from Hibbitt's cross, Gray nearly scored with a trademark diving header, at which point the Midlands side regained a smidgen of self-belief. Even so, with the final whistle imminent, they looked well-beaten. That was when Hibbitt, chasing a pass across the goal area, made marginal contact with Hoddle, fell flat on his face and rose, arms aloft in appeal.

After approximately a 500-year pause, Thomas pointed to the spot. Perhaps it was a case of rough justice, making amends for the contentiously awarded free-kick that brought Hoddle's goal. Carr had

the heart-stopping job of saving this semi-final for Wolves in what would almost certainly be his last kick of normal time. He did it.

Thirty minutes of extra-time failed to divide the teams. Richards had a decent chance for Wolves, setting off on a run that culminated in a shot swerving just wide of the far post. Spurs might have sucked in their breath in relief except that by then they – like their opponents – had very little of that commodity left. There was time only for Bradshaw to produce one marvellous save from a thunderous Hoddle shot before the whistle went. Wolves trooped off looking as though they had won. Spurs, meanwhile looked to be smarting as well as exhausted. Their skill and speed should have been enough to win handsomely long before Thomas broke their hearts with a penalty award that, especially with the hindsight offered by late-night analysis on *Match of the Day*, looked uncomfortably arbitrary.

A welcome note of post-match lightheartedness was struck by a small group advertising themselves as 'Welsh Spurs', who announced their intention of travelling to Mr Thomas' home town of Llanelli to seek reparation. The teams meet again on Wednesday at Highbury, where if any justice is left in the world, Spurs should clinch their place at Wembley at the home of their bitterest rivals.

Action Highlights

SPURS v WOLVERHAMPTON WANDERERS

MAIN PICTURE — STEVE PERRYMAN evades a tackle by WAYNE CLARKE of Wolves in the first of our two semi-final matches at Hillsborough.
INSET — STEVE ARCHIBALD tries a shot in the same match

100

SPURS

1 MILIJA ALEKSIC
2 CHRIS HUGHTON
3 PAUL MILLER
4 GRAHAM ROBERTS
5 STEVE PERRYMAN
6 OSVALDO ARDILES
7 STEVE ARCHIBALD
8 TONY GALVIN
9 GLEN HODDLE
10 GARTH CROOKS
11 GARRY BROOKE
12 GORDON SMITH

WOLVES

PAUL BRADSHAW 1
GEOFF PALMER 2
DEREK PARKIN 3
WAYNE CLARKE 4
JOHN McALLE 5
GEORGE BERRY 6
KENNY HIBBITT 7
WILLIE CARR 8
ANDY GRAY 9
JOHN RICHARDS 10
MEL EVES 11
NORMAN BELL 12

The Men in Charge

REFEREE: Clive Thomas from Porthcawl started refereeing as a teenager after once being a ball boy on Norwich City's books. Graduated through local and Welsh leagues to the Football League full list. Has refereed several international and important European matches including two in the 1974 World Cup Finals. During 1976 he was in charge of the FA Cup Final, two international matches — England v Ireland and Germany v Greece — the Bayern Munich v Real Madrid European Cup Semi-Final and the European Nations Cup Final. In 1977 he was in charge of an FA Cup Semi-Final and European Cup matches. In 1978 he officiated in the World Cup in Argentina. Earlier this year he refereed the League Cup Final and the subsequent replay between West Ham United and Liverpool. A married man, with two daughters, he is a group executive, and attends functions as guest speaker, to speak on football refereeing and his other interests include table tennis and basketball.

LINESMEN
Red Flag: **D. B. Allison** (Lancaster)
Orange Flag: **R. F. Nixon** (Stockport)

Match Ball:
kindly donated by
Mitre Sports of Huddersfield.

Today's entertainment provided by the:
BAND OF THE IRISH GUARDS
by permission of
Colonel R. T. P. Hume
Lt. Colonel Commanding
Director of Music
Major M. G. Lane, A.R.C.M. p.s.m.

Magazine Production Team
Designed and Printed by:
J. W. Northend Ltd., Sheffield
Editorial: Les Comer, Jon Culley and Derek Knight
Colour Plates: Quad Repro, Pinxton, Notts.
Pictures: Wolverhampton Express & Star, Match Weekly, Sheffield Newspapers, Tommy Hindley and Steve Ellis.

Tottenham Hotspur Football & Athletic Co. Ltd.

F.A. CUP
Semi-Final 1981
BALLOT CARD

N

(For explanatory notes—see over)
(To be retained until result of Ballot is announced)

NAME ....

ADDRESS ....

POSTAL CODE ....

No 2032

For and on behalf of the
Tottenham Hotspur
Football & Athletic Co. Ltd.

Secretary

WHOOPEE! □ WHEN it was all going right Hoddle hugs scorer Archibald.

So nearly Tottenham's match winner — as Glenn Hoddle's shot already rests at the back of the Wolves' net, to put Spurs 2-1 up in the first semi-final. Inset (left) aerial action as Wolves' John Richards vies with Graham Roberts (top) and Chris Hughton. (Above) Steve Archibald puts away Tottenham's first after only four minutes.

SEMI-FINAL ACTION

SHEFFIELD WEDNESDAY F.C. LTD.
HILLSBOROUGH, SHEFFIELD
Football Association Challenge Cup

SEMI-FINAL
Saturday, 11th April, 1981
KICK-OFF 3.0 p.m.

A.England.
Secretary

RESERVED SEAT £6.00
INCLUDING VAT

Issued subject to the Rules,
Regulations and Bye-Laws of the
Football Association.
No Tickets exchanged nor
money refunded.
THIS PORTION TO BE RETAINED

NORTH STAND
Leppings Lane

ENTRANCE
A

GANGWAY
J

TO THE LEFT
ROW   SEAT
48   89
You are Requested to
Take up your Position
Thirty Minutes Before
Kick-off

■ STEVE ARCHIBALD puts Spurs ahead in their semi-final against Wolves.

Lessons not learned

In a chilling portent of tragic future events, the Spurs fans on Hillsborough's Leppings Lane terrace experienced a terrifying crush due to overcrowding

The overcrowding in the Leppings Lane stand at Hillsborough that resulted in the deaths of 95 – subsequently 97 – people on 15th April 1989 was one of the most tragic episodes in British football history.

But it wasn't the first time that this stand had been dangerously overcrowded. Exactly eight years earlier came a stark – and unheeded – warning of what could happen when 38 Spurs supporters were injured in near-identical circumstances.

'We were in the ground around two o'clock,' remembers Ian Meth, who had travelled to Sheffield with his father and three Spurs-supporting friends. 'We were in the seats opposite the main stand, with Leppings Lane to our right. The team came out in their suits and I remember Steve Archibald walking back towards the dressing room and Andy Gray coming out, and the two of them, Scottish internationals, shaking hands. There were only about eight of us in there at that point but you could see from about half past two that there were going to be problems because the Leppings Lane end was already incredibly crowded. There was a corner bit where you could see over the top and there were thousands of Spurs supporters – you could hear them, still outside, with the terrace already packed. Yet the Kop end on our left – the Wolves end – was still pretty empty. You could see the crush barriers.'

A disregard for fans' safety was already a reality of football supporting in the 1980s. The game's public image had been tainted by the hooliganism of the previous decade, no matter that for the majority of fans going to a game was an innocent and pleasurably enthralling activity. But why was the larger group of supporters given the smaller Leppings Lane end and the smaller club given the big Kop end?

'I got in there and looked around and the first thing I thought was, "This end is too small," says Alan Fisher. 'The Leppings Lane end then had seats behind the goal and a terrace below that. The other end was a big open terrace. But you looked around your end and thought there wasn't enough room for all the Spurs fans you knew were coming.'

From the press box, supporters could be seen climbing over fences to reach the seating area above. In an act born of expediency, police made what we

now know to be probably a life-saving decision when they opened two of the gates in front of the terrace and helped people onto the pitch. By the time the game started there were large numbers of Spurs fans on the cinder track around the pitch. It was obvious that some people had quite serious injuries and were being helped away by St John's Ambulance and the police. They then escorted some Spurs fans round the track to space in another part of the ground.

'I decided to stand not in the middle of the terrace where there would be a greater crush but to the right-hand side,' says Fisher. 'Just before kick-off it started to get very, very busy even where I was, and although I was trying to get out of the way it was the section that was nearest to the entrances. I think that was one of the problems when Liverpool were there later on. I was getting pushed further and further down the terrace and it started to get crowded, and you started to hear, before and after kick-off, people shouting - shouting for help, from the police and St John's Ambulance workers. You saw people being carted towards the front in order to get some help. You also saw large numbers of people being pulled up into the seats above. You needed to make some effort to get up there, and people weren't doing it for a better view but because they were trying to get out.'

Throughout this process the crowd was strikingly orderly. Nobody invaded the pitch, nor was there any trouble between Spurs and Wolves fans who were close to each other. All fans were well-behaved, and any attempt to paint it as a pitch invasion caused by hooliganism would have been unjustifiable.

'Towards the end of the game I'd been pushed down to probably about 10 yards from the front of the

A Spurs fan implores referee Clive Thomas, as chaos ensues in the Spurs end of the ground

Spurs fans sit bewildered on the touchline, having clambered over the perimeter fences to escape the crush on the Leppings Lane terrace

terrace,' continues Alan Fisher. 'You couldn't move at all. I had my arms pinned to my sides. My feet were below the level of the pitch, so you were really quite low down, and, I have to be honest, I do remember a feeling of excitement because you were in the sway of the crowd, you couldn't move but – this was pre-Heysel, pre-Bradford, pre-Hillsborough '89 – you had no sense of the danger that you were in.

'I wasn't afraid because you had no concept of what could go wrong on terraces in those days. It was only in later years that you realised you had actually

been in enormous danger because there was no escape. I just thought, "Well, this is uncomfortable". It's very difficult to explain to people but in that situation it's impossible to move. You can't do anything. You're completely helpless.'

One fan approached after the game said, 'It was the most terrified for my life I've ever been at a match. Thankfully I managed to duck under a barrier and get to the other side.'

'I was one of the first to get onto the pitch,' said another. 'It was before they realised what was really happening, and I was pulled to the ground and punched in the head by the police who thought I was causing trouble. They pushed me back into the pen.'

It was a frightening experience even for those

"It was only in later years that you realised you had actually been in enormous danger because there was no escape"

not caught up in the original crush. 'We saw it and, like most people in the other areas of the ground, didn't know what the hell was going on,' confirms Jill Lewis. 'Then as we left we filed through these big cast iron gates, huge things, and everybody was being funneled into this narrow gap, and that was probably up there with the most worried I have ever been at a football match, because we were getting completely crushed. Scary. Really scary. So obviously later when you found out what had happened you felt that fear, because you were part of that fear.'

'When the Hillsborough disaster happened in 1989 my first thought was probably that of many,' says Ian Meth. 'Oh my God, that could have been us. It really was that close.'

'I emerged from that crushed but unhurt,' reflects Alan Fisher, 'but there's absolutely no doubt in my mind that if they hadn't opened the gates to the pitch that day that Spurs fans would have died. And I'm not being maudlin but frankly that could have been me because I was right down the front and there was no escape, you couldn't move at all. You couldn't move your arms to protect yourself or lift yourself up, you couldn't shift yourself. Tragedy was averted only because somebody decided to open the gates to the pitch when we were in there. When Liverpool were there they never opened the gates.'

SEMI-FINAL REPLAY SPURS v WOLVES

A night to remember

The penalty that took our semi-final against Wolves to a replay may have been a shocker, but it set up one of our greatest nights at the home of our biggest rivals

Terry Dyson, part of the 1960/61 Double side, once said that he didn't know what it was like to be a fan. As a footballer, you look at situations a bit differently. When Arsenal won the first half of the 1971 Double at White Hart Lane it hurt, obviously, but we'd fought from the first minute to the last to protect the history of our club. So we were embarrassed, but not for the wrong reasons. We were embarrassed because of what it meant to the fans.

But that was 10 years back, and I didn't actually connect the prospect of winning at Highbury with what had happened in 1971. That was then, a historical fact. This was now. We'd been through relegation and promotion and we were on a charge to becoming a big team again. That didn't mean we were indifferent to the prospect of getting to Wembley on enemy territory. We certainly thought about how good it would be to get to a final by winning at Highbury, and part of that feeling was how much our supporters would enjoy it, because your fans are your brothers-in-arms.

Spurs manager Keith Burkinshaw in unfamiliar territory, sitting in the home dugout at Highbury

On the other hand, I can't imagine Wolves and their fans being too pleased that the replay was going to be in North London. In their eyes it would have been a home game for us, just down the road, whereas for them there was a motorway in between. That gave us the feeling that things had started to turn in our favour. Maybe we didn't look at it that way as we travelled home on the bus from Hillsborough, but very soon it felt like it was our year again. Then, come the day of the replay, there was a second sign that the fates were on our side. Before kick-off the team-sheets came in. Andy Gray was out injured. That definitely hurt their attacking threat. But even with him in the team I don't think anything would have stopped us that night. We just felt the adrenaline running through us all match.

That semi-final replay was Tottenham Hotspur at its best. Imagine a kid in Scunthorpe or Southend being allowed to stay up to watch the highlights on television. The quality we showed must have made him or her Spurs for life. Fans still talk about Glenn's pass and Garth's pace for our second goal, calling it one of the most perfect they've ever seen. If you'd ask me to describe the definitive goal that great early '80s side ever scored, it would be that goal. But our first goal also illustrated the incredible link between the pair of them – the way that chip Glenn supplied sailed over George Berry and Emlyn Hughes and bounced up perfectly for Garth. So many of our goals began with getting the ball to Glenn in either the inside-right or inside-left position, where he was so dangerous. Glenn was always looking for the space in behind, and how he could get it there best. He'd prefer to get

Garth Crooks scores the second of his two goals, using a lethal burst of pace to latch on to Glenn Hoddle's imperious through ball

it there along the floor so it didn't give the man receiving it a problem, but sometimes the only way he could get it there was to lift it. For the second goal, Glenn hit the perfect through-ball along the ground and Garth just went *whoosh!* When I watch it now, I always think it's speeded up. It's not just Garth's pace but the purposeful manner of his run – you only do that it you know the ball's going to arrive. And Glenn gave you the certainty that the perfect ball was going to be delivered. Garth knew he wasn't wasting his energy. It's like before you fire a gun, you cock the trigger. The bullet is coming, and it's coming from Glenn Hoddle. It's worth running for.

I'm not sure we won many games at Highbury, so this was one hell of a night for our supporters. They were unbelievable all the way through, and they got rewarded for their passion and desire. They would have celebrated any kind of win, not just because of where it was but because of how we'd had victory stolen from us four days earlier. That alone made the feeling more intense, and 10 times more worth celebrating that if we'd done it at Hillsborough, but the fact we

did it in such good style, building up an unassailable three-goal lead with so much time left on the clock, made it even better. Imagine if the goal that got us to Wembley had been scored in the last minute – that would have been amazing enough in itself for the crowd to be celebrating for however much longer they were in the stadium, but our crowd had the last 35 minutes to celebrate, because we had won the game early and in such an unforgettable way. We deserved to beat Wolves in the first game. We certainly deserved to beat Wolves in the second game, with Garth's goal-taking and that spectacular finish of Ricky's. We were elated. Of course, there was such an important prize at the end of it that no one was taking any liberties, and there was no showboating, but it's always good when you play such a crucial game and it's virtually over with that much time to go. You can never say it's over, but we were already on our way to Wembley and deep down we all knew it.

And do you know how I felt at the end? I felt a bit sorry for Wolves. Should I have done? Probably not. But in my time we seemed to have a sort of hex over them. We always seemed to have the beating of them in the games that mattered. Going back to that night in 1971 when Arsenal won the title at White Hart Lane, if you look at it impartially, that season as a whole hadn't been a bad one for us. We finished third in the table but, more importantly, we had won the League Cup, which got us a place in Europe. And in one of those odd coincidences you sometimes get in football, the team we beat to win the 1972 UEFA Cup had been Wolves.

At the end of the second leg of that final, Bill famously said they

Right: Glenn Hoddle acclaims Garth Crooks after the midfielder's sublime pass set up the striker to score and put Tottenham in command

Facing: The celebrations are repeated after Ricky Villa's spectacular long-range shot makes the game safe. Spurs are on their way to Wembley

"What a few days followed. You'd go into training and be on a high; you'd go home from training, and still be on a high"

deserved to win. It wasn't unusual for him to be critical of the way we played, and I have to say there was some truth in what he said – we had had to hang on a bit in the closing stages, so we didn't win in the style that a manager like Bill Nicholson demanded. But ever since then, in my eyes – perhaps because we'd beaten them even though we hadn't been at our best – they were never a top club. They weren't as good a team as us. They were a genuine team, very competitive, but even so their good players weren't as well-known as the ones we had, with Ossie and Ricky, both proven big-game players, and Glenn, the greatest midfield player in England. Of course Wolves had good players, but they weren't regarded as being in the same class as our people.

But even before that we always seemed to have the edge on them when it came to the big prizes. If you delve into history, who did Tottenham beat to win the 1921 FA Cup? Wolves. At the end of the 1950s they were tipped to win the first Double. Guess what, within two years we were the ones that did it. We always seemed to have the beating of them when it came to the very end. Decent team, decent ethics – Hibbitt's dive notwithstanding – but 60 years on from the

1921 FA Cup, they still didn't have quite enough to beat us. It was just like they were always trying to get there but not arriving. So in a way I felt sad for them because we weren't only beating them, we were getting the trophies and making history while they weren't.

What a few days followed. You'd go into training and be on a high; you'd go home from training and still be on a high. Of course, we couldn't sit back and relax in that situation, we had to get on with completing the league programme, not to mention deal with all the extra stuff going on, like sorting out who gets what from your allocation of tickets and taking part in the non-football activities we got involved with for the players' pool. And, of course, we had a song to sing. On *Top of the Pops*.

It was good to be surrounded by people who were well-known, like Chas 'n' Dave, and the making and performing of *Ossie's Dream* did tell you a lot about professionalism; about people who were proper musicians, knew what they were doing and were able to tow us along with them, although what they must have thought of football teams messing about, I don't know. But it was fun, and there was nothing wrong with that. Everyone was in high spirits, weren't they? Because in the very near future we had the chance of a long-awaited trophy.

And that was the all-important thing. You don't win the FA Cup by winning at Highbury but it was satisfying for our collective ego that we'd got to Wembley by winning on enemy territory. Now we had to make sure that that win didn't fade into oblivion. Who'd give a shit about winning at Highbury if we went and lost the final?

Spurs 3 Wolves 0

15th April 1981, Highbury. Att: 52,539

Spurs goalscorers: Crooks (2), Villa

By Julie Welch

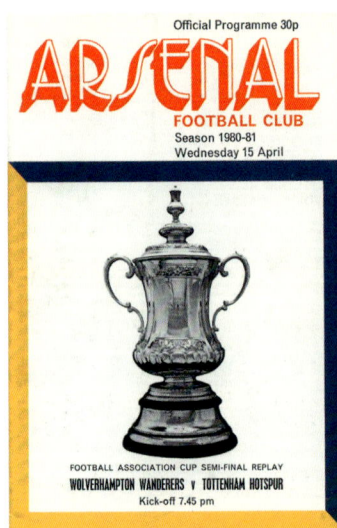

Ricky Villa tussles with former Liverpool legend Emlyn Hughes. Fired up by the sense of being unfairly denied in the first game, Spurs matched Wolves physically and surpassed them in flair

It ended in euphoria. A decision that felt all wrong as soon as it happened seemed a lifetime away as Spurs ran rampant at Highbury to defeat a Wolves side which didn't deserve to be there in the first place. They had got a reprieve through a penalty that should never have been awarded, and the chasm in class was manifest – Wolves a moderate side hovering just above the relegation struggle in the First Division; Tottenham a team which, if they produce a show like this, will make the 100th FA Cup Final one hell of an occasion. 'Where was the turning point in the game?' the press asked John Barnwell, the Wolves manager, afterwards. 'The turning point was when we turned up,' he said.

Although they hadn't planned on meeting the Midlands side for the second time in four days, it was worth it just to get Spurs playing the way they were meant to play – Glenn Hoddle more of an icon than ever before, two-goal Garth Crooks his willing partner in excellence and Ricky Villa with a belter from 25 yards out to wrap it up. 'It was good to win in the style I like,' said Keith Burkinshaw. 'I prefer to win playing like that.' Oh mate, don't we all…

With Kenny Hibbitt the most boo-able individual in sight, an injustice to deal with and a team strengthened last summer and getting it right at the perfect moment, this was also the ideal place for it to happen as far as the Spurs fans were concerned – at the home of their bitterest enemy. 'The best football seen from a London team at Highbury this season,' they said. They had waited a long time for this moment, not just 120 exhausting and ultimately futile minutes at Hillsborough, but 14 years – the gulf in time since Alf Ramsey had become a Knight of the Realm, Jimi Hendrix had set fire to his first guitar, The Beatles were still together and Tottenham beat Chelsea at Wembley with their braveheart of a captain Dave Mackay lifting the FA Cup.

Almost from kick-off Wolves were where they had been for most of the Saturday afternoon just past – trying to save the tie. Their centre-backs had trouble reading the bounce of the ball on a bumpy pitch, and the game had only been going 10 minutes when Ossie Ardiles found Hoddle in space midway inside the Wolves half. The outcome was almost inevitable. Hoddle's delicate lob – how does he do these things, does he have tongs for feet? – travelled up and down over the mesmerised George Berry into the goalmouth where it sat up and said please for Crooks to dart in and head home.

After that, Wolves embarked on their most dogged spell, hampered by the absence of striker Andy Gray, a last-minute absentee through a suspect hamstring tested to near-destruction by the ferocity of his Hillsborough battle with Steve Perryman. Wolves plugged away manfully with their long-ball game, as if they were closing their eyes and pretending he was still there rather than Mel Eves, a taller but much less threatening target than the man he had replaced. Even so, this was the only period of the game in which they looked capable of clawing their way back. With 20 minutes gone, after Emlyn Hughes nodded back a centre from Derek Parkin, Hughton had to clear Richards' well-aimed header off the line. Wolves came even closer to scoring 10 minutes before half-time when Tottenham's defensive uncertainty nearly bit them on the backside, with Willie Carr's corner kick from the right being touched on by Richards. Eves tried a diving header before Berry's shot rebounded from the underside of the bar.

In between all that, Spurs took turns rattling off shots, the contrast between both sides becoming increasingly marked. Tottenham's play was primarily short and possessive, with Perryman picking out the options from the back and Ardiles, Villa and Hoddle carrying the ball to the opposition and searching for space near goal with imaginative passing and running. They had a Plan B, too, which involved a Spur (almost always Hoddle) opening up the Wolves rearguard with a potent long pass for Archibald and Crooks to outpace Berry and John McAlle.

That said, for all their superiority and near-misses Spurs could have done with a second goal. They got it at a killer time, in the last minute of the first half. As ever it owed everything to the vision of Hoddle, who whisked the ball away from Eves near the right-hand touchline. With Crooks up and running already he split the Wolves defence with a marvel of a pass that Crooks pasted joyfully past the advancing Paul Bradshaw.

They weren't done yet. Eight minutes into the second half came a pass from Crooks followed by a screamer of a goal from Villa – 25 yards out, left-footed and at an angle of 45 degrees. It was unexpected, un-bloody-stoppable, wow, wow, wow – 3–0! There was no coming back from that. Highbury was lilywhite for the night and with the tie not yet over but so clearly won, a good three sides of the ground gave in to 35 minutes of joyful madness.

So, 'Hello Wembley', where Tottenham will go head to head with Manchester City, a team transformed by John Bond – thanks to the addition of a few grizzled campaigners – from bottom-of-the-heap losers in autumn to the surprise contenders of spring. City, increasingly described as pragmatic – the game's euphemism for crude but effective – will be a lot harder to beat than Wolves, and for all that Tottenham have two World Cup winners and, in Perryman, a man who has won at Wembley before, they are a young side for whom this will be the first encounter with the big time. They're also prone to some precarious moments in defence. That said, it's hard to believe that Hoddle, Ardiles and Villa won't flourish in Wembley's wide-open spaces, or that Crooks and Steve Archibald will forget where the net is located. This will be Tottenham Hotspur's sixth FA Cup Final in their history. They've never yet been the losing side in one of those.

Ricky Villa takes flight as his shot rockets beyond the helpless Wolves defence

Inspired Tottenham overwhelm Wolves with their quality

Garth Crooks beats Wolves defender ... Palmer to score the first goal.

WOLVERHAMPTON 0 (0)

Colours:
Shirts: Gold
Shorts: Black
Stockings: Gold

TOTTENHAM 3 (2)

Colours:
Shirts: White
Shorts: Navy Blue
Stockings: White

WOLVERHAMPTON		TOTTENHAM
(B) PAUL BRADSHAW	1	MILIJA ALEKSIC (B)
GEOFF PALMER	2	CHRIS HUGHTON
DEREK PARKIN EMLYN HUGHES	3	PAUL MILLER
WAYNE ~~CLARKE~~	4	GRAHAM ROBERTS
JOHN McALLE	5	GARRY BROOKE Ricardo Villa (1)
GEORGE BERRY	6	STEVE PERRYMAN
KENNY HIBBITT	7	OSVALDO ARDILES
WILLIE CARR NORMAN BELL	8	STEVE ARCHIBALD
ANDY ~~GRAY~~	9	TONY GALVIN
JOHN RICHARDS	10	GLENN HODDLE
MEL EVES WAYNE CLARKE	11	GARTH CROOKS (2)
	12	GARY BROOKE (for 7).

Referee Mr G Courtney (Durham)

Linesmen
Red Flag: **Mr D Hedges** (Oxford)
Yellow Flag: **Mr R L Hamer** (Bristol)

PROGRAMME OF MUSIC
THE BAND OF THE METROPOLITAN POLICE
(by permission of the Commissioner of Police of the Metropolis)
Conductor: Captain Chris Taylor, LRAM, ARCM, LGSM

Printed in England by Harrison & Sons (London) Limited

Nº 3815 C

F.A. CUP
SEMI-FINAL REPLAY

WOLVERHAMPTON WANDERERS
v
TOTTENHAM HOTSPUR

Wednesday, 15th April 1981
K.O. 7.45 p.m.

£2.50p

THIS PORTION
TO BE RETAINED

CROOKS IS CROWING

HALLELUJAH

Our next stop, Wembley

THAT'S FINAL ... Spurs midfielder Glenn Hoddle rushes to congratulate Garth Crooks after the black striker's second goal of the night eclipsed Wolves FA Cup hopes and started the "Glory, Glory" chants ringing.

Two-go...

Glory, glory, Garth
is Spurs cup king

Spurs' Wembley wonders

SPURS are back at Wembley — and no one can deny them the right to meet Manchester City at Wembley on May 9 after their super show against cup specialists Wolves in last week's semi-final replay at Highbury.

Two goals from razor-sharp Garth Crooks and a left foot thunderbolt from Argentinian ace Ricky Villa finished the job that Spurs came so close to completing in the first incident-packed game at Hillsborough, Sheffield.

The agony of seeing victory snatched away by a Willie Carr penalty in the last minute of normal time turned to ecstacy as Spurs blasted their way into their first FA Cup Final since 1967 when they beat Chelsea 2-1.

Above left: Spurs central defender Paul Miller heads clear from Wolves striker Norman Bell, who was deputising for the injured Andy Gray.
Above: Spurs' Wembley Wonders celebrate after Villa had sealed Wolves fate with its third goal. From the right — Glenn Hoddle, who laid on two of the goals,
Ricky Villa, scorer of a crashing left-footer, and Garth Crooks, scorer of the other two goals. Chris Hughton (2) runs over to add his congratulations.
Left: Wolves warhorse Emlyn Hughes battles for a ball with Ricky Villa, but couldn't prevent his team losing 3-0.

NEXT WEEK

50 FA Cup posters to be won FREE

STEVE MORAN
'My big test'
JIM CANNON and MICK LYONS
'Why we've stayed loyal'
STAR CHOICE
More than 150 players reveal their likes and dislikes

FA CUP COUNTDOWN
Features on the Wembley finalists
AND IN COLOUR
SOUTHEND team group
JOE GALLAGHER pull-out poster
TOM RITCHIE
RAY WILKINS

Behind enemy lines

The decision to play the semi-final replay against Wolves at Highbury allowed Spurs fans to turn the home of their arch-rivals blue and white on a famous night

An FA Cup semi-final replay in enemy territory, a Glenn Hoddle masterclass, three unforgettable goals, and an evening game that turned into a carnival celebration of what it meant to be Spurs. If anyone still scoffed at the idea that Tottenham Hotspur's name was on the cup, this was the night that put them right.

'Highbury was three sides Tottenham,' remembers Mike Leigh, who was 14 years old on that famous night. 'My God, it was like a home game. It was like White Hart Lane for the night.'

'It was one of the great games that stay in the memory,' says Ian Meth. 'From where we were sitting in the East Stand we could see that the North Bank on our right was a sea of blue and white. Spurs probably had three-quarters of the Clock End, too, and the whole of the West Stand. It was almost worth it to go to Highbury. We put in what was probably our best performance of the season. Forty-one years ago and it seems as fresh as ever. Even though it was only a semi-final, give me most Tottenham fans' top 10 Spurs games ever and will be right up there – the atmosphere, the noise, three great goals.'

'That was a lot of fun, being in the North Bank,' says Alan Fisher. 'That was where the Arsenal fans went, so that was their spot, a place that was sacred to them and here we were, allowed in. We were completely in control of this sacred territory. It had fantastic acoustics because it had a low roof and you had 90 minutes of singing, noise and joy. Of course there was merciless taunting of Kenny Hibbitt – "Hibbitt, Hibbitt, what's the score?" That was stick of the highest order and he deserved it because of what happened at Hillsborough.'

Euphoria alternated with anxiety during the first half. 'We were approaching half-time and I felt we were on top but we weren't quite making the most of our dominance,' recalls Simon Lipson. 'I was looking at my watch, 45 minutes, let's go in in front, let's not concede now – blow the whistle, blow it – and then the ball arrived at Glenn's foot and I remember thinking, "Hang on a sec, don't blow."'

'Hoddle played a beautiful 30 yard through-ball,' continues Alan Fisher. 'Crooks was going full pelt and the ball ends up right at his feet as he's in full stride – what a perfect, perfect pass. Hoddle encapsulated in one immaculate movement.'

'And then it was 2-0 and the whistle went shortly after that,' adds Simon Lipson. 'It was just the most perfect moment. For so many years Glenn was passing to Ian Moores and Chris Jones, and with all due respect he was now passing to Crooks and Archibald, players of his capability. Then in the second half, there was that spectacular finish from

Man of the match Garth Crooks receives the acclaim of ecstatic fans on the Highbury pitch

"My God, it was like a home game. It was like White Hart Lane for the night"

Villa. We hadn't had the team, we hadn't had the players for so long. And now we all knew we had, and we were in the final. It didn't feel very Spurs-like.'

'I don't remember getting too excited until then, because so much was going on in my life at the time,' says Pete Haine, whose marriage was in its final throes. 'But I took the lucky coin I had found just before the third round replay with me to Highbury. I rubbed it all the way until the third goal went in and we were safely on our way to Wembley. I was almost directly behind Ricky's shot. It screamed into the top corner – you could see it just slightly curl and go in. An incredible night, and I think that's when the excitement really kicked in, thinking, "Ah, brilliant, we're going to Wembley for the FA Cup final."'

'On the morning of the replay I took my car and parked in one of the roads near Highbury on my way to work, so it was there for the evening,' says Jill Lewis. 'I went to the match with my friend Claud, and when we came out we realised there had been parking restrictions. They'd cleared all the roads, but my car was still there, this little white mini in deserted streets. I was euphoric. I guess this is incomprehensible to younger supporters, but I'd seen the 1967 FA Cup win, I'd seen the 1971 League Cup win, so as far as I was concerned if we were in any final we were going to win it. I was nervous, but I had absolute confidence. We've got through that semi-final – we are going to win.'

133

"An incredible night, and I think that's when the excitement really kicked in, thinking, 'Ah, brilliant, going to Wembley for the FA Cup final'"

Tottenham are back: the joy of fans and players alike is unconfined in scenes of happy bedlam after the final whistle at Highbury

In the run-up to the 1921 FA Cup Final between Tottenham Hotspur and Wolverhampton Wanderers, cards printed with the following verse circulated around London:

The Wolves came wandering from their lair,
To grab the cup and make it theirs,
But 'ere the victory occurs,
They have to beat the gallant Spurs

As it turned out, Wolves failed to beat the 'gallant' Spurs, and it wasn't the first time that Tottenham Hotspur had lifted the trophy, either. A key component of FA Cup magic is when the big boys slip up against what are popularly known as 'minnows'. By the time of the victory against Wolves, Spurs were in the First Division, but it wasn't like that 20 years before when they pulled off a feat that has so far not been emulated. In 1901 they became the first, and remain the only, non-league side to lift the FA Cup.

The FA Cup was 30 years old by then – the first-ever ties were played on 11th November 1871. The competition was christened The Football Association Challenge Cup, and the final held in the spring of 1872 at the Kennington Oval, where Royal Engineers lost to Wanderers.

The competition was the brainchild of FA Secretary Charles Alcock, who got the idea from his days at Harrow School, where its numerous boarding houses would – in more innocent times - compete for the title of 'Cock House'. Many of the names on Wanderers' teamsheet were those of Old Harrovians, which figured because Charles Alcock owned the club. Another Old Harroviann was Lord Kinnaird, who also turned out for Old Etonians for whom he scored the first ever own goal in an FA Cup Final, against Oxford University in 1877. It didn't stop Old Etonians winning 3-1.

But the young bucks and their amateur teams clad in knickerbockers and silky shirts soon started to be outnumbered by the hardboiled professional northern clubs of the newly-hatched Football League. The FA Cup evolved into a knockout competition involving every club in the country – a money-spinner peddling the dream that any club, even the smallest and most obscure, had a chance. No one can say for sure when the phrase 'the magic of the cup' was minted but it could easily have been on 6th October 1888 when Warwick County became the first non-league side to beat a First Division club by winning 2-1 away to Stoke.

Back then the trophy was an 18-inch tall slimline number topped with a solid silver footballer. But following Aston Villa's 1-0 victory over West Bromwich Albion in 1895, the trophy was put on display in the window of William Shillcock's football equipment shop in central Birmingham. It was promptly nicked, never to be recovered. In the 1950s a geriatric petty thief came forward to claim responsibility for the crime. He'd had the trophy melted down to make counterfeit coins. The trophy Spurs took home in 1901 was a replica.

At that time, only one London club was a member of the

The magic of the cup

Back in 1981, reaching the FA Cup Final was considered the pinnacle of English football and the build-up lasted for weeks, leading up to an unprecedented day of blanket television coverage

By Julie Welch

Football League, and that was Arsenal. When Spurs had applied for entry, they were turned down, as the northern clubs didn't fancy the bother of travelling down to the capital twice in a season. Spurs joined the Southern League instead, and having been swatted aside by mighty Preston North End in 1899/1900, no one was expecting glory the following season when they drew Preston again in the first round. Yet Spurs held the northerners to a 1-1 draw at their new ground, White Hart Lane, and won 4-2 at Deepdale. After that they disposed of the holders, Bury, who had nine internationals in their side, and lucked out at Reading when they equalised with a handball which everyone saw except the referee, then won the replay. The semi-final was at Villa Park where they wiped out West Bromwich Albion.

This was romance. This was unprecedented – non-leaguers contesting the cup final. The final was played at Crystal Palace and went to a replay after Sheffield United scored an equaliser that wasn't. Tottenham keeper George Clawley saved, the linesman signalled for a corner but the referee blew for a goal. As it happened, this was the first FA Cup Final ever to be filmed, and the footage showed clearly that the ball was a foot in front of the line when Clawley got to it. But Spurs got what was due to them in the replay at Bolton's ground, Burnden Park. If you've ever wondered where the tradition of tying ribbons in the winning club's colours onto the trophy started, it was when the wife of Tottenham director Morton Cadman prettied up the handles with blue and white ones. According to eyewitnesses, when the team arrived back in North London they were met by a crowd bigger than the one that cheered news of the Relief of Mafeking, a decisive victory for Britain in the Second Boer War the previous year. This was how big the FA Cup had become.

There is another 'first' connected with that 1901 win. Tottenham's Sandy Brown was the first player to score in every round. And Spurs feature in other diverting bits of cup trivia. The highest score draw in the FA Cup was in January 1914 when Leicester against Tottenham Hotspur finished 5-5. Spurs also lie fourth in the table of record wins with their 13-2 fourth round demolition of Crewe Alexandra in 1960. The first trainer to lift

Danny Blanchflower carries the cup down the Wembley steps in 1961. It was Tottenham's third FA Cup success when the year ended in a '1', but set a high and often frustratingly elusive bar for future Spurs teams

"There's nothing that says 'big-time' like having the reigning monarch rock up to watch your event and present the prizes"

the FA Cup was Billy Minter. This was after Spurs beat Wolves in the 1921 final at Stamford Bridge when the captain, Arthur Grimsdell, simply abandoned the team and set off home to Watford after the final whistle. Nobody has ever found out why.

Two years later, the FA Cup Final had a permanent home. The Empire Stadium at Wembley opened in 1923 and the cup final was its inaugural event, played in the presence of the King. There's nothing that says 'big time' like having the reigning monarch rock up to watch your event and present the prizes.

The match itself is remembered less than the chaotic crowd scenes that preceded it. The official attendance at Bolton Wanderers v West Ham was 126,047 but it was more like 300,000, and spectators in the lower tier spilled onto the pitch to avoid the crush. Among the mounted police deployed to disperse them was PC George Scorey on his white horse, 'Billy'. Inevitably the event has passed into legend as the 'White Horse Final'. Astonishingly, no serious casualties were reported that day.

With the Wembley factor, the magic of the FA Cup really took hold: the big occasion; the thrill of stepping out onto what would become known as the 'hallowed turf'; the winning side climbing exhaustedly up those steps to receive the trophy from top-tier royalty, then finding the energy to cavort round the pitch in front of their besotted fans. To underline its importance in the national calendar, the 1938 final between Preston and Huddersfield was broadcast on live television, thereby ensuring that the gaffe committed by the commentator, Thomas Woodroffe, lives on. With the game goalless with only two minutes of time left, Woodroffe uttered the words that would haunt him till his last

Above right: Led by captain Arthur Grimsdell (seated, third from left) and managed by Peter McWilliam, Spurs won their second FA Cup in 1921

Right: The press speculate that Tottenham Hotspur's famous lucky omen will come true again in 1981

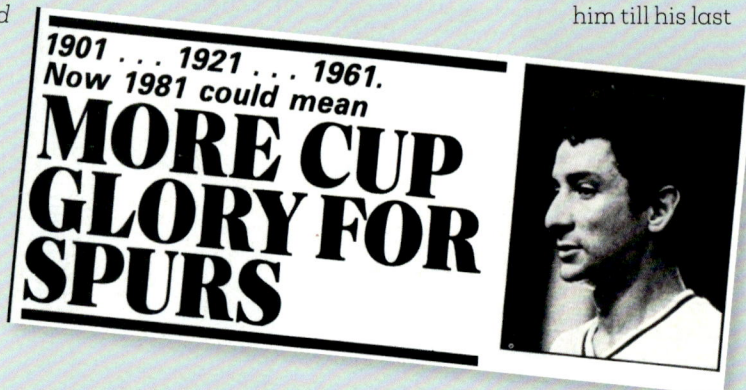

1901 . . . 1921 . . . 1961.
Now 1981 could mean
MORE CUP GLORY FOR SPURS

breath – 'I'll eat my hat if there's any score before the final whistle goes.' Obviously this was the signal for George Mutch to bulge the netting from the penalty spot to win the cup for Preston. Woodroffe did get a hat to eat, incidentally, even though it was one made of cake and marzipan.

The FA Cup and television were made for each other. In the decades that followed, footage of those David-triumphing-over-Goliath battles have become a potent part of cup magic; Liverpool losing 2-1 to Worcester City in 1959; non-league Wimbledon drawing with champions Leeds in 1977; Bournemouth knocking out Man Utd in the third round in 1984. Television, too, has preserved the 'Matthews Final' of 1953, when Blackpool came back from 3-1 down to beat Bolton Wanderers 4-3. Stanley Matthews' main contribution was the cross from which Bill Perry netted late on. It was an injury-time winner, but the real hero of the afternoon was Stan Mortensen with his hat-trick. Mortensen used to say that when he died the burial ceremony would be known as the 'Matthews Funeral'.

As the 1960s went on, more and more TV sets arrived in the nation's lounges, cementing the FA Cup into the national consciousness. The final – one of the only football matches televised live all season – was talked about all week in the run up. If your club wasn't involved, you'd pick who to support. People asked whether you were going to watch on BBC or ITV. There are moments from more than half a century back that, if you were around then, you can still see in your mind's eye: there's the fan running onto the pitch chased by two policemen after Everton got back to 2-2 against Sheffield Wednesday in 1966. Everton went on to win 3-2. There's the 1970 final, Chelsea v Leeds, the first to go to a replay, which had to be switched to Old Trafford because the pitch had been churned up from the *Horse of the Year Show*. There's Ronnie Radford's equalising long range-strike for Hereford United against Newcastle in a third-round replay in 1972 – poor Ricky George, who scored the winner, hardly ever gets a mention. There's Bob Stokoe in 1973 running onto the Wembley pitch in his coat, tracksuit trousers and trilby hat to hug his goalkeeper Jim Montgomery, hero of the match when Second Division Sunderland beat Leeds to win the cup.

And as the decade wore on, there was *Cup Final Grandstand*. This was an era in which hardly any live football was on the box. Now you had a whole day devoted to the match. Coverage would start in the morning with any BBC light entertainment that could be hung on a football theme, and it wouldn't only be kids who were glued to *Cup Final Swap Shop* – featuring Noel Edmonds wearing a scarf – or *Cup Final It's A Knockout*. There would be a montage of highlights from earlier rounds, coverage from the team hotel, Tony Gubba riding on the team bus to the stadium, and *vox pops* as the cameras dwelt on fans walking up Wembley Way towards the Twin Towers. You'd be treated to the pre-match entertainment, which generally entailed dogs jumping over and through things, a military brass band, and the community singing of *Abide With Me*, which once television got in on the act guaranteed that for a few minutes on every late spring Saturday the entire nation got something in its eye.

In 1980 another giant-killing featured, though not by Tottenham Hotspur. Their cup run had ended in the quarter-final at Anfield when Ossie got penned in near the corner flag. A lesser player would have walloped the ball up and over the touchline but he tried to make a constructive pass. It went straight to the feet of Terry McDermott. You could have sworn that ball rose

of its own accord for McDermott to volley it into the net from 30 yards out. The giant killing was supplied by West Ham, who became the first Second Division club in modern times to win the trophy. So for Spurs, the only magic about the cup that year was that West Ham's beaten opponents were Arsenal.

No one can say for certain when the legend sprang up that if there was a '1' in the year the name on the cup would be Tottenham Hotspur. Maybe it was in 1961 when Danny Blanchflower lifted the trophy in front of the royal box after Spurs had clinched the Double. In 1967 they jumped the gun, and when 1971 came around it was the other team in North London that claimed it.

But now it was 1981, and it would bring the most magical moment of them all.

Reflecting the status of the competition, the Radio Times' Centenary FA Cup Special devotes its front page and exhaustive coverage to the match. The TV coverage started a full three-and-a-half hours before kick off

Chartbusting cockerels

With cockney Lilywhite combo Chas 'n' Dave on board, Spurs' Wembley preparations culminated in an assault on the hit parade with classic cup final song *Ossie's Dream*

By Julie Welch

'**I** don't know that any of us could sing, apart possibly from Glenn,' says Steve Perryman. 'Chas 'n' Dave sort of pulled it along. The rest of us were just humming in the background.'

Ossie's Dream came about because Bob England, manager of Towerbell Records, was a mad Spurs fan. When it looked like they might get to Wembley, he begged one of his acts, the Spurs-supporting 'rockney' duo Chas 'n' Dave, to come up with a cup final anthem. The result is one of the best football songs ever written.

The duo were in the middle of a 35-day tour at the time and with Chas Hodges preoccupied with the musical arrangement, Dave Peacock was left to do the lyrics. As it turned out, that night his sister phoned and when he told her what he was doing she said, 'That's funny. I've just heard Ossie Ardiles on the radio. He doesn't say "Tottenham", he says "Tottingham."'

It was Dave's 'aha' moment, the kick-start for the song's famous line, 'In de cup for Tottingham'. 'It was the quickest song I ever wrote,' he recalled. 'It took about two minutes.'

Even so, when the team assembled to record it on 31st April at the Portland Studios in London's West End, they encountered a problem. Ossie didn't want to sing the line.

'One thing that was guaranteed to make me feel uneasy was the idea of singing on my own on a record that would be released to the general public,' he wrote in his autobiography, *Ossie's Dream*. 'I would actually have said anything to get myself out of doing the solo.'

SPURS . . . JUST FOR THE RECORD

FROM THE SPURS TEAM
TO OUR LOYAL SUPPORTERS
SHELF RECORDS PRESENT

"OSSIE'S DREAM . . .
(SPURS ARE ON THEIR WAY TO WEMBLEY)"
c/w
GLORY GLORY TOTTENHAM HOTSPUR

Performed by The Spurs F.A. Cup Final Squad
Written & Produced by Chas & Dave

AVAILABLE NOW IN SPECIAL SOUVENIR COLOUR BAG FROM
THE SPURS SHOP & ALL RECORD STORES

SHELF 1, SHELF RECORDS, 32-34 GONDAR GARDENS,
LONDON, N.W.6.

"Ossie wanted it to be about the whole team, not have the focus put on him"

'He wanted it to be about the whole team, not have the focus put on him,' explained Dave. 'He didn't realise how much he was loved by everybody.'

After a lengthy period of persuasion that included his being plied with a lot of beer, Ossie gave in, though his ordeal was only just beginning. 'You know what footballers are like, they were all taking the mickey out of him,' said Dave. 'I remember Chas saying, "Look at that clock on the wall, don't look at that lot. When your bit comes in, just say, 'In de cup for Tottingham'." Sure enough, when his turn came, he did it in one go, perfectly.'

The song was taped in one session and turned around in record time. Chas' wife, Bob England's wife and two other women, all dressed in Spurs kit, delivered them to record shops around North London.

Tottenham's stadium announcer, Willie Morgan – a record promotor in his day job – was tasked with getting it played on the radio. Two weeks later, *Ossie's Dream* – released under the 'Shelf' label – was in the charts and the players were asked to appear on *Top of the Pops*.

'It was the week of the FA Cup Final,' says Morgan, 'but the snag was that, unusually for that time, *Top of the Pops* was to be a live edition on the Thursday and not pre-recorded. Keith Burkinshaw agreed to release the squad for the programme, but with the stipulation that they had to be back at the team hotel by 6.30pm, which meant that appearing live would be impossible. So the producer was persuaded to tape the Spurs players singing the song during the final dress rehearsal at 4.15pm and slot it into the show.'

It was Chas 'n' Dave's second Top 10 hit, entering the charts higher than their breakthrough single *Rabbit* and peaking at number five when Spurs won the FA Cup after a replay. It turned Ossie into a national treasure, and people still sing it to him to this day.

Spurs' vintage vinyl. The single reached number 5 in the charts and led to an appearances on Top Of The Pops with Chas 'n' Dave (right)

FA CUP FINAL SPURS v MANCHESTER CITY

Wembley and we nearly blew it

When the big Wembley occasion arrived, for whatever reason – perhaps the pressure or too many distractions – none of us showed up (although Ricky took all the headlines)

When I joined the famous Tottenham Hotspur, the team had just won the FA Cup. Now, 14 years on, I was leading my team out at Wembley to bring the FA Cup back home. It was one of the most important games I was going to play in my whole life. It's not important to any team if they lose the cup, but if you win it'll be talked about forever. It's the difference between winning and losing. And we didn't win.

Manchester City didn't win either, but by getting a draw they won the day. They stopped us playing like Tottenham Hotspur. We deserved to beat Wolves in that first semi-final and we certainly deserved to beat them in the replay. Ricky came to the fore, and Glenn's passing and Garth's goalscoring were out of this world. But maybe the manner we got through the semi-final made us think we were a bit better than we were.

Keith would probably say that we overdid it with the record and the hype surrounding the final. Chas 'n' Dave, *Top of the Pops*, all that stuff. Was it a mistake to make *Ossie's Dream*? On the one hand, there was an element of, 'We're in this together. We're not good singers, but we're looking idiots together.' Doing things together was always a positive thing. But the problem you've got is how much focus you put on that sort of silly stuff. When it's one of the most important games you're going to play in your life, you're thinking about all the people who've got you to this point, you're thinking about the fans, you're thinking about

> "I wonder if we were temporarily more of a collection of individuals than a team"

your responsibilities, and yet you're on the telly singing a song. And I wonder if, because we'd been on telly – because we'd been watched by millions of people all over the world – that we were temporarily more of a collection of individuals than a team. That we went out there self-conscious. That we were worried about how we looked.

An error in the match programme had me listed at number five, instead of my usual six. It was an honest mistake, but it made me feel as though things were slightly out of kilter.

Worse than that, of course, was the fact that it was a big day for us and we struggled to live up to it. John Bond, City's manager, had brought in journeymen, hard-working, gritty players who could run out a result. The final had been talked up as the workers against the flair players, and the way we'd won at Highbury made that an easy comparison to make. That might be another way of saying 'Spursy'. The way we tried to play counted for too much. It counted for us as much as the actual result.

You always have to be careful against a hard-working team because it's easier to produce work than it is to produce flowing football. Their midfield did a real job on us that day. They were nasty with it. It's easier to destroy than create. They were also helped by being cast as the underdogs. That meant that they got a lift every time they did a number on us. They went for Ossie, they went for Glenn, which gave them a bit of extra success to cling to. Even without being a goal

Captain's pride – Steve Perryman realises a lifetime's ambition and leads his team out at Wembley for the first time

"Saved by a freak free-kick. That's how close we were to being the first Tottenham team to lose at Wembley"

up, that helped them. But then with half an hour gone they took the lead through a great header by Tommy Hutchison, which made them even more confident, and that made it even more difficult for us to get the equalising goal. They did what they could do better than we did what we could do, and they nearly won it.

In the dressing room at half-time, I'd have been saying, 'It's one v one. Somebody's got to get the first goal, and this time it's them. You know how important that first goal is but it's only important up to a point. The most important minute in football is the next minute. So if that goal affects you too badly, one minute becomes two minutes just like that. We might have to do something a bit different now but it's not the end of the world.'

What Keith did that made the difference was taking Ricky off in the second half. There's that famous image of him walking off around the track with his shoulders slumped, straight into the dressing room instead of going to sit on the bench. To be fair, at the end he was shaking everyone's hand and smiling, but in the heat and pressure of the moment I just felt he'd left us to get on with it.

Brookesy coming on in his place was what changed things, though. A lot of us were suffering from cramp by then, and his energy and movement drew play further into City's half, which led to us winning a free-kick on the edge of the box. That set-piece was something we'd rehearsed countless times in training – a little touch from Ossie, then me putting my foot on the ball for a brief moment before I found Glenn. City were lined up with one body outside the post, thinking we can't bend it round there, but what we were doing was just changing the approach by a yard because Glenn would be clever enough to hit it into the top corner. But it was just so, so lucky. Joe Corrigan had it covered

Right: Relief is etched on the faces of Glenn Hoddle and Garry Brooke after the former's deflected free-kick equaliser rescued Spurs

but rather than trusting his goalkeeper Hutchison went to head the ball out and instead scored twice at Wembley – one for each side.

Saved by a freak free-kick. That's how close we were to being the first Tottenham team to lose a Wembley cup final.

Ossie once said that people shout and scream at the end of the game and what they're really saying is, 'Not my fault.' There's a lot of truth in that. It's like anything. If you're the manager and you're talking to the team after a bad result, you're not going to go too deep into how and why, you're not going to be too hurtful, but sometimes a player on a certain day – and I'm not naming anyone in particular – will, within his disappointment, hit back. 'Well, you're not out there, what do you know about it?' So then the manager comes back a bit stronger, and then things snowball from there. That's how it usually happens. But Keith and Peter were both sensible, down-to-earth people. They knew how disappointed we all were. There was no nastiness after the match. Instead they gave us words of encouragement. It was an even-tempered approach to give us a bit of hope.

'OK, you know, I know, 100,000 people know – we're better than that,' was the message. 'We're so much better than that. You have to think about why we didn't play our way, or why what they did stopped us playing our way. And how off the back of that they got the confidence to play a bit better than how they normally play. And on Thursday night there is no way, no possible way, that we can play as poorly again as we've just played.'

That night we did the 'big-hitters' dinner thing at the Hilton Hotel. We'd organised it ourselves and sold tickets, with the proceeds going to the players' pool. But no one there had anything to celebrate. It wasn't like after the draw at Hillsborough, because there was no way we could console ourselves with the thought that we were unlucky. Bill Nick was the designated speaker, and being Bill he gave us a slight roasting, with all the people who'd bought tables avidly listening. It was such a downer. Everyone was depressed, we knew we hadn't played well.

I'd felt sorry for Wolves when we beat them at Highbury but I've got to say if we hadn't got that freak goal from Glenn's free-kick, if City had gone on to win the cup that day, it wouldn't have been Wolves I'd have been sorry for – it would have been us.

In the dressing room after the match Keith asked me if I thought Ricky should play in the replay? I responded that I didn't think he should. I was still coming down from the game and at that point I felt angry. I felt he'd left us to get on with it and I hadn't been impressed by his body language when he walked off. Thank goodness Keith didn't take my advice. He told Ricky straight away he'd be playing on Thursday, and then went out to tell the gathering of journalists in the post-match press conference the very same thing. That immediately protected us from all the distracting questioning and speculation we would have been subject to. It was great man-management.

Looking back on our team at that stage, I can see we were as good as anyone on our day, but sometimes we needed a second chance to beat someone. In the league, you don't get any replays but in the FA Cup you do. Ricky had been given a second chance, and so had we. And we weren't going to let it slip away.

'See you back here on Thursday' – the two teams shake hands on the pitch after the final whistle

Spurs 1 Manchester City 1 aet

9th May 1981, Wembley Stadium. Att: 100,000
Spurs goalscorer: Own Goal (Hutchinson)
By Julie Welch

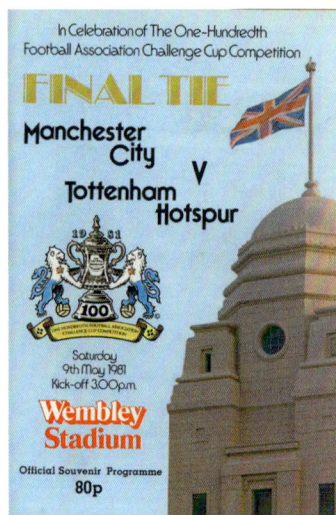

As Bill Shankly once put it, football is a game of 90 minutes and it's not over until the final whistle is blown. Except in this case it was a game of 120 minutes, and a hard, cruel one at that, and when the final whistle went it still wasn't over. Manchester City and Tottenham Hotspur will have to come back on Thursday and play the 100th FA Cup Final all over again.

By that time hopefully Tommy Hutchison will have recovered psychologically from scoring at both ends, and Graham Roberts will have been able to get to the dentist and get a couple of new teeth to replace the ones knocked out in a collision with his own team-mate, Chris Hughton, before half-time. Men of the match? For City it was their veteran goalkeeper Joe Corrigan, for Spurs it has to be Roberts for his sheer blinkered bravery, his insistence, though bleeding and concussed, on having a bucket of water poured over his head so he could carry on. 'He was Tottenham's outstanding player,' said Keith Burkinshaw. 'The doctor wanted to keep him off for the second half but he finished playing right through extra-time as well. He was magnificent.'

Tottenham as an outfit were not magnificent, but at least they were dogged, tasked with overcoming the twin obstacles of Corrigan's brilliant defiance and a goal by a player, Hutchison, who last scored with his head when there was a lace in the ball. This was a game nearly won and nearly lost in midfield, where Steve Mackenzie, Paul Power and Hutchison, often supported by Dave Bennett and Kevin Reeves, simply denied Tottenham space, thus depriving their big hitters – Ossie Ardiles, Ricky Villa and Glenn Hoddle – of the opportunity to string passes together and make penetrating moves.

For Spurs' fans, the boo-hiss villain of the afternoon was Gerry Gow.

The former Bristol City stalwart, who had plied his trade in the West Country for so long he was virtually an old lag, was obviously under orders to go after Ardiles, and it wasn't pretty. Villa looked as though he'd walked into the wrong wedding reception and was bewilderedly peering around for anyone he recognised. Hoddle had a mixed afternoon, often having to detach himself from the cluttered midfield battleground to find options for the placing of those trademark angled passes. Like Ardiles, he was forced to run backwards to find space, where he could have done with binoculars to locate the distant figures of Garth Crooks, Steve Archibald and Tony Galvin.

City were spoilers. They had wrecked Ipswich Town's chances of winning the league title and now they weren't reluctant to trample all over Ossie's Dream either. But in between the blocks and bone-crunching tackles they were good enough to take the lead on the half-hour when Bennett barged in from the left and set up an exchange of passes with Reeves near the right-hand edge of the Tottenham penalty area. Hughton slipped on a damp pitch as he tried to follow the ball's trajectory, leaving Reeves time to pass back to Bennett. The winger centred rapidly for Hutchison to beat Milija Aleksic with a sharp header inside the near post, leaving Tottenham to chase the game.

Which they did with increasing – if at first unrewarded – success in a second half when City found that the energy expended in keeping their opponents quiet for 45 minutes had taken more out of them than anticipated. Spurs got more of a look-in, although Villa, it has to be said, continued to have a stinker. Eventually, a bouncer in the form of Burkinshaw removed him, and the image will linger in the mind for a long time. The Argentinian left the arena by the route

favoured 15 years earlier by his fellow countryman Antonio Rattin after his infamous dismissal against England in 1966, although while Rattin's departure was all Latino flounce and imprecations, Villa trudged away as heartbreakingly as a whipped hound.

Spurs fans had spent the last few weeks chanting that their name was on the cup. Now, a goal down with the clock remorselessly ticking, they would have been deliriously happy to settle for a draw. And the replacement of Villa by Garry Brooke, diminutive, stocky and urgent, changed the game favourably enough to give them just that. Suddenly City were having to stop Tottenham nearer to their own penalty area than the halfway line, and with nine minutes remaining, Ardiles dispossessed Gow, whose predictable response was to bring him down.

Everybody thought Hoddle would try to score directly from the free-kick. It didn't happen quite that way. Ardiles tapped the ball to his right and Steve Perryman stopped it dead. In the two seconds that this was happening the defensive wall broke up with Hutchison darting to cover the far post. You don't give Hoddle that kind of opportunity. Corrigan had the shot covered but by the time Hoddle shot his line of vision was obliterated by his team-mate. Hutchison went to chest the ball down but it had a mind of its own, skidding merrily off his right shoulder, out of Corrigan's reach and into the net.

From match-winning hero to Hoddle's stooge. You had to feel sorry for Hutchison. Well, you did if you were an impartial witness, though if you were Spurs the emotion would have been more on the lines of 'Ha, ha, haaaaa'. And to be fair, it was the only way Corrigan was going to get beaten that day.

And so into extra-time. That last half-hour was pretty painful to watch, and must have been excruciating to play. Brooke was already limping from an ankle injury. Players on both sides dragged cramping, protesting legs after the ball and collapsed with sheer exhaustion. City, slightly the less knackered and wounded of the two sides, still managed the occasional twitch of life, though. When Reeves hoisted the ball high beyond the Tottenham defence it fell to Gow's left foot, and a younger, fresher player might have done something with that. But a winning goal then would have been an act of inhumanity.

Afterwards Burkinshaw said nice things about Villa and stated he would feature in the replay. 'South Americans are more emotional than us,' he commented, 'and he showed it a little bit more. But he shook hands at the end and smiled and perhaps more than an English bloke would have done in the same circumstances.' Meanwhile, spare a thought for Barry Daines. Tottenham's first-choice keeper until injury robbed him of that position in March is due to have his testimonial on Monday, so the timing couldn't be worse. Never mind Hutchison, if anyone's unlucky it's him.

Left: Glenn Hoddle's free-kick, just before it hits the unfortunate Tommy Hutchison to gift Spurs a late equaliser

Below: Graham Roberts had to battle through the pain of cramp – and losing teeth thanks to an accidental kick from team-mate Chris Hughton!

On our way to Wembley!

The thrill of seeing their team in an FA Cup Final at Wembley was only slightly tempered for the Spurs faithful by the disappointing performance

'Bang – it was the final,' reminsces Kev Clark. 'For the first time in the cup run, our group couldn't get tickets all together. The ones I got had Liverpool and Manchester FA stamped all over them. I was 20 and it was the first final I'd been to, and my mum said, "Why are you paying all that money for a ticket for a game?" My dad, who was an avid Spurs fan, said, "This might be the only cup final he ever gets to".'

As it turned out, it wasn't. In the words of Mike Leigh, 'We all showed up that Saturday with the attitude that the trophy was in the bag. Let's face it, we were lucky to get a draw.'

'I was watching it on television,' says Theo Delaney. 'I was living with my mum. We were a one-parent family in a council house in Chiswick, and I had been an obsessive Tottenham fan as long as I could remember. I went to my first game when I was about five, taken by an uncle. So when you're 15 and you get to the FA Cup Final… My God, I had waited my whole life for the moment. Since I was small, Tottenham had been nothing. We even went down, never finished above mid-table. And suddenly we were in the biggest thing in the world, the cup final.

'I was beside myself, contorted with excitement and anticipation in the run-up. Because the cup final was always the best day ever even if you weren't in it, so when you were actually in it…

'I was sitting in the front room with my brothers who were big football fans but not Tottenham. They wanted to watch the game, and there were a few stragglers – people coming in and out all the time – and my mum. I was the oldest brother, the next ones were 14 and 13, so we were all slightly feral teenagers, and we had another brother who at that point was five or six. I was thinking, "How am I going to do this?" So I just got some cans of lager, and I had 12 ready-rolled cigarettes on the arm of the sofa.

'I just remember sitting there chain-smoking. And then the horror when City scored, the sheer horror. I thought I'd prepared myself for the prospect of defeat, but this is football for me. You think you're ready for defeat and then when the other team scores… Spurs

> "Spurs in the FA Cup Final, I couldn't believe they were in it, and then to go behind – it was just unbearable"

in the FA Cup Final, I couldn't believe they were in it, and then to go behind… it was just unbearable. And I was chain-smoking, drinking, chain-smoking, drinking… I was so tense with the enormity of what was going on.'

'We'd built up to this,' continues Alan Fisher. 'I know there are Buddhist monks who spend 35 years halfway up Everest trying to get in touch with another plane of consciousness but frankly all I needed was that replay at Highbury. I was in a different world, buoyed by the delirium of the fans, the singing, the occasion itself. And then I suddenly realised about halfway through the second half of the final that we might actually lose. On the pitch it felt as if that feeling had got into the players' legs. They were moving and running and trying and passing but it suddenly all looked a bit stiff and stilted – moves were breaking down, things weren't quite working out, people were despairing, trying hard to get back into the game but it wasn't working.

'Then Ricky went off. He was on his own. None of the staff came out to be with him, to put a consoling arm round him. He carried the weight of the world on his shoulders as he trudged off. And I thought, "We'll never see him again. He can't come back from that." You felt all our hopes were disappearing with him.

"Oh, that game. It was just so depressing. We had this complete belief that we were going to win it"

You thought, just give him a hug. I would have given him a hug if they'd let me.'

'I was arguing with people,' counters Ivan Cohen. 'I was saying he should be substituted. He was anonymous. We all loved Ricky Villa. That magnificent shot at Highbury – that's what Ricky did. But you can't do that for 90 minutes. Ossie was an engine, he was the Duracell Bunny, but Ricky had good and bad days at the office, and he was having a bad one that afternoon. I thought the manager made the right decision. And even if I didn't think it was the right one, it's the manager who's paid the big bucks to make these difficult calls.'

'Ricky trudging off, behind the goal,' remembers Ian Meth. 'A forlorn figure, looking like, "Why me? I've come all this way, I'm miles from home, I've been in the World Cup and I'm substituted." It was actually quite sad.'

'He was like a sulky teenager,' says Theo Delaney. 'He'd really not done what he was supposed to do, and then when he got punished he went into a real sulk about it.'

Pete Haine's lucky coin had been with him all the way through the cup run. Had it lost its power? 'One-nil down with 15 minutes to go. Things were getting desperate. I got the lucky coin out and started rubbing it,' he remembers.

'And then,' says Delaney, 'there was that glorious moment when Glenn hit the free-kick. I don't think it would would have gone in but it hit poor old Tommy Hutchinson. I went absolutely insane – lagers, tobacco flying everywhere – and my mum, who'd been oblivious to the whole thing up to that point, is shouting, "What the hell's going on?"'

'We were a group of four,' recalls Jill Lewis, 'my friend Neil, who was a very, very tall bloke; Claud, who shall we say was not svelte; my dad, who was just shy of 6ft, and me, all driving to Wembley in my little white mini. Oh, that first game. It was just so depressing. We had this complete belief that we were going to win it. I don't remember much about it,

Right: Steve Perryman leads his team in thanking the fans after a tough game ended with the teams level

just that we didn't play well. Added to which was the Ricky Villa thing. I loved Ricky, absolutely loved him. I thought he was an incredibly underrated player and I loved the swashbuckling look, the hair, the touch, I just loved it. So I was not in a good mood, and my three passengers were given a mad journey home.'

'I do remember interviewing one of the players on *The Spurs Show*,' says Theo Delaney, 'and he said that when they were leaving one of them looked up at the City coach as they were pulling out and a couple of City players looked at him, and there was something in their eyes that said, "We've blown it. That was our chance, we know it."'

'I can remember the feeling of frustration that we had to come back,' concludes Pete Haine. 'And the big question was, "Am I going to get a ticket? What do I do? Where do I go?"'

Welcome to our Royal Guest

Her Majesty Queen Elizabeth
The Queen Mother

Time Table and Programme of Events

1.10 p.m. to 1.35 p.m.	SELECTIONS BY THE MASSED BANDS OF THE ROYAL MARINES (Under the direction of Lt.-Col. J. R. Mason, M.V.O., L.R.A.M., A.R.C.M., L.G.S.M., R.M., Principal Director of Music, Royal Marines.)
	DISPLAY BY THE WONDERWINGS
1.35 p.m. to 2.00 p.m.	PITCH INSPECTION AND 'WALK ABOUT' BY THE TWO CUP FINAL TEAMS
2.00 p.m. to 2.10 p.m.	INTRODUCTION OF CAPTAINS OF PAST WINNING FINALISTS
2.10 p.m. to 2.30 p.m.	MUSIC BY THE MASSED BANDS OF THE ROYAL MARINES
2.30 p.m. to 2.45 p.m.	Singing of the Traditional Cup Final Hymn 'Abide With Me' (see below) Accompanied by the Derek Taverner Singers
2.45 p.m.	THE NATIONAL ANTHEM PRESENTATION OF THE TEAMS TO HER MAJESTY THE QUEEN MOTHER
2.50 p.m.	KICK-OFF
3.00 p.m.	Half-Time MARCHING DISPLAY BY THE MASSED BANDS OF THE ROYAL MARINES
3.45 p.m.	END OF MATCH
4.40 p.m.	PRESENTATION OF THE F.A. CUP AND MEDALS BY HER MAJESTY QUEEN ELIZABETH THE QUEEN MOTHER

EXTRA TIME: If scores are level after 90 minutes, an extra half-hour will be played

ABIDE WITH: Abide with me: fast falls the eventide; The darkness deepens; Lord with me abide! When other helpers fail; and comforts flee. Help of the helpless, O abide with me.

I need Thy presence every passing hour; What but Thy grace can foil the tempter's power? Who like Thyself my guide and stay can be? Through cloud and sunshine, Lord, abide with me.

MANCHESTER CITY

(Colours: Sky Blue Shirts, Blue shorts, Blue Stockings)

1. JOE CORRIGAN
2. RAY RANSOM
3. BOBBY McDONALD
4. NICKY REID
5. PAUL POWER (Captain)
6. TOMMY CATON
7. DAVID BENNETT
8. GERRY GOW
9. STEVE MACKENZIE
10. TOMMY HUTCHISON (1)
11. KEVIN REEVES

Substitute: TOMMY BOOTH

Manager: JOHN BOND

EXTRA TIME: If scores are level after 90 minutes play, an extra half-hour will be played.
REPLAY: If necessary it will take place at this stadium on Thursday May 14th, Kick-off 7.30 p.m.

REFE...
KEITH S.
(Sheff...

Commenced refere... Sheffield and then... and N... gressed to the Footb... and full list. Has refere... Premier Cup Finals. 1975 Boys' Club Fina... Also lined for the Fin... game in 1976. Refere... Debenhams Cup match... an F.A. Cup Final... referee two Footbal... Semi-Finals and an F.A... Final in 1980. Married, and with two s... Sales Manager and his in... caravanning and all sp... walking.

LINESMEN
DAVID HUTCHIN... (Harrogate)
ALAN JONES (Wirral)

Reserve Linesme...
JOHN PENROSE (Hull)

FA CUP FINAL

WEMBLEY SHOWDOWN

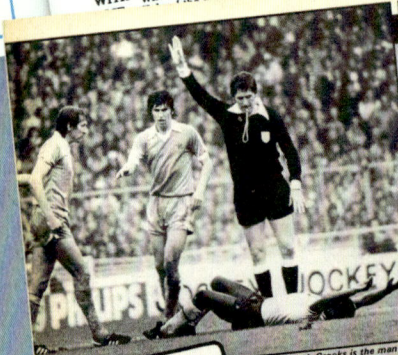

Above left: Garth Crooks is the man on the deck, but City's Tommy Hutchison, fist clenched, isn't happy with the Spurs striker's tackle.

Above: Spurs' Glenn Hoddle tussles for the ball with City's grounded Dave Bennett.

THEY RAN until they dropped at Wembley on Saturday. The tackles came in hard and fast . . . the pitch soaked up stamina like a sponge — but no-one shirked the challenge. Graham Roberts' blood-stained shirt was a banner for the fighting spirit.

It was totally of commitment. The picture's of Match photographer Duncan Cubitt tell their own story.

City's Ray Ranson (2) stretches out to rob the charging Tony Galvin of Spurs.

"I just felt sick for the lads and I felt I let them down a bit with the own goal. As for my goal it was just instinct really. Given the choice I would probably have preferred to bring the ball down instead." Manchester City's TOMMY HUTCHISON.

"Spurs deserved what they got but at the same time I felt the only way JOE CORRIGAN was going to be beaten was with something like a deflection. We have been climbing mountains since last October and there was no reason why we can't continue to do that . . ." City manager JOHN BOND

"I had Hoddle's free-kick covered and there was no way... have gone in...

COURAGE OF THE CUP

CUP FINAL '81

"We have more talented players throughout the side and I think we are in with a great chance in the replay." . . . Spurs manager KEITH BURKINSHAW

"I enjoyed every minute of the match, but I was disappointed with our midfield in the first half, and that's why City looked the stronger side then." . . . Spurs' OSSIE ARDILES

A momentary breather for the two leg-weary teams at the end of normal time as the managers offer words of encouragement and the treatment boys go into action.

Top: Spurs' Garth Crooks leaps to avoid the lunging tackle of City's midfield aggressor Gerry Gow.

Right: Draped in Spurs favours, Ossie Ardiles gives a wave of thanks to the adoring Tottenham fans.

TOTTENHAM HOTSPUR

(Colours: White Shirts, Dark Blue Shorts, White Stockings)

1. MILIJA ALEKSIC
2. CHRIS HUGHTON
3. PAUL MILLER
4. GRAHAM ROBERTS
5. STEVE PERRYMAN (Captain)
6. RICARDO VILLA
7. OSVALDO ARDILES
8. STEVE ARCHIBALD
9. TONY GALVIN
10. GLENN HODDLE (1)
11. GARTH CROOKS

Substitute: GARRY BROOKE (for 6)

Manager: KEITH BURKINSHAW

REPLAY TICKETS: If a replay is necessary, the Final Teams will each receive 30,000 tickets and supporters should apply to their respective clubs. Also, 20,000 Replay Final Tickets will be on sale at the Wembley Arena Box Office, Wembley, from 10a on Sunday, May 10th.

33

ps the field

...d amateur alike for style and stamina on the soccer pit...

...g stamp to cover postage).

...nksway, Stockport, SK4 1ED.

Hutchison's
sweet and sour

Saturday, May 7
FA CUP FINAL
MANCHESTER CITY (1) 1 TOTTENHAM (0) 1
Hutchison 29 og 80
After Extra Time
Attendance: 100,000
(At Wembley)
Receipts: £703,250

Manchester City
Corrigan 9
Ranson 6
McDonald 8
Reid 7
Power 7
Caton 7
Bennett 8
Gow 7
Mackenzie 6
Hutchison 7 (sub. Henry)
Reeves 6

Spurs
Aleksic 6
Hughton 7
Miller 7
ROBERTS 8
Perryman 8
Villa (sub. Brooke 7)
Ardiles 7
Archibald 6
Galvin 6
Hoddle 6
Crooks 7

Match Rating:
Referee: K. Hack...

Spurs
escape—
and City's
old-timer
takes
the rap

I'LL STAND
BY RICKY,
PLEDGES
THE BOSS

CUP FINAL
SPECIAL
1981 F.A. CUP CENTENARY FINAL SOUVENIR - 60p
SPURS v MAN.CITY

WEMBLEY STADIUM
No ticket genuine unless it carries
the Lion's Head watermark below
FOOTBALL ASSOCIATION
Challenge Cup
Competition
FINAL TIE
REPLAY
THURS., MAY 14, 1981
KICK-OFF 7.30 p.m.
YOU ARE ADVISED TO TAKE UP
YOUR POSITION BY 7 p.m.
1. This ticket is not transferable.
2. This counterfoil must be retained
   for at least 6 months.
V. Stella
CHAIRMAN
WEMBLEY STADIUM Ltd.
TO BE RETAINED
STANDING
£2.50
ISSUED SUBJECT TO THE CONDITIONS ON BACK
TURNSTILES
G
ENTRANCE
51
WEST
LOWER
STANDING
ENCLOSURE
565
REPLAY

81

MOMENT IN TIME

9th May 1981, 6pm, Wembley dressing room
Tottenham Hotspur v Manchester City
FA Cup Final

"Keith takes me to one side and says, 'Would you play Ricky on Thursday?'

I say, 'No, Keith, I don't think you can.'"

Steve Perryman

The golden ticket

For the Spurs supporters, the rush for tickets for the FA Cup Final replay began as soon as the final whistle had been blown at the end of the first match

There were two options for getting tickets for the replay, scheduled for the Thursday after the first match. Either way, you weren't going to get much sleep. Some fans bedded down at Wembley wherever they could find a flat surface so they could be there when the box office opened on the morning after the game. Others set their alarms for a trip to White Hart Lane at brutal o'clock after what for many had been a late return from Wembley. Many more skipped sleep and went straight to Tottenham.

Jill Lewis got up at 4am on the Sunday morning and joined the queue at the White Hart Lane. 'It was only two tickets per person, so I needed someone to go with me. It turned out to be Claud. My dad decided not to, and I think Neil had been so terrified by my driving on Saturday that he opted out.'

'I never thought I was going to get to the replay,' says Theo Delaney. 'I hadn't got a season ticket, I had no vouchers. It would have been like when Charlie from *Charlie and the Chocolate Factory* gets the ticket. But then one of my uncles – Simon – phones me up and says, "Look, they're doing tickets where if you

queue up they're just selling them because the game's on Thursday. There's no vouchers, there's no anything. You just queue up and get them."

'I had to be somewhere else so my brother Caspar, who was two years younger and supported QPR, was going to queue. My uncle said, "We're going to get four tickets – you, me, Caspar and Greg, and we'll all go." And I thought, "That can't be right, can it? I can't go to the cup final. I can't even imagine such a thing."

'Anyway, Cas and Simon went to Tottenham, and I think they queued for six hours. They just queued and queued. And they got the tickets! I couldn't believe it. I don't think I believed it till the day of the game,' he remembers.

> "That can't be. Can it? It can't be right. I can't go to the cup final. I can't even imagine such a thing"

'When I got home after the first game, my wife was nowhere to be seen,' remembers Pete Haine. 'I thought, "I'll worry about that tomorrow. I've got to get in the queue. I've got to be there early because I'm due to be playing cricket in the afternoon."

'It must have been 10 o'clock by the time I got back from Wembley, and I must have left home around 3.30 in the morning and driven all the way to Tottenham. To my amazement, at 4 o'clock when I arrived, there were already around 10,000 people in the queue. Loads of debris, mattresses strewn along Tottenham High Road. The queue went all the way from the ticket office in Paxton Road back to Park Lane, down Park Lane and round to Worcester Avenue. I joined it about halfway along there. It was miserable and drizzling and everybody was a little bit tired after the day before. The ticket office opened at 10 and I probably got through at around half eleven. I was well happy till I got home and was faced with, "I think the marriage is over, divorce proceedings etc etc." So I was brought back down to earth very quickly and it was just, "Gawd, here we go." But at least I had my ticket!'

The effort to secure precious tickets for the replay has passed into Spurs fan folklore. Thousands braved the rain to queue patiently at White Hart Lane

FA CUP FINAL REPLAY SPURS v MANCHESTER CITY

The night that changed our lives

We put in a proper Spurs performance in the replay to win the cup on an unforgettable Thursday night at Wembley, after which none of our lives would ever be the same again

August 1980, The Bull's Head, Cheshunt. It's an early season team meeting and things are looking good. We've beaten Nottingham Forest 2-0 at home, Crystal Palace 4-3 away and drawn 2-2 with Brighton. That's eight goals for – which is great – but five against, and I'm getting the feeling that one or two of us have got a bit carried away. 'Listen,' I say, 'if we score a stack of goals and still finish third from bottom that won't be a lot of help to us. Guess what, there's a bit more to do yet.' I pause to let it sink in. 'We've got to win something.'

I once suggested to Keith that maybe, just maybe, we should consider playing a bit more like Arsenal.

'What do you mean?' he said.

'Well, their ethic is, "On a bad day, we get a draw." They play in a way you could say isn't as exciting as us. You could say it's more consistent than us. On a bad day we get beat by three, on a good day we win by three. The fans love you, they'll go along with anything you decide. Why don't we go a bit more away from entertainment at all times? Why don't we scale it down a bit, to become a better league team, a better points team? Instead of being Spursy all the time, why don't we become a bit more, erm, Arsey?'

'You would never say that if you were sat behind this desk,' he replied.

The point he was making was that if you are manager of Tott-

Right: Redemption – Ricky Villa wheels away in unbridled delight after getting Spurs off to a flying start, scoring after just seven minutes

enham Hotspur, you can't think like that. And that Thursday night at Wembley we played like *Tottenham* and it brought us glory.

In the aftermath of our draw on the Saturday, I had told Keith I wouldn't pick Ricky for the replay because I didn't think his head would be right. That was all it was, advice. He didn't have to take it, he didn't take it, and that was the right decision. There were just seven minutes on the clock when Ricky scored. Of course he did. That was Ricky for you. He was a confidence player. He was either a 10 or a four. Nothing in between.

We were now in the reverse of the position that we had been in on the Saturday – this time it was our turn to get the first goal. And after all the Spurs fans had finished jumping up and down I bet there were a few who started biting their nails because there were more than 80 minutes left. 'We've scored too early' is a traditional reaction among Spurs fans. The implication is that we're not capable of hanging on that long, and something negative is coming our way. That night it wasn't long coming, either, because Steve MacKenzie caught us napping with a volley from 20 yards out. Wow, what a strike that was. And destined to be all but forgotten because of what came later.

So we were in the lead, then we were level and after half-time we were losing 2-1 when Maxie fouled Gary Bennett and Kevin Reeves tucked the penalty past Alex. At that point, we had to deal with all

> **"That Thursday night at Wembley we played like Tottenham and it brought us glory"**

the fear of what losing meant. A lesser Tottenham team might have fallen apart but we were no longer that team. We weren't the Tottenham who lay down and died against Cardiff in our relegation season. We weren't the naive team that went to Anfield in Ossie and Ricky's first season and got embarrassed 7-0. We had the strength and togetherness forged in those two semi-finals against Wolves and the bottle to hold it together against City the previous Saturday. It's a huge thing, that winning mentality. Huge. It's living it right, doing it right, acting it right, saying it right, and the more of it you get right, the more the chance the eleven of you have got of winning. I always go back to Bill Nick's maxim – 'Just do it right.' This was Keith's era now, but the same rules applied.

Garth's goal drew us level. We were back. Both sides were now in with a chance. That goal was as important to us as anything, because if you don't get back level you can't get a winner. We all had the same mindset. Now, let's get after it. How much time left? All except Garth. Everyone was running back to the centre circle except him. Garth wasn't getting after anything. He was gazing up at the scoreboard. 'My name in lights!' he breathed. But that was Garth. I suppose you'd call it *joie de vivre* and it was completely in character.

And Ricky's next goal was absolutely in character too. Ricky grew up on a massive ranch miles away from anywhere. There weren't any children around, so whereas I'd have been outside the house with

Garth Crooks wheels away in delight after scoring to make it 2-2 and ensuring his name would go up in lights

the other kids playing in the street or kicking a ball against a wall, he spent a lot of time on his own, just running with a ball in and out of the trees. He didn't get to play 11-a-side until he was 13, and when he did he was still that solitary boy running the ball in and out. The teacher would be shouting, 'Ricky. Ricky, pass!' And Ricky would be like, 'What is this "pass"? What's he talking about?'

When a game's got to that stage of intensity you're so locked in the moment you're barely aware of the crowd noise – all I could hear was Archie screaming for the ball at the far post – but every Spurs fan at Wembley must have been shouting, 'Pass! Pass!' But that night he didn't pass and it won us the cup.

As Ricky weaved his way through the City defence and got ready to shoot, I glanced quickly at Garth. He should have been running towards goal in case there was a rebound. Then he could have knocked it in and he would have been the hero. But he just stood transfixed, and gave a little synchronised air kick as Ricky shot. Maybe he was exhausted because, like everyone else, he'd put in a shift, and just wanted a breather. He had the energy to sprint and congratulate Ricky mind you!

As I climbed those steps and lifted the trophy, my first as Tottenham captain, I thought of the number of years it had taken us to win it. I thought of all those people who followed us through the relegation season. I thought of all those people who committed to us the day we went down, who followed us to places like Mansfield when we were in the Second Division, and celebrated when we got promoted back up. The club came together then, and this FA Cup win was another of those moments. Of course I was proud for myself. I'm one of the few people who has had the honour of lifting the FA Cup, so there was that element of selfishness, because it was some special feeling. But I was even more proud of representing all those people I cared about; people who had helped me live my life. You're a product of who you're surrounded by, and for me playing for Tottenham Hotspur was inextricably connected with the people who lived and worked in and around the club. They were pure, genuine people who loved the club – top-class, North London people – and they were probably all at Wembley that night. This was reward for all their efforts. This was their night, and we were there representing them.

"We did it the 'Spurs Way' – thrilling, entertaining, romantic and finishing with a goal that owed more to the Estadio Monumental in Buenos Aires than Wembley Stadium"

I took the mickey out of Garth afterwards for the way he'd just stood there watching Ricky, like one of the trees Ricky used to dribble around. And yet his character was something that made us a team. I was the only one who had been there all along. I've always believed I was shaped by Bill Nicholson, and what I had learned from him was evident in our team. The ethics of the game, the fairness, the relentlessness of play. Just get on with it. Which is the attitude typified by what I said in that team meeting – 'There's a bit more to do yet.'

We were a very honest team, a band of brothers, made up of all different tastes and colours and abilities and techniques, and all thrown in the mix to make *us*. Archie's awareness, Garth's pace, Glenn's vision, Tony Galvin's work-rate and never-give-up spirit, Roberts' front. This was a big day for *me*, and I'd been there a few times already. So you can imagine what it was like for Tony Galvin from Goole Town; Milija Aleksic from the north of England via Luton Town; and Graham Roberts from Weymouth. Think of the impact on Paul Miller from the East End, just 20 years old, and Chrissie Hughton, who'd trained as a lift engineer because he wasn't judged quite good enough to make the cut when he was a teenager. Never underestimate the worth of homegrown talent. Take Glenn Hoddle, the best, most technically gifted footballer in the land, a player with skills any club would pay a fortune for. Yet Tottenham Hotspur didn't have to because he was one of our own, a boy from Harlow. Ok, Ossie and Ricky won the World Cup and all that went with that, but this was a new country where they had to learn a new language and make

themselves part of a new football family and prove themselves all over again. That was courage and daring in itself.

We could have sailed through it like we did at Highbury. That would have been more comfortable. But there was something about the way we did it, riding that rollercoaster of winning, then losing, then winning again, that showed this was a special team, one that didn't fold, one that did it the 'Spurs Way' – thrilling, entertaining, romantic and finishing with a goal that owed more to the Estadio Monumental in Buenos Aires than Wembley Stadium.

You're not going to play great every game. It's not always going to go your way. It's down to whether you've got the feeling and the faith and the belief to drive on and make it happen. Make it happen. Don't wait for it to happen. *Make it happen.*

Above: Ricky Villa writes his name into football's history books, slotting the ball under Joe Corrigan to give Spurs a cup-winning 3-2 lead

Following pages: 'Villa... and still Ricky Villa! What a fantastic run – he's scored! Amazing goal!' The words of BBC commentator John Motson perfectly describe the greatest FA Cup Final goal of all time

Spurs 3 Manchester City 2

14th May 1981, Wembley Stadium. Att: 96,000
Spurs goalscorers: Villa (2), Crooks
By Julie Welch

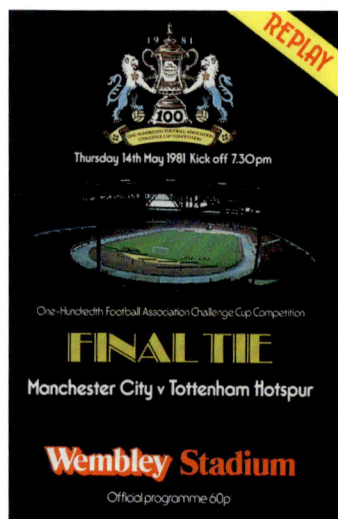

As Spurs push for an equaliser, Garth Crooks' prodded finish brings huge relief

Steve Archibald was on the floor, Garth Crooks kicking thin air and Tony Galvin seemingly frozen to the spot in exhausted incredulity. Only Steve Perryman was still on patrol, waiting at the back, anticipating what might come next – a last-gasp save by Joe Corrigan, a rebound maybe, a counter-attack. But as the fans shouted in unison for Ricky Villa to pull the trigger, what did come next, in the 76th minute, was the most glorious goal in FA Cup history. The Spurs Double team did it their way and the Spurs 1981 team did it theirs, and when it came to an ending no one had done it better.

The 100th FA Cup Final: Part Two, a sequel to Saturday's gruelling draw, was bookended by goals scored by Ricky Villa. This was the player who four days earlier had been the forlorn symbol of Tottenham's failure, Keith Burkinshaw's ceremonial sacrifice as he trudged towards the dressing room after being hooked with nearly half an hour of normal time still on the clock. On Saturday there had been plenty who declared he was finished in the English game, plenty more who questioned whether he should start in this replay because the man surely had to be an emotional wreck, but Burkinshaw didn't listen and what a decision that turned out to be.

What a game it turned out to be, too. With the FA dignitaries less in evidence and no Queen Mum to hand over the trophy, it was more like a proper football crowd at Wembley and they were treated to a match in which the lead changed hands three times, and which culminated in a redemption story straight out of Hollywood. Villa was not the only hero, though. Every single Spur was, and not the least of them Glenn Hoddle, who had spent most of the season hinting it was to be his last at White Hart Lane, saying he wanted to go where he

was properly appreciated financially. If this was his last appearance in a Spurs shirt it was one of his greatest and most committed.

Chris Hughton's contribution shouldn't be overlooked, either. It could all have gone the other way if he hadn't saved Tottenham twice at the beginning with timely interceptions. Instead, Spurs took the lead in the seventh minute with a goal created and finished by the Argentinians. First it was Ossie Ardiles, swerving in from the left and spotting a gap. The shot hit Archibald, who turned quickly on the ball for his own shot, only for it to be blocked by Joe Corrigan, but Tommy Caton was powerless to do anything as Villa pounced on the rebound.

Three minutes of delirium for the Spurs fans were followed by corresponding ecstasy from the Manchester cohort as City put themselves on level terms, Spurs failing completely to clear Ray Ranson's

long upfield punt with the inevitable consequences. Tommy Hutchison headed square across the face of the Tottenham penalty area and Steve Mackenzie met the ball with a rocket of a right-foot volley that beat Milija Aleksic from 20 yards out. Poor Mackenzie. He wasn't to know that what was undeniably the finest goal ever scored in an FA Cup Final would have lost its status in under an hour.

That was still to come, though. Four minutes into the second half, City seemed to have their fingertips on the trophy again after a square Spurs defence was caught napping by Dave Bennett's acceleration, prompting Paul Miller to close in from behind and topple the young City forward to the ground. Kevin Reeves' no-frills penalty put City back in the lead and for a while the emotion of the evening boiled over, with Tony Galvin, Ardiles and Gerry Gow receiving cautions after a foul on Ardiles, while Corrigan pushed a shot from Hoddle over the bar. Spurs were on the march again, and City couldn't hold out. With 70 minutes gone, Archibald found space in the penalty area and Hoddle prodded the ball forward for him, but the Scot appeared to have lost the chance when the ball rolled off the end of his foot. Crooks, following up quickly, stretched out to push it past Corrigan.

There was time, just, for a euphoric Crooks to gaze almost dreamily up at the electronic scoreboard. All square, but it wouldn't stay like that for long. Within minutes, Graham Roberts was giving Galvin the ball just outside the City penalty box and the winger set off on one of his trademark runs towards the corner flag, where he stopped the ball and turned round, a tired man looking for someone to pass to because he was short of pitch and short of ideas. And then he saw Villa.

Villa's run began, the run that would go down in history, zig-zagging from the left, this way and that for what seemed to the fans to be an eternity as he swerved past Caton's lunge, cut in past the challenge from Ranson, swerved to evade Caton again and slipped the ball past Corrigan. This was redemption. This was vindication of Burkinshaw's judgment and resurrection of Villa's reputation. Here was a man who had been saying he wanted to leave Tottenham Hotspur, who wasn't having any luck there, who had been injured and out of the team so often, who had started to think he was a bad player. Everybody had been saying that Ardiles was brilliant but not him. Now he had scored the goal that would make him a Spurs immortal. 'I have never scored a goal like that in my life,' he said afterwards. 'I was very pleased.' Oh Ricky, you weren't the only one.

Meanwhile Perryman was shouting. It wasn't over yet. 'Don't blow it now.' There were some 14 minutes left of exquisite torture for Tottenham fans as John Bond brought on Dennis Tueart in place of Bobby McDonald to save the game, and he nearly did, hitting the bar. But that was all it was, a near thing. After the final whistle, Hoddle was crying. Some said it was because he thought it was his last game for Spurs but maybe it was out of sheer emotion. He had worked, run, chased, he had even tackled. He had put so much into this game and he hadn't been found wanting. None of them had.

But it was Perryman's day as much as anyone's. Two other great Spurs captains before him, Danny Blanchflower and Dave Mackay, had climbed those steps to lift the FA Cup and now it was his turn. He had been through the bad times and the nearly-good times, he had vowed to lead Spurs back to where they belonged, and he had kept his promise. For Steve Perryman, Tottenham Hotspur from boy to man, it was mission accomplished.

Glenn Hoddle manages to achieve what the City defenders failed to do and hinders a Ricky Villa run, this time in joyous celebration after the Argentinian's amazing winning goal

*Steve Perryman alongside Pat
Mullery and Martin Peters,
who replaced Jimmy Greaves
in the Spurs side of 1970*

81

BASKING IN THE GLORY

Following their exhilarating victory, the Spurs players and supporters celebrated together as the cup was paraded round the Wembley pitch on the traditional lap of honour

Right: Double goalscoring hero Ricky Villa gives Ossie Ardiles a lift, presumably because his friend and countryman's knees have gone 'all trembly'

Far right: Maximum happiness for Maxie – Paul Miller lifts the trophy towards the Spurs fans and beams in delight

Winners! Chris Hughton (far left) and Graham Robers (above) celebrate in a supporter's homemade hat, while an emotional Glenn Hoddle clutches his winners' medal (left)

Right: Paul Miller, Chris Hughton, Tony Galvin and Garth Crooks bask in FA Cup-winning glory

Above and below left: Ossie Ardiles is the focus of the media attention following the fulfilment of his dream

Far left: 'The General' in victory – even the usually unassuming Keith Burkinshaw put on a supporter's hat for the victory lap

The cup that cheers – Garth Crooks gets his chance to kiss the FA Cup (above) while Steve Perryman and Ossie Ardiles share a moment (above right)

Right: Glenn Hoddle kisses the famous trophy while Ricky Villa admires it from up close

RICK'S A DREAM!

Villa goals

make it a Spurs glory night

FINAL FACTS

FREEKICKS
SPURS 15
MAN CITY 17

OFF SIDES
SPURS 4
MAN CITY 4

SHOTS
SPURS 14
MAN CITY 8

ON TARGET
SPURS 10
MAN CITY 5

CORNERS
SPURS 9
MAN CITY 5

BOOKINGS
SPURS: Galvin (foul, Archibald (dissent).
MAN CITY: Caton, Ranson, Gow (fouls).

MANCHESTER CITY

(Colours: Sky Blue Shirts, Blue shorts, Blue Stockings)

1. JOE CORRIGAN
2. RAY RANSON (8)
3. BOBBY McDONALD
4. NICKY REID
5. PAUL POWER (Captain)
6. TOMMY CATON (6)
7. DAVID BENNETT
8. GERRY GOW (6)
9. STEVE MACKENZIE (4)
10. TOMMY HUTCHISON
11. KEVIN REEVES (1 pen)

Substitute: DENNIS TUEART

Manager: JOHN BOND

REFEREE
KEITH S. HACKETT
(Sheffield)

LINESMEN
DAVID HUTCHINSON
(Harrogate)
ALAN JONES
(Wirral)
Reserve Linesman
JOHN PENROSE
(Hull)

EXTRA-TIME: If scores are le
after 90 minutes play, an e
half-hour will be played
scores are still level at the e
extra-time the match wil
decided on penalties.

Bukta
SPORTWEAR

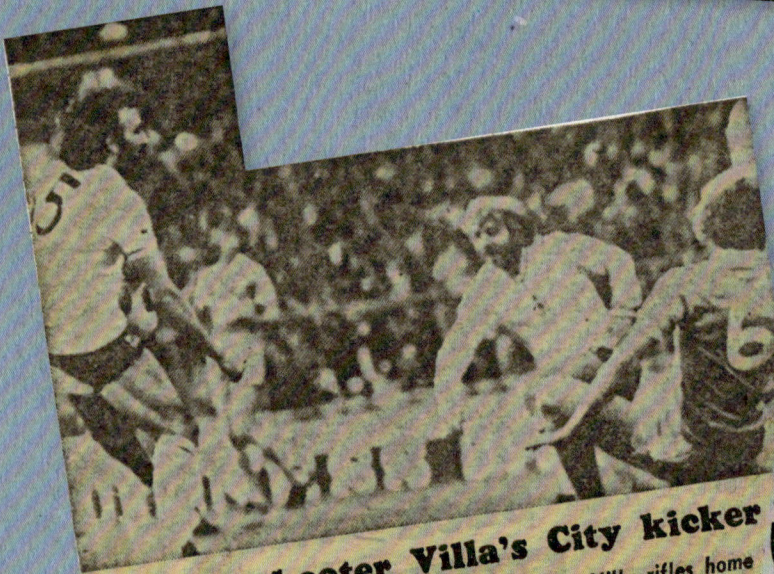

Sharp shooter Villa's City kicker

THAT'S TRICKY RICKY . . . Argentinian Ricardo Villa rifles home
first goal after Steve Archibald's shot had been blocked by City keeper Jo
Corrigan

FAIRY TALE FINISH FOR SPURS!

Villa back with two-goal blast

SPURS' WEMBLEY TEAM IN THE YEAR OF THE COCKEREL

Viva Villa! . . . Ricky holds high the FA Cup

Fantastico!

FA CUP FINAL REPLAY . . . THE SAGA ENDS

It's viva Villa for hot Spurs

THE EMPIRE STADIUM, WEMBLEY

No ticket genuine unless it carries a Lion's Head watermark below

Football Association
Challenge Cup
Competition

FINAL TIE

REPLAY

THURS., MAY 14, 1981

KICK-OFF 7.30 p.m.

YOU ARE ADVISED TO TAKE UP
YOUR POSITION BY 7 p.m.

1. This ticket is not transferable.
2. This counterfoil must be retained
   for at least 6 months.

TURNSTILES
F

ENTRANCE
78

ROW
5

SEAT
35

CHAIRMAN:
WEMBLEY STADIUM LTD

NORTH STAND SEAT

£10.00

SEE PLAN AND CONDITIONS ON BACK

TO BE RETAINED

Oh what a night!

For the thousands of Spurs fans who made it to Wembley for the cup final replay, it was a seminal moment in their lives and the memories still burn brightly

The big unknown surrounding the replay was, 'Which Ricky Villa is going to turn up?' The question had dominated the back pages. It was so huge that there had been a national debate about whether or not he should be picked. 'He had been absolutely hopeless, he'd forgotten to turn up for the first game completely,' remembers Theo Delaney. 'But Keith Burkinshaw was never in any doubt that he was going to pick him. I suppose that was because Villa was the personification of Tottenham Hotspur. He was either useless or he was unbelievable. And Burkinshaw knew that, and that there was every chance he'd be unbelievable on Thursday because he was useless on Saturday.

'On the day, we got in the car and drove to Harrow, where we parked and then got on the tube from there. I was pinching myself all the way because I'm 15 years old and this is the FA Cup Final I'm going to and I can't believe it. I had my Tottenham scarf on, obviously. We got there, and where we had tickets turned out to be a mixed section along the sides, with City fans all over the place. It was a bit tasty, as you'd expect. It was 1981 and City were a big urban club like Tottenham. So there were all sorts of vibes going down, and an atmosphere. But once the game got going, everyone was absorbed because of course it was the most absorbing game.

'We were at the end where Villa scored his first goal. I was right there! Only a few minutes after kick-off and he scored. If we'd won the cup 1-0 with just that goal, it still would have been a massive story that no one would ever forget – Villa on the Saturday trudges off and then he wins the cup 1-0 for Tottenham with that goal. Spurs shut up shop and they win the cup, and the whole story's about Ricky Villa. *Without* what happened after that.

'But of course so much more happened after that. Steve Mackenzie scored. I once interviewed Simon Hattenstone for my *Life Goals* podcast – such a brilliant bloke, huge Manchester City fan, and he's so

> "I'm pinching myself all the way because I'm 15 years old and this is the FA Cup Final I'm going to and I can't believe it"

bitter, a lot of them are, about '81. He says that the greatest FA Cup Final goal ever scored was in that game and it was Steve MacKenzie's goal.'

'I remember clapping that goal,' says Simon Lipson, 'even though it sucked.'

'And then early in the second half Reeves scored a penalty, right in front of us,' continues Delaney. 'And I thought, "Oh my God, we're back to square one, we're back to where we were in the first game." But the difference was, Spurs were playing really well.

'Looking back at that game now, because it was the Ricky Villa final, I don't think Glenn Hoddle got anything like the credit he should have. He was just on a different level in what he was doing. The way he played, it wasn't just that he had this incredible talent, touch, and ability to do things no one else could do – there was something about his demeanour and his attitude. He looked like the grown-up and all the other players were kids. It wasn't arrogant, he just knew he was better. It was all about him having more time on the ball, looking at options, assessing them and then stroking it here and there. He was just great. Well, everyone played brilliantly.'

But Spurs were losing.

'I was on the edge, tearing my hair out,' recalls Delaney. 'And then Crooks scored. And the relief was so immense. And then it happened. Ricky's goal. Built up on the left-hand side where I was. Every Spurs fan, wherever they were in the stadium, was screaming exactly the same thing. "Pass it you idiot, just pass the ball!" He didn't do anything on the Saturday, and now he had the perfect opportunity to set someone up to score, and win it for us, and he was refusing to pass the ball. And then he put it in the net. And it was absolute bedlam.'

'I just remember that moment going on forever,' recalls Jill Lewis. 'When you see the replay it's not long but it seemed like an absolute eternity with him going one way then another way – and then Claud and I were in each other's arms crying and laughing. It was just unbelievably ecstatic, just the kind of moment you don't get, it was that special.'

'There weren't many British players who could have scored that goal,' agrees Ian Meth. 'When we were kids a foreign player came from Scotland and an overseas player came from Ireland. This was a piece of Argentinian genius.'

'You realise you have seen one of the greatest moments in football history,' adds Theo Delaney. 'It's not one of those things that only sinks in afterwards. Straight away after that goal you

think, "That's one of the biggest things that's ever happened. And I've just seen it. For real. Right here." I was actually there when it happened. Of course, Simon Hattenstone describes it as, "A fat bloke, pissed, after the pub's closed, trying to negotiate his way home – and accidentally kicking a ball over a line." So furiously bitter.'

'I watched it on video later,' says Ivan Cohen, 'and even now when I think about that goal I hear the BBC commentary in my head – "Tony Galvin down the left…" – and I do remember shouting, "Pull the trigger! Pull the effing trigger!", thinking it's one swerve too many, and I think everyone felt that at the time. And then he tucked it away and it was pandemonium. The

crowd were going mad and I got separated from my friends. You just all jumped up and kissed the person next to you and I found myself in the arms of this six-foot-three bloke. I've no idea who he was, but that goal, that event, just brought you together. That's what football's about, it's a sense of community, a common cause – and it was just the unbridled joy because you knew from that moment on that Manchester City were not going to come back.'

'That game took you to a higher level,' agrees Delaney. 'All my life I'd worshipped the FA Cup, I'd worshipped Tottenham Hotspur, I'd worshipped Glenn Hoddle – and there it all came together. I've watched all these teams winning all these cup finals,

"All my life I'd worshipped the FA Cup, I'd worshipped Tottenham Hotspur, I'd worshipped Glenn Hoddle – and there it all came together"

doing laps of honour, wearing those scarves, putting silly hats on their heads, putting the FA Cup on their heads – and it was my team doing it. It was my captain going up to lift the FA Cup.'

'A bunch of us had driven down from Sheffield in my Vauxhall Viva,' says Ivan Cohen. 'It was only working on three cylinders at the time and it broke down on the North Circular, near a pub called The Pantiles, which is a McDonald's now. We just pushed the car into a side street and I said, "Sod it, I'll call the AA after the match." So after the game we went back to the pub and while one of my friends got the round in I phoned the AA. The place was full of Spurs supporters, a mass of people most of whom you'd never seen before and would never see again. I didn't drink much because maybe the AA would fix the car and I'd have to drive back to Sheffield, so for me it was a feeling of, "We've won the cup and we've won the cup in style!" tinged with, "When's the AA going to get here?" because the next day – which soon became the day itself – I had a job interview in Loughborough.

'The AA man arrived. My car was beyond roadside repair so he called the AA Relay team to tow it. My car was put on the back of a truck and I sat up front with the driver just going though the game in my head because it was a four-hour drive back to Sheffield and you couldn't go very fast. I was so in

the moment of that joy that everything else going on around was in soft focus. I got back to Sheffield, had a shower, put a suit and tie on, and went to Loughborough for my interview.

'I didn't get the job, but it's given me a superstition that when something goes wrong on the way to a match, we're going to win.'

'We went to Trafalgar Square afterwards,' explains Alan Fisher. 'I was with my old friend Ian, and this bloke from work called Pete. He was from New Zealand and I don't think he'd seen an English football match before. He had a camper van so we drove to Trafalgar Square. I just remember the sound of horns and people dancing in the fountains. It's this glorious thing when you win and everybody goes to the same place – you feel like you've taken it over. We were driving around Trafalgar Square when we came across this Spurs fan trying to hitch a lift. He was holding a tree. So he and the tree got in the camper van and we drove around Trafalgar Square some more, and then he said, "Cheers, mate," and we dropped him and his tree off in another part of the square.

'So then we stopped and joined in and sang a few songs. And in the weeks afterwards, when I was on the tube or whatever , I'd be wearing my Spurs Supporters Club badge, and sometimes a scarf, and people would come up to me and say, "Just wanted to

tell you what a fantastic game that was." You'd never get that now, you'd just get abuse. But it was amazing the number of people who stopped me to say, "Were you there? You are so lucky."'

Mike Leigh says: 'I remember Ossie saying on *The Spurs Show* that he and Ricky had no idea when they joined that this was a relegated side just coming back. It would have made a difference to their decision to come to Tottenham. "Mansfield Town? What is this thing?" We got promoted on goal difference, literally those nine goals against Bristol City. If we hadn't gone back up, Ossie and Ricky wouldn't even have been signed. Hoddle wouldn't have stayed. If Keith hadn't brought Bill back, we'd never have got Graham Roberts or Tony Galvin. So many stars aligned for this to happen.'

'I was wearing my special Spurs jumper, as modelled by Garry Brooke in one of the Spurs programmes,' concludes Pete Haine. 'I was on my own. I didn't go in the pub pre-match, I didn't go in the pub post-match, I didn't celebrate in any way, shape or form apart from being quite happy in the car on the way home, singing and shouting to myself. That replay was one of the greatest games I've ever seen, topped off by such a brilliant goal as well. Ricky and my lucky coin had done the business. My marriage was over, but we'd won the cup.'

81
VIEW FROM THE TERRACES

Photographer Frank Herrmann mixed with the Spurs fans at Wembley to capture the night of the replay from a unique, monochrome perspective

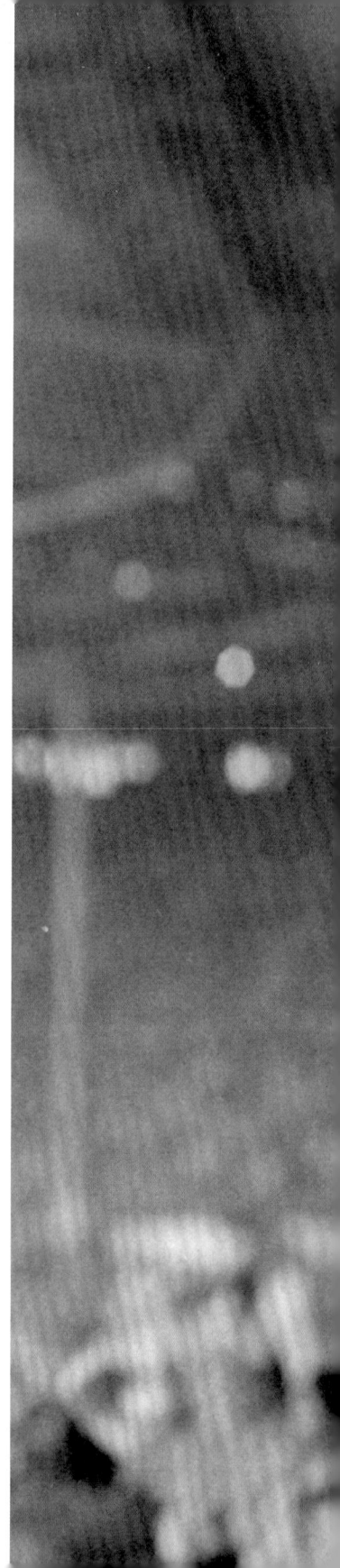

Let the party begin

With the FA Cup in pride of place at the front of the team coach, the Spurs squad left Wembley and a night of serious celebrations kicked off in the N17 corner of North London

"This was Tottenham Hotspur. They knew how to celebrate"

Right: An unforgettable night of celebration on a packed High Road saw the team and fans unified in joy. The players held the trophy out from the famous Red House to the delight of the ecstatic supporters below

If you ever get to see the old FA Cup trophy, the one that was used before it was replaced by a replica in 1992, you might spot not just the number of times 'Tottenham Hotspur' is engraved on it, but also a small dent in the lid. That was caused by Ossie diving into the communal bath with the trophy in his hands. He had never celebrated the English way before but wow, we certainly showed him how it was done that night.

In the dressing room everyone was there who had a right to be there – players, the management team, coaches and physios – just like you'd have after a normal game, except that this time it wasn't so normal because we were sharing the space with a big, shining trophy. We were exhausted, our stomachs were empty, so any drink taken was bound to make us light-headed, or even more light-headed I should maybe say because we were already that way out of sheer elation...

Our bus left the stadium with the FA Cup propped up against the front windscreen where everyone could see it. We went out through a tunnel which instead of having light at the end of it had thousands of Spurs supporters, all cheering and shouting. On the North Circular it was party time. People were lined up on bridges, hanging out of their car windows, sounding their horns. Some were dancing on top of buses. This was Tottenham Hotspur. They knew how to celebrate.

There had been no time to arrange another formal dinner, of course. So what did we do? We went to our *home*. Win, lose or draw, that would have been our destination. It must have been past midnight by the time we got there, and Tottenham High Road was jam-packed. There must have been around 60-70,000 people already there. It was just amazing. The place had come alive and it was thronging with people thinking exactly the same as us – 'We've done it.'

In the Chanticleer, the famous restaurant on the Paxton Road, there was a sit-down buffet. Nothing over the top, because if we'd lost it wouldn't have warranted being over the top. The place was filled to bursting. Chas 'n' Dave were on stage, doing a set. People didn't have to pay to be in there, and we had so many guests ourselves. Everyone I seem to meet these days tells me they were there that night.

I have to say that one of my strongest emotions was relief. It had been like a contract that had taken us three years to fulfil. We were a big club looking big again. We stood for the real Tottenham Hotspur, winning things, being in Europe. I can't say for certain but I have a feeling Ricky's goal probably gained us 200,000 people who liked Spurs a bit more than they had done before. Many of them are still hanging on today. So there was a lot to be happy about. Keith had justified the board's decision to keep him on rather than sack him when we went down. Peter Shreeve had proved that he'd made some difference, not least by bringing on all our young players. Garth and Archie had done what they were supposed to do, which was to turn this middle-of-the-road team into a trophy-winning side. Ossie and Ricky now knew they'd been right to sign for us, whereas in 1978 they'd joined, unknowingly, a team that had just come up and when they discovered that they must have thought, 'What have we done?' Roberts, Miller, Galvin and Chrissie had come from nothing and now they'd been on the Wembley pitch, running round with the FA Cup with people adoring them.

I remember being on stage singing *Ossie's Dream* and stuff like that. I must have made a speech, though I've no recollection of what I said – probably something soppy about not forgetting the players who had earned us promotion back into the First Division, and something stirring like how it's a long, big step to winning your first trophy but once you've done that you're halfway to your the second one. No one would remember a word of that but I would make sure I reminded them when we came back in for pre-season.

By the time we left, dawn had broken. It was six o'clock in the morning. I don't even know how drunk we were, but some of us must have been. Garth claims now that he lost three days of his life and Archie says he can't remember anything. But it was all right to let our hair down, and not only because that replay was the last game of the season. We'd achieved what we'd dreamed of for so long. It had taken a dodgy goal to force us into a replay against Wolves. Then a

The celebratory party at the Chanticleer has become one of those events at which thousands claim 'I was there'. Goalscoring heroes Garth Crooks and Ricky Villa certainly were...

dodgy goal kept us in the cup. In terms of luck, this was the other side of the coin – we were fortunate to get out of that with something intact. And I think the way it happened just emphasises the fact that we knew we were going to win. We knew after Exeter, we knew after Wolves. Maybe all that stuff about the year having the number '1' in it and our name being on the cup is nonsense, but it was almost as if it was our destiny to win it.

The open-top bus parade that weekend was just special. Everything glowed. When you lose a cup final, you don't want to see anyone. When you win a cup final, you want to see every person on Earth. You want to put yourself out in front of everyone that's moving. And the way to do that is on top of a bus. The official number at the civic parade was a quarter of a million and I don't think that estimation is over the top. As we went along the High Road through Edmonton, everyone was out on the balconies of their flats. *Everyone.* There were people standing on top of places you didn't think people could possibly stand on, like bus stops, so they could get a better view – or maybe because they wanted us to notice them!

On the top deck of the bus we were on Cloud Nine – Cloud 10, even. We had Chas 'n' Dave with us, and the other poor bloke who never got a mention – the drummer. I sometimes wonder how he felt. 'Chas 'n' Dave' this, 'Chas 'n' Dave' that – any chance of giving me a mention? But it was wonderful. This was the place where I'd virtually been brought up, the road that I'd driven along so many times, sometimes in despair after a defeat, other times so overjoyed after a win that I'd want to wind down the car windows and shout and sing. This was the Town Hall that I'd never noticed for the last 10 years, I just drove past it, and suddenly it had come alive. It was the focal point of what we'd wanted and dreamed about for so long. Aah, so this is the Town Hall! And then we were on that balcony, with Ossie messing about, being chirpy, just being Ossie really, because he was so happy, and beneath us it was like a river had burst its banks and flowed all over the road except instead of water it was floods of people swirling underneath.

Sometimes after you've achieved what you set out to do life can seem flat, but I never felt that way. There was no comedown. No, 'It's over, what do I do now?' Maybe that's a me thing, but I was just so

"On the top deck of the bus we were on Cloud Nine – Cloud 10, even"

happy it had all happened, and then my attitude was, 'It's done.' On to the next thing. Holiday time. Maybe a tour. I did my usual two weeks in Steve Perryman Sports while my brother Bill was away. As always, it was the worst time ever. I would be like a caged tiger, because my life was about being outdoors, on the move, and doing something where I knew what I was doing. In the shop, I didn't know anything at all, apart maybe from how to sell a pair of football boots. But when it came to things like restringing tennis rackets, oh dear me. What an amateur. I really wanted to say to customers, 'Look, if you want me to kid you, I will, but I honestly don't know what I'm talking about.' On the other hand, it was good fun in a way, because at the end of the day I felt I'd achieved something that didn't come naturally to me. It put me in touch with normal life. If we hadn't had the shop, I would have been less of a captain.

We had around six weeks in all between the end of the season and starting training for the next. That was good enough. The longer you get off, the more they put you through it when you get back, so you pay for it. Ugh, dear me. They absolutely batter you. The players talk about tough managers battering them now, but it has always been like that. It isn't anything new or different.

For the last week before you went back, you probably needed to go out jogging or running every day just to prepare yourself, but you'd end up doing it for a day or so and then give up. You'd tell yourself, 'Well, that's something under my belt, anyway.' But it wasn't. You'd kid yourself that a day and a half was enough, but it really wasn't.

When we returned we had a new keeper. Ray Clemence joined us from Liverpool, and Glenn had decided to stay. We were back at Cheshunt, getting ready for the start of the new season, having our team meetings in the Bull's Head, talking through what we were going to do. 1981 was over. Tottenham Hotspur were ready to go again.

Welcome home cup heroes

Massive crowds give Spurs a welcome they'll never forget

- All the family turned out to cheer on the heroes.
- Massive crowds herald the 1981 FA Cup winners.
- Climbing to get a view.
- Broad smiles from fellow defenders Paul Miller and Graham Roberts.
- Viva the Argentinian duo.
- A wave from the rooftops.

81

'EE-AYE-ADDIO WE WON THE CUP'

Previous pages: Glenn Hoddle
and goalkeeper Milija Aleksic
show off the cup from the
window of the Red House to
the delirious fans below

Right: Keith Burkinshaw
(above right) makes a speech,
with the FA Cup trophy
perched on a stand behind
him, while (right) the players
have a sing-a-long with Dave
Peacock from Chas 'n' Dave

Far right: The skipper and
his great pal, Ossie Ardiles,
proudly parade the trophy
just one more time

Goal of the Century

Ricky Villa's extraordinary goal – heralded as the 'Goal of the Century' – gets the full treatment in the press

GILLETTE GOALS OF THE CENTURY

1 The replay of the 100th F.A. Cup Final between Tottenham Hotspur and Manchester City produced the greatest solo goal ever seen at Wembley.

The score was 2-2 with the game swinging violently one way then the other when Tottenham's GALVIN received a pass out of defence. Evading a GOW tackle GALVIN set off down the left where his path was barred by City's REID. GALVIN checked then knocked the ball to VILLA who accelerated towards the City box, controlling the ball with his instep — a technique more difficult that controlling with the inside of the foot, the area of contact with the ball being much smaller, but it has the added advantage of allowing a more natural running position.

SIDE OF FOOT

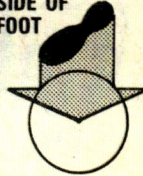

INSTEP

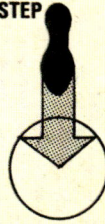

A VILLA

B VILLA

C VILLA

2 DIAGRAM A — Surging forward, VILLA was soon at the City penalty box.
DIAGRAM B — Darting to his left, VILLA evaded City defenders RANSON and CATON.
DIAGRAM C — Suddenly VILLA turned back inside, dodged three tackles and netted.

3 When VILLA received the ball from GALVIN a goal seemed impossible, but a magical combination of power, daring, skill and technique carried VILLA onwards to score the Wembley goal of the century.

SPURS 3 — MAN CITY 2

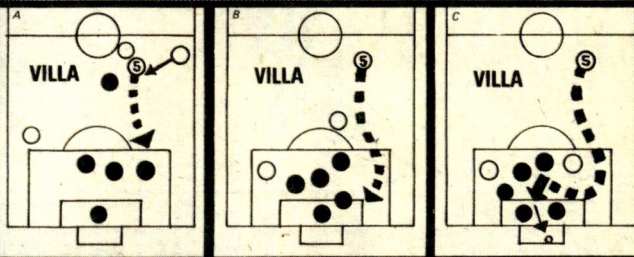

RICKY'S WEMBLEY WONDER GOAL

76 mins

3 He then cuts back inside beating Caton again and leaving Ranson unable to reach him, before slotting the ball home

2 He beats Tommy Caton then Ray Ranson after turning brilliantly to his left

1 Ricky Villa collects the ball 35 yards from goal and makes his way towards the penalty area

Villa
Caton
Caton
Ranson
Galvin
Villa

← Pass/Shot
← Run with the ball
← Run without the ball

FA Cup Final Replay
May 14, 1981
Tottenham **3-2** Manchester City
Wembley

Over the years, graphic artists and illustrators have analysed Villa's goal. It even made a postage stamp on the island of Jersey

81

MOMENT IN TIME

27th January 1968, White Hart Lane
Tottenham Hotspur v Manchester United
FA Cup third round

"It's the third round of the cup and Spurs are playing Manchester United. I'm sat on the benches so my view is at leg level, watching George Best get in from the halfway line. He's bearing down on Pat Jennings, one on one, and it isn't like George Best in 1967/68 is a mug. And my impression is that the whole crowd stands up, not just the people in the seats in the East Stand where I'm looking but all of the 55,000 people there, all on their feet as George tries to beat him. And Pat just gets his fingers on the ball.

This is theatre, pure theatre. This is the save. I've never seen that moment matched in all my time. That's how heroes are made. In one single brilliant moment."

Steve Perryman

Behind every great team...

More than 40 years on, when I look back on the events of 1981, more and more I am drawn to the bigger picture and the wider efforts of club and community that was behind the achievement

What made that game against United in 1968 even better was knowing that we apprentices had helped stage it. We'd got a draw up in Manchester and the club started selling tickets for the replay straight away, but on the Monday it snowed. Half of us were sent out to clear the pitch, and the other half were in Bill Beeby's office opening letters containing applications for tickets. That taught us that we were part of things, that we belonged. There was absolute unity, from Dave Mackay and Jimmy Greaves, Alan Gilzean and Pat Jennings, to the youngest members of the ground staff. We were all in the frame. It made you want to do the best you could for Tottenham Hotspur. It was a great, great feeling.

Pat Jennings was the ideal role model for a 17-year old starting his career. It was just the way he conducted himself. I don't really understand a lot about goalkeepers but I know what I like. I saw Pat in good and bad teams and what did it for me was his mental resilience and his clarity about what he wanted from his defence. In the dressing room he was quiet, but if you were in front of 65,000 people at Old Trafford and he wanted you to move, you'd hear him all right. This was serious. This was what real life was about.

What a pinnacle for young players to look up to. It wasn't only the messages and the techniques Pat passed on – as far as I'm concerned his greatest value was and still is his manner. He's straight, upright and dignified. A lot of football talk is childish, it's banter or whatever you want to call it. Pat would just smile. Meaning, 'That's for you, not for me.'

But back then there were so many good people to teach you about life. When it comes to Alan Gilzean, all I can say is, 'What a great man.' Bill Nick was the man who taught me football, but Gilly could add the sort of life experience within that framework that you wouldn't ever get from your manager. He was a top player, so why Bill made him and I room-mates, I do not know. It was as if he nodded his head towards Gilly and said, 'Here. He'll lead you the right way. He might lead you slightly astray, but it'll be the right kind of astray'.

It wasn't just the older players, either. It was the people in and around the club that made such an impression on me. What characters they were. Johnny Wallis was in charge of the youth players when I joined Spurs. He could be fun. He was one of those types I've met in football at every club I've been at. On a good day he was a fair man. On a bad day he was an absolute bastard. He made everything competitive. We'd have to race to see who got dressed first. All

> **"You were all in the frame. It made you want to do the best you could for Tottenham Hotspur. It was a great, great feeling"**

Spurs goalkeeping legend Pat Jennings strides out at White Hart Lane in 1968. The Northern Irishman was a key role model for the young Steve Perryman and an important helping hand in his development

the kit would be jumbled up on a table in the middle of the dressing room, everyone had to scramble for theirs, and if it wasn't theirs they'd throw it onto the radiator on the far side, and if you were the last guy you'd be going out with only one sock on.

Johnny didn't like Charlie Faulkner, the chief scout. Before I signed for Spurs, Charlie arranged for me to train with them, and because I lived in a totally different area to anyone else he would sometimes take me to Tottenham in his car. To Johnny, it wasn't right that he was taking me at the expense of others. I think he looked on it as Charlie dictating something over his head. So if the traffic was bad on the North Circular, Charlie would be jumping red lights to get me there on time to join the team bus going to Cheshunt, because if I was late it wouldn't be Charlie who got the grief, it would be me. The number of times I'd jump out and run that last little bit past Bill Nick's house to the lights. The others would be on the bus and Johnny would wave at me as the bus pulled off. He could have stopped. He didn't. So I'd have to make my own way to Cheshunt.

Then there was Cecil Poynton, the physio. He was born in 1901 and had been a pro in his own right, though I'm not sure he had any qualifications. Someone who's young now might not take to a guy like that, but back in the day you'd think what he had was wisdom. He was a bridge between me and my parents. Parents have a certain

The reserves and backroom staff such as Johnny Wallis (far right) were all a vital part of the backroom team, and deservedly celebrated their part in the FA Cup success

"These were real, dyed-in-the-wool North Londoners and Tottenham Hotspur dominated their lives"

wisdom that at that age you don't necessarily listen to. My mum used to remind me about a lot of stuff I ignored, as we all do. And then later on, I'd think, 'She was right!' With Cecil, it was a case of him having a superior knowledge about his world of treatment. He and Johnny Wallis had opinions about everything. To me, they were like tribal elders and I would be metaphorically sitting at their feet, listening to those opinions. They'd been there in the Double years, and maybe through the '50s. They would tell me about Tottenham players of the past. In their eyes, Ron Burgess was the greatest Tottenham player ever, in a different class even to Dave Mackay, and I'd think, 'Wow, what a player he must have been.' It was as though they were passing on a kind of historical thread. I would get to know about Bill and Eddie not as manager and coach, but as the brilliant players they had been in years gone by. I would hear about Alf Ramsey, who'd gone from winning the title for Spurs in 1951 to being England's World Cup-winning manager.

The same went for the ground staff, the office staff and the people who worked on the High Road, at Doll's Café and Tony's Café, at the Bell and Hare, the White Hart and the Coolbury Club. These were real, dyed-in-the-wool North Londoners. Tottenham Hotspur had dominated their lives and created most of their greatest experiences. Like Bill and Eddie, they dedicated their lives to the club, and they thrived on that much-used word 'banter'. But they were just as brilliant when it came to not overdoing it with us as players. They treated us exactly the way we were being treated in the dressing room and on the training field. If you want to call it care, the only bit of care from Tottenham Hotspur in those days was from Mrs Wallis, Bill's secretary, and Mrs Bick, who worked in the office. They would greet you nicely – 'Good morning, Steve, how are you?' If you had a problem, it would be, 'Leave it with me.' Everywhere else, it was basically, 'Eff off. Just eff off. Who do you think you are?' It was a sort of continuation from the dressing room, really, and we all bought into it. I don't know if I thought it was more brilliant than anyone else did, but I still laugh about events from that time.

For instance, if you were on the High Road, two of the ground staff might walk past you and say, 'Where you going? Oh, are you going to buy some new shoes? Any chance of your old ones?' There'd always be some comeback. God forbid if you were mentioned by name in the paper. If you'd played well, you'd never hear the end of it. And God forbid, too, that you arrived in a new car. 'Oh. Still drive on the same roads, do you?' All that. Just non-stop. But it was brilliant. It gave you the club feeling, the one every club's got to have. We're special. You're not special because you're Tottenham Hotspur, you're special because you're one of us. This is us. The fact that it's Tottenham Hotspur makes it even better. But don't gloat. Because if you gloat you'll soon come crashing down.

It was as if they were pointing you all in the same direction. Everybody was like that. And you thought, if these people enjoy working at the club after all these years, it can't be a bad place. Not that you ever thought it was, but this was the evidence, out there every day in front of your very eyes. You might have had a bad game and the crowd got at you, but they were caring in those situations. They wouldn't add to your grief. They'd rather go quiet than do that. But when you were on top, oh my God. That was the red rag to the bull. 'Oh – scored two goals, did you? You must have had two shots to score. How did you have two shots? You never have two shots in a season, let alone two shots in a game.'

That's the ethos I'm talking about – these were people who embedded you into Tottenham ways. You weren't just there on the ground, it was as if you were being planted. They were all of a kind, whether they worked at the club or around it. They all had this Tottenham imprint. I don't think the people on the staff were very well paid, but their humour and the love of their club was blindingly obvious. If anyone could pass that on to you, it was them. Bill Nicholson

Steve is pictured before a home game in December 1969 at the start of his lifelong love affair with Tottenham Hotspur Football Club

gave you the desire and Eddie Baily the grit, but these people taught you about love of a place, of a stadium, of an ethic. Of a banner in the sky above us all, saying, 'We're Tottenham. Be proud.' And for me, it was heaven. Heaven on Earth.

It was that deep connection I felt for the club that drove me on as I led us back from relegation and helped put Tottenham Hotspur on the big stage again. I never get together with the team which was relegated. There's nothing to glue you together. It's what we achieved in '81 that you want to recreate – the struggle of the first game, the rollercoaster of the replay. Goal up, goal down, win it. And then the reward when you've all done what you set out to do, when you can finally enjoy yourself.

When I look back on my days as an apprentice, I think of Cecil and Johnny encouraging me to think about Ron Burgess, about Alf Ramsey, about Bill and Eddie in their playing days. The game has changed so much since then. These days players come and go, and so do staff. It's the way the world is now. Of course, they can see for themselves on YouTube what a great player Glenn Hoddle was, and how Ricky Villa's goal won us the cup in 1981. But they're not going to be lying in the treatment room being told about Dave Mackay and Danny Blanchflower. There won't be those tribal elders making them understand how it used to be in the way we apprentices were. I don't think that kind of historical thread is passed down to young players now, and to me that's a loss. As Pat Jennings once put it, 'Stevie, those who drink the water should remember who dug the well.'

81

TAKING THE HIGH ROAD

On the Sunday after the replay triumph, Spurs' victory bus made its way along the packed High Road to Haringey Town Hall for a civic reception and another chance for a glimpse of the famous trophy

*Mounted police escort
the open-top bus down
Tottenham High Road, with
fans gaining any and every
vantage point available*

GREY-GREEN

St.Tropez - Corfu - Costa Brava

The bus is surrounded by a sea of happy Spurs supporters as it slowly makes its way towards the Town Hall

Left: At the Town Hall, goalscoring hero Ricky Villa – looking slightly sheepish – delivers a speech to dignitaries and assorted friends and family

Below left: Glenn Hoddle and Ossie Ardiles pose with the youngest member of the Spurs family sitting in the cup

Right: Keith Burkinshaw treats himself to a suitably huge and well-deserved celebratory cigar

Special scenes from a special
day. Even a spot of rain
failed to dampen the sense
of excitement and collective
happiness, while bus-stop
roofs provided a unique if
precarious vantage point
spot to view all the fun

*Left: Thousands of fans
wait outside the Town Hall
for the players to emerge
and show off the trophy*

*Above: Garth Crooks
and Ricky Villa give the
crowd what they have
been waiting for*

Right: Civic pride – a formal photo for the archives as the Mayor, Haringey councillors and various local and club officials join the players on the Town Hall staircase

Far right: 'We did it!' Ossie and Steve lift the trophy one last time – for this year at least!

(Cup) final thoughts

Spurs supporter Mo Keenan looks back on her 1981 experience as a 13-year-old fan who got to go to Wembley and never looked back

I grew up with two older brothers. My dad was a Spurs fan, and my memories of growing up were very much of him taking first my oldest brother and then my next brother to White Hart Lane. But when it came to me, the girl in the family, I had to wait for my brothers to come home then quiz them about what went on. I was 13 the year we got to the final and I remember those two going off to Wembley. We lived quite near the North Circular Road in North London so I went down there with the Tottenham flag and hung it over a bridge, and of course that was the route to Wembley so everyone was tooting their horns at the flag while I was there. And then I ran back home, probably about twenty to three, just in time for kick-off.

I remember my older brother coming home and saying, 'I'm going to go down and get a ticket for the replay, can I take Mo with me?' and straightaway my parents said, 'No.' But I said, 'Pleeease, you've got to let me go!' And fair play to my brother, Dave, he kept saying, 'I'll look after her, she'll be perfectly safe.' Finally my mum relented.

We left at 10 o'clock at night, went down to Tottenham and slept for a couple of hours in my brother's Ford Capri. It was around half-one when we joined the queue, which was already quite long. Everyone was chatting and excited and being so friendly. A lot had sleeping bags and tents. Gradually dawn broke and everyone was getting a bit more excited, and then all of a sudden gaps appeared and there was this big rush for everyone in the queue to catch up. We got in there, got our tickets, and I just remember the sheer excitement of what was going to come in four days' time.

I don't think I slept that week. I was obviously at school at the time, and I drove everyone nuts telling them about it but I kept it from the teachers because on the day my mum wrote a letter saying that I had to go to the dentist and I had to leave at half-two.

So I left, got home, got changed. I didn't have much memorabilia at the time, just a scarf, plus a white T-shirt and jeans, but then from the moment

> "Once we got on the tube gradually more and more Spurs fans appeared. It was feeling part of something, it was wonderful"

we got to the bus-stop to travel up to Highgate the sheer excitement was incredible. Once we got on the tube gradually more and more Spurs fans appeared. Feeling part of something was wonderful. My dad had stopped going regularly by then because he was concerned there was quite a lot of trouble creeping into the game. But on the tube there were Man City fans and Tottenham fans sharing crates of lager and everyone was so friendly. One of the conversations was, 'Who's going to be the Royal giving out the trophy tonight?' and it was decided that it was going to be the Queen Mum.

Once we got to Wembley Park and came out of the tube station, I looked up at those towers and it was like walking towards a castle. It was such a light evening, and I remember the brightness of the light blue of Man City and the white of Spurs. It was just amazing, I couldn't believe my luck. We walked to our gate, which had those big steps going up to it, and the entrance had only just opened so it took a while to get in, but we just gradually worked our way up those steps. And then we were inside Wembley.

My brother said, 'Come on, I'll show you the pitch.' We were in the upper tier, and quite a way back, but the sheer size of the pitch, with the greyhound track around it, was incredible, and I remember not just the

excitement but the belief we were going to win. I had nothing to base that on, I was 13, it was just naivety, but just knew everything was going to be great. The terraces at Wembley were very steep and when you jumped up to celebrate, like we did after Ricky's first goal, all of a sudden you could find yourself two or three steps down. And then came the equaliser, and then the penalty, and my brother said, 'That's it, you'd better prepare yourself, we're not going to win.'

But I had no negativity at that age. I said, 'We're going to be fine.' Then we got the equaliser, and then Ricky's goal, him weaving in and out and everybody shouting, 'For God's sake, shoot!'

That sheer joy when that goal went in was just incredible. We were hanging on for the last 10 minutes till the final whistle. And that was it. Steve was going to go up and get the FA Cup.

Although we were a long way back I remember the trophy glistened. You could see it shining. Steve lifted it up, and the players were coming down the steps and bringing it round in front of the fans. I just wanted that night to last forever.

Above left: Mo Keenan flies the Spurs flag at the victory parade
Left: The queue for replay tickets extends down Tottenham High Road

"And though we were a long way back I remember the trophy glistened. You could see it shining"

Going home was just full of joy. It took ages to get out of Wembley, and in those days you had to go through a tunnel to get back up to Wembley Park Station, which was quite stifling. But I never felt safer. I was just a little 13-year-old girl but everyone was looking out for the kids and making sure they were safe. I still had to go to school the next day, no matter what time I got back, that was part of the agreement with my mum. I actually went to a posh Catholic grammar convent, so I was a bit of an anomaly – the girl from the council estate that loved football – and I just went round all that day singing, 'When Steve, went up, to lift the FA Cup, we were there.'

That song was in my head for weeks. It was just crazy to think that that was my first ever live game. How lucky was I? It was 40-years ago but those things, they stay in your mind, they never leave.

SPURS F.A. CUP FINAL 1981

S.ARCHIBALD   M.ALEKSIC   C.HUGHTON   D.McALLISTER   G.ROBERTS   G.BROOKS   S.PERRYMAN   T.GALVIN
G.CROOKS   B.DAINES   G.HODDLE   R.VILLA   K.BURKINSHAW (MANAGER)   O.ARDILES   J.LACY   G.SMITH   P.MILLER

Cover stars

Spurs winning the FA Cup was front page news

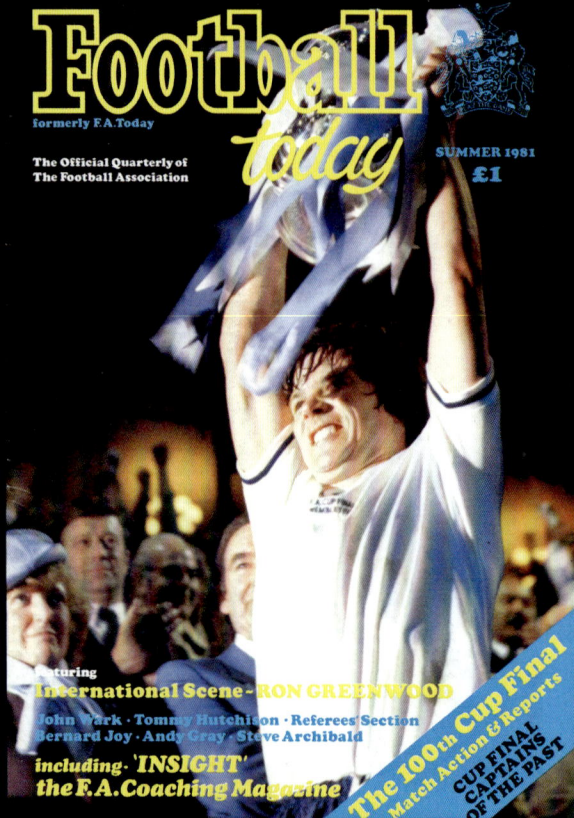

Football today
formerly F.A.Today
SUMMER 1981
£1
The Official Quarterly of
The Football Association
featuring
International Scene · RON GREENWOOD
John Wark · Tommy Hutchison · Referees Section
Bernard Joy · Andy Gray · Steve Archibald
including: 'INSIGHT'
the F.A. Coaching Magazine
The 100th Cup Final
Match Action & Reports
CUP FINAL
CAPTAINS
OF THE PAST

MATCH
weekly
IT'S SPURS
Saturday May 23
1981 30p
INSIDE
CUP FINAL
COLOUR
ACTION
Kevin Keegan's
Action Replay
FREE INSIDE
Your super
KEVIN KEEGAN
transfer gift

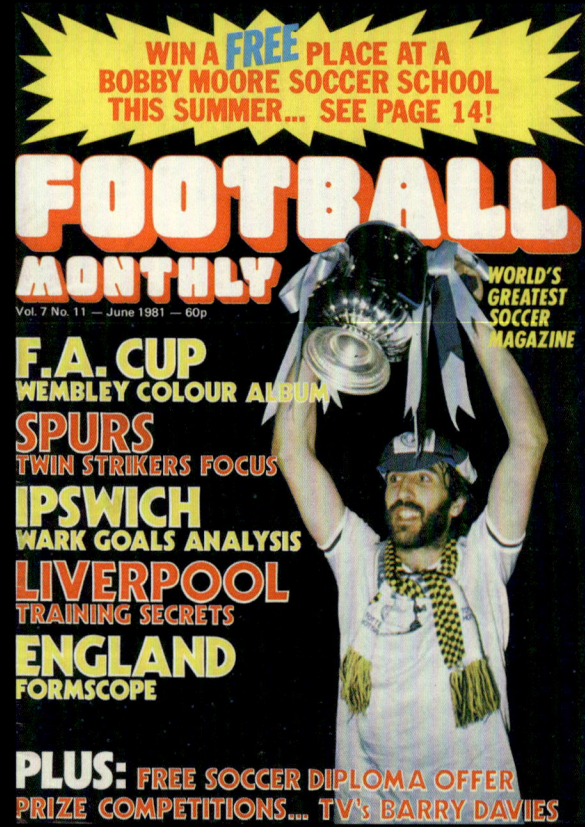

WIN A **FREE** PLACE AT A
BOBBY MOORE SOCCER SCHOOL
THIS SUMMER... SEE PAGE 14!
FOOTBALL MONTHLY
WORLD'S
GREATEST
SOCCER
MAGAZINE
Vol. 7 No. 11 — June 1981 - 60p
F.A. CUP
WEMBLEY COLOUR ALBUM
SPURS
TWIN STRIKERS FOCUS
IPSWICH
WARK GOALS ANALYSIS
LIVERPOOL
TRAINING SECRETS
ENGLAND
FORMSCOPE
PLUS: FREE SOCCER DIPLOMA OFFER
PRIZE COMPETITIONS... TV's BARRY DAVIES

CUP FINAL SOUVENIR POSTER

GLORY, GLORY SPURS

65p

GIANT COLOUR POSTER OF YOUR WEMBLEY HEROES!

THE GOAL IN A MILLION THAT WON THE 100th CUP FINAL!

Spurs 82

OFFICIAL ANNUAL 1982

Compiled and Edited by: Harry Harris

Super Colour Action on your Favourite Stars

Tottenham Hotspur 82

A Weekly Herald souvenir

SUPER SPURS

FA Cup winners 1981

Eight pages full of action from Spurs historic cup win

• Glenn Hoddle acknowledges the cheering fans outside Tottenham Town Hall on Sunday.   • Steve Perryman victoriously lifts the FA Cup

SEE INSIDE PAGES

Hallelujah - glory again
page 15

How they won — report and photos
pages 16 & 57

Welcome home
page 62

Burkinshaw's next battle

Big match photo action

• The winning line-up: back row — Steve Archibald, Peter Shreeves (coach), Paul Miller, Tony Galvin, Glenn Hoddle, Keith Burkinshaw, Garry Brooke, Milija Aleksic (deputy), Ricky Villa. Front row — Graham Roberts, Steve Perryman, Chris Hughton, Garth Crooks, Ossie Ardiles, Milija Aleksic.

Just the beginning

Although the 1981 FA Cup-winning team never won the league title, further trophies and triumphs confirmed that the Wembley victory had been the start of something special

By Julie Welch

Below: Spurs returned to Wembley in 1982, with Steve Perrymam on the cover of the Radio Times

Right: Keith Burkinshaw congratulates 1984 UEFA Cup Final hero Tony Parks

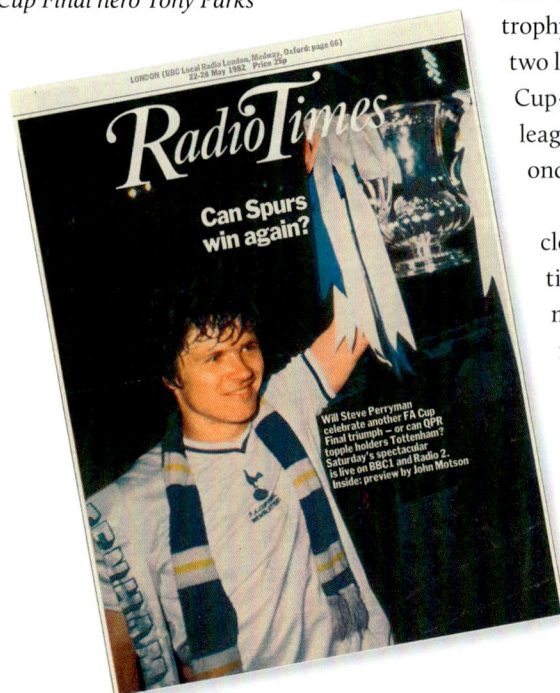

Steve Perryman had said winning that first big prize was only the beginning, and he got that right. When the 1981/82 season got underway, Spurs found themselves in line for four trophies and chasing an unprecedented treble. With a relatively small squad, such a feat proved beyond them; that March they lost to Liverpool at Wembley in the League Cup Final – the first time a Spurs team had come away from a Wembley final without the trophy in their hands – and in April they went out over two legs to Barcelona in the semi-final of the European Cup-Winners' Cup. But they also finished fourth in the league and were back at Wembley in May for their second FA Cup Final in two seasons.

Along the way they had an unexpected obstacle to overcome. 'World events overtake us sometimes,' said Burkinshaw, who had woken up on the morning of the semi-final against Leicester to the news that Argentina had invaded the Falklands. Politics was one of the reasons Spurs' two Argentinians were missing from the team that contested the final against QPR, which once again went to a replay. A single goal from the penalty spot, scored by Hoddle, brought the cup back to North London.

The 1982/83 season brought drama right at the top of the club. The Wale family, for many years the main shareholders in Tottenham Hotspur, were bought out in a coup by Irving Scholar, a Monaco-based property developer and passionate Spurs fan. Tottenham Hotspur became a business, foreshadowing all the commercial developments in the game that were to come in the following years. On the pitch, Tottenham had what was now, for them, a mediocre run in the cups but produced another fourth-placed finish which entitled them to a UEFA Cup place for the upcoming season.

It was to be Keith Burkinshaw's last at Tottenham Hotspur. Scholar's enthusiastic support for his club stretched to an involvement in team matters which didn't sit well with him.

'Scholar wanted to run the club and the team,' Burkinshaw later explained. 'If I'm the manager, I manage.'

But the last trophy a Burkinshaw side collected was arguably its finest, and it was a victory for homegrown talent. Ricky Villa had already gone, leaving in 1983 to play in Florida. While the Falklands conflict was going on, Ossie Ardiles had been loaned to PSG, but returned before his 12-month period was up. Four games in, he was sidelined with a broken shin. By the time the second leg of the final against Anderlecht was due to be played, Glenn Hoddle was on the treatment table, both Ardiles and Ray Clemence were only just back from injuries, and Steve Perryman was sitting out a suspension incurred in the first leg.

'It's a fact of life that you can't have your best team available at all times,' says Steve now. 'The game had to be played. Television

"That great Spurs side never won a league title, but two domestic cups and a European trophy demonstrated their worth beyond doubt"

coverage had been booked. The tickets had been sold. It is what it is, you just get on with it. You put out the best team you can, you take a risk with youngsters if that's what's needed. I've won games, be it as a player, coach or manager, with a very, very weakened team and, guess what, that weakened team surprises you.'

The risk Burkinshaw took was to keep Tony Parks, Ray Clemence's understudy, in goal. A gripping final ended in a penalty shoot-out, where Parks made the save, from Arnór Gudjohnsen, that won Spurs the UEFA Cup.

It was the last hurrah. As Ardiles said later, 'We won the UEFA Cup, but the team was finishing its life.' Burkinshaw left to coach the Bahrain national side and though Peter Shreeve's elevation to manager meant continuity, he was replaced after two seasons by David Pleat. And after 654 league appearances, 69 FA Cup appearances, 66 in the League Cup and 63 in Europe, Steve Perryman's career at Tottenham Hotspur came to an end in March 1986 when he joined Oxford United.

That great Spurs side of the early 1980s never won a league title, but two domestic cups and a European trophy demonstrated their worth beyond doubt. There have been few better legacies, and no Tottenham manager since then has achieved anything comparable. And maybe the architect of it all should have the last word.

'I tell you what,' said Keith Burkinshaw, 'During that period I would have paid to watch us play. Even as a manager, I would have gone through a turnstile with my money.'

Acknowledgments

My first thank you must go to Steve Perryman. Without him this book wouldn't have happened and as far as I'm concerned without his leadership Spurs wouldn't have achieved all they did between 1981 and 1984 when that great side was at its peak. It's been a privilege to work with him. His honesty, integrity, straightforwardness and sense of fun have made it an honour and a pleasure.

Most fans have a favourite season and for me it's always been 1980/81, when Tottenham's FA Cup win – the club's first for 14 years – brought the glory days back to White Hart Lane, and as a reporter I had the good luck to be there to chronicle some of the big moments. There is a rule in the press box that you have to leave your fandom behind and be strictly impartial, which was a very hard ask when Kenny Hibbitt dived at Hillsborough. Of course, I wasn't so high up in the pecking order that I could pick and choose which match I was sent to cover, and would sometimes find myself at Highbury or Portman Road when my heart and soul was at the Lane, so I'm enormously grateful to all the fans who have come forward to share their fantastic recollections and anecdotes, notably Kev Clark, Ivan Cohen, Alan Fisher, Pete Haine, Mo Keenan, Jill Lewis, Simon Lipson and Ian Meth. Willie Morgan gave me some lovely recollections from his years as stadium announcer at White Hart Lane and a special mention has to go to Mike Leigh and Theo Delaney, not just for sharing their memories of that cup run but for allowing me to plunder the fantastic archives of *The Spurs Show*.

I would also like to thank Tottenham Hotspur Football Club for supporting this project, especially Jon Rayner, Zoe Richardson and Gary Jacobson. In addition, huge thanks to club statistician Bob Goodwin for access to his archive and to Lee Hermitage of *nwmfootball.com* for the kind loan of his 1980s magazine collection as well as Adam Powley for his editing skills.

Lastly, Jim Drewett, Toby Trotman, Doug Cheeseman and Ed Davis at Vision Sports Publishing have been brilliant at getting this project off the ground from what began as a thought bubble in my head: 'That 1980/81 cup run was the best-ever and Ricky Villa's winning goal will never be matched. Wouldn't it be great if Steve and I could write about it?' Their hard work, patience and support are what has made it possible.

Julie Welch, October 2022

ROUND-BY-ROUND TO WEMBLEY

Third Round (Jan. 3)

*Q.P.R.	0 1
TOTTENHAM H.	0 3
*Hull City	1
Doncaster Rovers	0
*Leeds United	1 0
Coventry City	1 1
*Birmingham City	1 2
Sunderland	1 1
*Newcastle United	2
Sheffield Wednesday	1
*Orient	1
Luton Town	3
*Leicester City	3
Cardiff City	0
*Maidstone United	2
Exeter City	4
*Swansea City	0
Middlesbrough	5
*West Bromwich A.	3
Grimsby Town	0
*Barnsley	2
Torquay United	1
*Port Vale	1 0
Enfield Town	1 3
*Colchester United	0
Watford	1
*Stoke City	2 1
Wolverhampton W.	2 2
*West Ham Utd. +	1 0 0
Wrexham	1 0 1
*Wimbledon	0 1
Oldham Athletic	0 0
*Nottingham Forest	3 1
Bolton Wanderers	3 0
*Manchester United	2 2
Brighton & H.A.	2 0
*Mansfield Town	2 1
Carlisle United	2 2
*Derby County	0 0
Bristol City	0 2
*Huddersfield Town	0
Shrewsbury Town	3
*Ipswich Town	
Aston Villa	0
*Bury§	1 0 0
Fulham	1 0 1
*Plymouth	
Charlton Athletic	2
*Southampton	3
Chelsea	
*Preston North End	3
Bristol Rovers	4
*Everton	2
Arsenal	0
*Liverpool	4
Altrincham	1
*Notts County	
Blackburn Rovers	1
*Peterborough United	1 2
Chesterfield	1 1
*MANCHESTER C.	4
Crystal Palace	
*Norwich City	1
Cambridge United	

Fourth Round (Jan. 24)

*TOTTENHAM H.	2
Hull City	0
*Coventry City	3
Birmingham City	1
*Newcastle United	
Luton Town	1
*Leicester City	1 1
Exeter City	1 3
*Middlesbrough	
West Bromwich A.	1
*Barnsley + +	1 3
Enfield	1 0
*Watford	1 1
Wolverhampton W.	1 2
*Wrexham	2
Wimbledon	1
*Nottingham Forest	
Manchester United	0
*Carlisle United	1 0
Bristol City	1 5
*Shrewsbury Town	0 0
Ipswich Town	0 3
*Fulham	1
Charlton Athletic	2
*Southampton	3
Bristol Rovers	
*Everton	2
Liverpool	1
*Notts County	0
Peterborough United	1
*MANCHESTER C.	6
Norwich City	0

Fifth Round (Feb. 14)

*TOTTENHAM H.	3
Coventry City	1
*Newcastle United	1 0
Exeter City	1 4
*Middlesbrough	2
Barnsley	1
*Wolverhampton W.	3
Wrexham	1
*Nottingham Forest	2
Bristol City	1
*Ipswich Town	2
Charlton Athletic	0
*Southampton	0 0
Everton	0 1
*Peterborough United	0
MANCHESTER C.	1

Sixth Round (Mar. 7)

*TOTTENHAM H.	2
Exeter City	0
*Middlesbrough	1 1
Wolverhampton W.	1 3
*Nottingham Forest	3 0
Ipswich Town	3 1
*Everton	2 1
MANCHESTER C.	2 3

Semi-Finals (Apr. 11)

TOTTENHAM H.	2 3
Wolverhampton W.	2 0

(Hillsborough) Replay at Highbury

TOTTENHAM HOTSPUR

Ipswich Town	0
MANCHESTER C.	1

(Villa Park)

MANCHESTER CITY

*Denotes home side.   + 2nd replay at Wrexham   + + replay at Tottenham   §2nd replay at West Bromwich.